Big Small Plates

Big Small
Plates

Cindy Pawlcyn

with Pablo Jacinto and Erasto Jacinto

photography by
Laurie Smith

TEN SPEED PRESS
Berkeley | Toronto

Some of the recipes in this book include raw eggs, meat, or fish. When these foods are consumed raw, there is always the risk that bacteria, which is killed by proper cooking, may be present. For this reason, when serving these foods raw, always buy certified salmonella-free eggs and the freshest meat and fish available from a reliable grocer, storing them in the refrigerator until they are served. Because of the health risks associated with the consumption of bacteria that can be present in raw eggs, meat, and fish, these foods should not be consumed by infants, small children, pregnant women, the elderly, or any persons who may be immunocompromised.

Ten Speed Press
Box 7123
Berkeley, California 94707
www.tenspeed.com

Distributed in Australia by Simon and Schuster Australia, in Canada by Ten Speed Press Canada, in New Zealand by Southern Publishers Group, in South Africa by Real Books, and in the United Kingdom and Europe by Publishers Group UK.

Jacket and text design by Toni Tajima
Food styling by Erica McNeish
Photographs on pages 204, 232, 234, and 240 by Heidi Swanson. All other photographs by Laurie Smith.

Library of Congress Cataloging-in-Publication Data
Pawlcyn, Cindy.
    Big small plates / Cindy Pawlcyn with Pablo Jacinto and Erasto Jacinto.
        p. cm.
    Includes index.
    ISBN-13: 978-1-58008-523-6
    ISBN-10: 1-58008-523-7
    1. Appetizers. 2. Cookery, International. I. Jacinto, Pablo. II. Jacinto, Erasto. III.
  Title.
TX740.P37 2006
641.8'12—dc22   2006040446

Printed in China
First printing, 2006

1 2 3 4 5 6 7 8 9 10 — 10 09 08 07 06

To Marshall Fairbanks, for making me love to cook
at home again and about a million other little things.

—Cindy Pawlcyn

contents

chapter 4: On a Raft 176

chapter 5: Knife and Fork 246

chapter 6: Something Sweet 314

acknowledgments

Cindy's Acknowledgments

My most heartfelt thanks to Erasto and Pablo for being such wonderful business partners, cooks, chefs, critical taste buds, now published authors, and big time good humor guys. We've been through a lot together and I know I would never have made it without their support, encouragement, laughter, and incredible hard work. I would also like to thank Maria and Adriana Jacinto—being a chef's wife is a much more difficult job than being a chef!

Without Sherry Fournier's determination and drive this book would never have gotten started, let alone finished. Thank you, thank you!! Many thanks as well to Michael Wolf; in the end, we didn't include a beverage chapter, but he wrote the most beautiful one I have ever seen.

Thank you to all the recipe testers: Maxine Bloom, Sid Bloom, Kelly Cash, Kate Curnes, Kathy Dennett, Sherry Fournier, David Graham, LouAnne Hackett, Nancy Johnson, Marilyn Marchi, Gail Monahan, Aimee Newberry, Sylvia Guenza Pestoni, Valerie Presten, Ann Putnam, Shanti Singh, Sally Tantau, Garth Waters, Kris Waters, Michael Wolf, and Lynn Zachreson. It's so important that the book works in the home kitchen.

Thanks to Lorena Jones for once again thinking I could write a cookbook—you are so patient. What did it take, three years?!

Many thanks to Nancy Austin, Carrie Rodrigues, and Toni Tajima for making it look good and read well.

To Jackie Wan for every comment she made, and every battle she fought and won, thank you!

To the incredible dashing duo of Laurie Smith and Erica McNeish (aka, Robin Hood and Little John), thank you for making our food so beautiful, with buckets of love and good humor to boot!

Martha Navarrette, without your making all the hard work easy, we never would have made it. We love you!

Erasto's Acknowledgments

This book is dedicated to my mother and my father, Sara and Filiberto Jacinto and my wife Maria Jacinto. And to all my brothers and sisters.

A special thank-you to Cindy Pawlcyn for her belief and trust in me. And thank you to my whole team at Mustards Grill, for all of their hard work.

Pablo's Acknowledgments

I dedicate this book to my mother, Sara Jacinto, and my grandmother Benita Gutierrez, because they have cooked all of their lives and they were the first to teach me the difference in the food when you use the very best ingredients. They have had a profound influence on my career as a chef and I am grateful to them. I also dedicate this book to my father, who worked very hard to raise his family.

Others have supported my career and inspired me, namely, my two daughters, Jacqueline and Vivian, and my wife, Adriana. Adriana keeps Jacqueline and Vivian on track while I am working long hours. I know it's not easy being a chef's wife.

Many many thanks to chef Cindy Pawlcyn for giving me the opportunity, enthusiasm, and criticism to help me grow in this career.

Finally, I would like to give thanks to my team of talented cooks at Cindy's Backstreet Kitchen.

introduction

I sold out of my big restaurant company in 2000. It really wasn't very big compared to McDonald's but it was large enough, as it included Fog City Diner in San Francisco, Buckeye Roadhouse in Marin, and Mustards Grill in Napa Valley. I'd had it with the three- and four-hour commutes from Napa Valley to San Francisco and Marin. Then one day I got caught up in a thirty-six-car pileup on Highway 101, and had a really close call when a car flipped up in the air, sailed over me, and landed on the car behind me. That was it! A clear sign for me to make some changes!

I sold my interests in the Bay Area restaurants to my partners, Bill Upson and Bill Higgins, and took over as the sole owner of Mustards Grill. Mustards was close to home, and I had been managing it since it opened in 1983 anyway. It was a perfect solution.

It was lucky for me that the Jacinto brothers, Erasto and Pablo, stuck with me through this changeover. I first met these two young men in 1984 when they came into Mustards looking for work; fortunately I had the good sense to hire them both. Over the years they have taken on more and more responsibilities, to the point where they can run things on their own. Erasto has *never* left Mustards, and he is now chef-partner of that restaurant. Pablo did leave Mustards after a while, but he came back to work for me when I was doing the Buckeye Roadhouse. Then, when I gave up Buckeye, Pablo stayed with me and helped me develop a new restaurant in St. Helena. He became chef-partner there.

This restaurant, the Miramonte, was the first one I'd ever done without my former partners, the two Bills. It featured Mexican and Central and South American food. Unfortunately, to put it bluntly, it wasn't a big hit. People in the wine country want wine-friendly food, and although the food was great and actually did go well with wine, people were intimidated by it.

Within a couple of years, funds were running low, and we needed to do something in a hurry. Pablo and I put our heads together, and once we'd made our plans, we turned Miramonte into Cindy's Backstreet Kitchen. A complete makeover in just sixteen days—it was quite a feat, and it worked! We kept the Latin dishes that we loved and couldn't part with, but gave most of them new Anglo names; then we added a few unintimidating, wine-friendly dishes to the menu, and we were off. The new restaurant's name told people that we were off the main drag and that we were serving up the kinds of dishes we had been known for in the past. (Regarding names, there's no doubt they make a huge difference: after Pablo's Oysters Raza became Oysters Pablo, that dish tripled in sales.)

Looking back over the years, I can see how our focus has changed. Back in the mid-1980s, we were doing foods from the Pacific Rim and from Italy. Gradually we broadened our horizons to include all of the Mediterranean countries, with a heavy emphasis on foods from Spain. At the same time, food from Mexico and Central and South America became more important. We also went less for fusion, and concentrated more on authentic techniques and culturally accurate dishes. In recent years, Erasto, Pablo, and I have traveled to Oaxaca, their home state in Mexico, and to New York and Spain, and what we learned on those trips influenced our work in the restaurant kitchens.

There are a million things that get our creative juices flowing. Travel does it, of course, but closer to home there are always the daily specials we need to work up, or the pastry chef may say we're in a rut, or someone may come in with a new cookbook, or an old recipe they've just rediscovered. It's a combination of all that, plus where we've been recently, or what's in season, what's in the walk-in refrigerator or in the garden. I have to admit that we are very ingredient-driven, which is why certain ingredients make repeat appearances in this book.

In the 1990s, a movie came out called *Mermaids*. In it, Cher played the part of a mom who knew how to do only appetizers. As a chef, this just cracked me up. It also made me want to do a book about our own appetizers and small tasty dishes. It took a while to pull that book together, but it's probably a good thing. I'm a much better cook now than I was back in 1990, plus I've learned so much from cooking with the Jacinto brothers over the years. Most important of all, because Erasto and Pablo were standing by running the restaurants, I was able to steal away enough time to work on this book.

As I've said before, it's tough for chefs to write a cookbook, as we hardly ever measure or take notes or, for that matter, make the same dish the same way twice! If a dish is good enough to go on the menu during one of our seasonal menu changes or was developed for a special event, we usually have some written record, but I could kick myself for all the dishes that have slipped through our fingers. Still, there were plenty in our files, and we re-created or reinvented several more. So here it is, a collection of the small plates the three of us love to eat, cook, and share with family and friends.

First, a few words on how to use this book: All the recipes are "small plates," and you need to put three or four of them together to make up a whole meal (or what I call a "small-plates meal"). The dishes are meant to be shared, so that each person can enjoy a few bites of this dish, and a few of that, and not come away feeling stuffed. When the recipe yield says "Serves 6," it means it will serve six people as part of a small-plates meal. If this thought is confusing to you, try one or two of the suggested menus on pages 349–51 for a start.

If you want to stick with a more traditional meal plan, you can double any recipe, which will yield entrée-size servings. (You'd cut down on the number of dishes served, of course.) Most of the dishes can be served as passed hors d'oeuvres, too. Just cut the food up into bite-size pieces so your guests don't have to do a juggling act. For cocktail parties, I often place the messier items on tables around the room to get people moving, and to give them a place to rest their drinks while they attend to the more serious business of eating.

All the recipes in here are "small plates," and you need to put three or four of them together to make up a whole meal (or what I call a "small-plates meal"). The dishes are meant to be shared, so that each person can enjoy a few bites of this dish, and a few of that, and not come away feeling stuffed.

You will notice that in a lot of these recipes, I've called for a quantity range for certain ingredients, rather than specifying just one amount. This means you should use more or less of something according to your taste. For example, in the Chile-Garlic Peanuts, you could use more or less dried chile depending on how much you like chile. Or, in the Sunday Supper Burgers, the patties will be a tiny bit bigger or smaller depending on the amount of ground beef you use. The recipes will work either way, so trust your own instincts and taste buds!

When it comes to cooking, the little extras make a huge difference, so sweat the details. Otherwise it's just airline food, and you know what has happened to that! Always stick with produce that is in season and at its peak of flavor, and spend an extra minute or two to make each plate of food visually appealing. Look for interesting serving platters, bowls, dishes, spoons. I almost called this book *Life Off a Long Oval Platter* because small bites of food look so good on them!

Pablo Says . . .

Whether I'm entertaining or just putting today's dinner on the table, I think everything tastes better when I cook surrounded by friends and family. Even better, I like a congenial atmosphere where I can eat and cook at the same time, and prepare each new dish as people are finishing the previous one. That's why I love small plates. From the Stuffed Piquillo Peppers to the Oysters Pablo (my personal favorite) to our Rabbit Tostadas, I can satisfy everyone with a small-plates meal.

Another reason I love small plates is that they look so beautiful. With just one main ingredient per plate, they lend themselves to a variety of pottery and silverware, and other novel serving options. They are also a great way to feature the freshest in-season ingredients.

Erasto Says . . .

When I think of small plates, I think of variety and flavor. Fresh meats, poultry, and seafood; salads made with fresh, locally grown, organic produce and seasonal vegetables and herbs from Mustards' garden—all uniquely presented with flair and style. And when you're dining with friends or family, how cool is it that these dishes lend themselves perfectly to sharing? Then, when the small plates are all gone, you still have room for dessert. For me, the two words *small plates* represent one simple thing—fun, fun, fun!

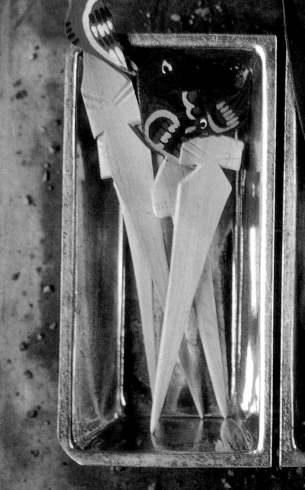

sticks, picks,

and with fingers

Of all the chapters in this book, this one is my favorite.

chapter 1: Sticks, Picks, and with Fingers

Of all the chapters in this book, this one is my favorite because everything in it is meant to be eaten out of hand, without the benefit of knife and fork, and that's the way I like to eat. My poor mom tried to teach me better; however, she didn't have much success. When food was put before me, my first instinct was always to dig in with my hands. It still is.

This chapter has more recipes in it than any of the others, so there's a lot to explore. The recipes range from very simple (Chile Garlic Peanuts and Grilled "Street" Corn, for example) to very challenging (like the Salt Cod Cakes with Aioli or the Smoked Duck Spring Rolls). There are several dishes that are served in edible lettuce cups (just pick up the whole thing and enjoy). Some come on skewers (My Very First Beef Satay and the Serrano Ham–Wrapped Prawns, among others). Three quick tips on using skewers: (a) bamboo or wooden skewers should be soaked in enough water to cover at least thirty minutes to keep them from burning up on the grill; (b) you can break long skewers to any length that will work best for you; and (c) to keep food from twirling around or curling up on the grill, thread the food on two parallel skewers.

Any dish in this group would make a good starter for a small-plates meal, or you could serve three or four of them together for an all-appetizer, no-knives-and-forks-needed meal. They would all be excellent for cocktail parties, wine tastings, or buffets, as well. Just remember that for passed hors d'oeuvres, you want bite-size morsels of food and short skewers (three or four inches at most). Put out plenty of napkins or wipes for your guests.

There are choices for every season here, so come back to this chapter often.

4 or 5 large eggs

Pinch of salt, plus ¼ teaspoon for the gougères

¾ cup water

⅓ cup butter

¾ cup flour

¾ cup finely grated Gruyère cheese

Gougères

Serves 6 (makes about 60)

Jennifer Palmer is one of the best pastry chefs I've ever worked with. She makes these cheese puffs every Christmas Eve, and I look forward to them each year. Her trick is to place a small slice of cheese on top of each one before she bakes them. Delicious! Hot out of the oven, they are addictive . . . and one of my favorite Christmas treats.

You are completely dependent on an excellent cheese to make this dish memorable, so don't cut corners on the cheese. Inexpensive Gruyère often has an odd gym-sock aroma that just ruins anything you make with it. Try one of the many wonderful cave-aged Gruyères from Switzerland. Tomales Bay Foods carries one called Emmi that has a wonderful nutty taste. Just be sure to get the tastiest Gruyère you can.

Preheat the oven to 375°F to 400°F.

To make an egg wash, beat 1 of the eggs with a pinch of salt and set it aside. For the *gougères*, combine the water, butter, and ¼ teaspoon salt in a saucepan and bring it to a boil. Reduce the heat, add the flour, and whisk until the batter comes away from the sides of the pan. Cook for 1 to 2 minutes longer. Transfer to a mixer bowl and beat in 3 of the eggs, 1 at a time, beating till smooth after each addition. Add the last egg only if the batter seems too thick. The dough should be like a thick cookie dough. Stir in the Gruyère, saving a little to sprinkle on the top before baking.

To finish the *gougères*, line a baking sheet with parchment paper and pipe or spoon the batter onto it, about a teaspoon of batter for each. Brush with the egg wash and sprinkle with the remaining cheese. Bake until golden and puffed, 12 to 16 minutes.

Cheesy Wonder Crackers

Makes 30 crackers (serves 6)

Once you start munching on these crispy, cheesy crackers, you will not be able to stop. They are that good. At the restaurant, we use them to garnish soups. They are great floated on or served alongside pureed soups of all kinds. The dough keeps well in the refrigerator and unbaked frozen crackers will keep for 3 months, so these are great to have around to handle those situations when you have unexpected guests.

You can roll the dough out flat and cut the crackers into any interesting or fun shape you wish. Or you can roll the dough into a log and slice it up. If you want to add a little extra, roll the log in some seeds, nuts, or spices.

8 ounces white Cheddar cheese, grated

2 ounces blue cheese

½ cup butter

1 cup flour

¼ cup whipping cream

1 teaspoon sugar

½ teaspoon salt

optional extras (pick one)

Aniseed and fennel seeds, coarsely crushed

1 tablespoon sea salt plus ½ teaspoon cayenne pepper

Poppy seeds

Freshly ground black pepper

Sesame seeds, black or white

Sliced almonds

Place the cheeses, butter, flour, cream, sugar, and salt in a food processor or mixer bowl and process or mix with the paddle attachment until a ball forms. Of course, this could also be done by hand, but it will take a bit more effort.

Roll the dough into a log and wrap it in plastic wrap. Tap and turn the log against the countertop a few times to form a triangle shape. Chill the dough for at least 1 hour (as long as overnight is okay). If you're going to dress the crackers up with seeds or nuts, spread them out on a baking sheet and press the dough into them. Cut the dough into $^1/_4$-inch-thick slices. Dipping the knife into hot water first will make the job easier.

Alternatively, chill the dough and roll it out to $^3/_8$-inch thickness and cut out 2-inch circles with a cookie cutter. Press the scraps together and roll them out to make more circles. If you're making these ahead, place the disks on a baking sheet and freeze.

When firm, put them in freezer bags and return them to the freezer.

To bake the crackers, preheat the oven to 375°F. Line a baking sheet with parchment paper and arrange the crackers on it, allowing some space between them because the dough will spread. Bake 8 to 10 minutes in a convection oven, 10 to 12 minutes in a conventional oven, until cooked through and crisp and brown around the edges.

Pan-Roasted Hazelnuts

Serves a crowd (makes 1 pound)

Olive oil

1 pound fresh hazelnuts

Coarse sea salt (Maldon flake salt is the best)

These are a great cocktail nibble, and they're quick and easy to make. I keep hazelnuts in my freezer and do this whenever my guests have the munchies and the meal isn't ready yet. Don't worry about removing the skins on the hazelnuts. You can get fancy by mixing a little cayenne pepper, toasted ground cumin seeds, or chipotle chile powder into the salt just before seasoning the nuts. Be sure to season them when they are hot. Almonds, walnuts, and pecans can also be pan-roasted; just reduce the cooking time.

Pour oil to a depth of ⅛ inch into a heavy-bottomed skillet. Heat over medium heat; when the oil is hot, add the nuts. Stir continuously but slowly till golden brown, 8 to 10 minutes. Drain on paper towels and sprinkle with sea salt while they're still hot. Best served warm.

Chile-Garlic Peanuts

Makes a big bowlful

2 whole heads garlic

¼ cup peanut or vegetable oil

2 pounds shelled raw Spanish peanuts, with skins

2 to 4 fiery-hot dried chiles, slightly crushed

1 tablespoon kosher salt

Grated zest and juice of 1 lime

The peanuts you want for this traditional Oaxacan bar snack are the short round guys with red skin that are known as Spanish peanuts. The American peanut is a bit longer than the Spanish peanut and has a brownish skin. It will work, too; it just doesn't quite have the look. For the chiles, any small hot dried chile will do, but I especially like chiles de árbol or chiles pequín for this.

Traditionally these are cooked in pork lard. Although we norteños eat them like crazy when we go south of the border, few of us cook with lard at home anymore. A peanut or vegetable oil would work well also. You just need something with a high smoke point, because you want the oil really hot when the peanuts, chiles, and garlic hit it. I often use a double-handled pan to make shaking the nuts easier as they're cooking. A wok would also work.

Two pounds of peanuts may sound like a lot, but I guarantee the whole batch will disappear quickly, especially if you serve them warm. You can make them in two batches if it is easier for you.

Separate the heads of garlic into cloves. Trim off the root ends, but don't peel the cloves. Put the oil in a pan large enough to hold everything, and heat it until it is almost rippling. Add the peanuts, garlic, and chiles; cook, stirring and shaking continuously, for 10 to 12 minutes, until the peanuts have darkened. Add the salt and lime zest and juice to the pan and give it another good stir and shake. Pour out into a serving bowl and watch them go!

Mustards' Famous Onion Rings with House-Made Ketchup

Serves 6

house-made ketchup

3½ pounds tomatoes, peeled and chopped

1 to 1¼ pounds apples, cored and chopped

3 onions, chopped

1½ cups sugar

2 cups cider vinegar

1 tablespoon sea salt

½ teaspoon cayenne pepper

6 black peppercorns

6 allspice berries

6 cloves

Peanut or vegetable oil, for frying

3 cups flour

1 tablespoon salt

6 large yellow onions, thinly sliced

3 tablespoons minced chives or scallions

Boy, do I get grief for having left this recipe out of the Mustards Grill cookbook! Who would have thought that people would actually want to make onion rings at home? Well, here's the recipe, along with directions for making a super ketchup that we always serve with them. This ketchup is also a great complement for hamburgers, meat loaf, and, of course, french fries.

Making good onion rings is mainly a matter of technique. First of all, you need to slice the onions very, very thinly; they should be thin enough so you can see through them, but not too thin. You may need to experiment on the thinness—too thin and they will burn, too thick and they will get soggy. Really, unless you are the best slicer in the world, you should use a mandoline or an electric slicer for the onion cutting. Timing with the flour coating is crucial, too: you can't let the onion rings sit too long in the flour or they will become gooey (not good). So don't flour more onions than you can fry in one batch. And this may be tricky, but you should have the oil ready—at 375°F—so the onion rings come out of the flour and go right into the hot oil. Finally, you need to keep the onion rings moving freely while they're frying, turning them gently with tongs.

As for the ketchup, I've been playing with ketchup recipes for at least twenty years. This is one of my favorites. The secret ingredient in this one is apples—they add sweetness to the ketchup, and the pectin in them adds texture and gives it a natural body so the ketchup really clings to fries and onion rings. We use Sierra Beauty apples or Granny Smiths. It's

Here's the equipment you will need for making perfect onion rings.

- Mandoline or electric slicer
- Large, stainless steel bowl
- Electric deep-fat fryer
- Wire basket or strainer
- Long-handled tongs

Note: If you don't have an electric fryer, you can use a heavy, straight-sided pot, but it should be deep enough that the top of the pot is three to four inches above the level of the oil, and your wire basket should fit at least three-fourths of the way into the pot. You'll also need a candy or deep-fry thermometer to monitor the temperature of the oil.

really wonderful with McIntosh apples, too, but their season is very short. Green apples should be peeled, but don't bother peeling the red-skinned ones. Use a high-quality, good-tasting vinegar that tastes and smells of apples. You could cut the recipe in half, but it's so good, you'll wish you hadn't.

For the ketchup, combine all the ingredients in a large stainless steel pot and bring to a boil. Reduce to a simmer and cook, uncovered, about 2 hours, until it is the consistency of commercial ketchup. Allow it to cool slightly, then puree in batches in a blender until very smooth. Return to the heat for several more minutes to thicken further. Stir often during this final cooking. Strain and cool.

For the onion rings, heat at least 3 inches of oil to 375°F in a heavy straight-sided pot. Combine the flour and salt in a large stainless steel bowl and mix well. Now toss in a few slices of onion and separate the slices by hand into individual rings. Get all the rings coated with some of the flour-salt mixture and transfer them to a strainer. Shake with abandon over the bowl to remove excess flour. Do this longer than you think you should, again separating any clumps with your fingertips.

Transfer some of the rings to the frying basket. It is very important not to overcrowd the pan, so start with just a few to get a feel for the process. Check the oil temperature to be sure it's at 375°F, then carefully lower the basket into the hot oil. Keep the rings moving almost constantly, using tongs to lift, separate, and turn the rings in the oil as they cook. Use a light touch here, as you don't want to mash the onion rings together, which would probably result in a gummy mess. Carefully remove the onion rings when they are golden brown and crisp. This takes us about 1 minute at the restaurant, but we are very practiced and can do 80 to 90 orders per shift. Shake the excess oil from the cooked onion rings onto paper towels, and pile them up on a big plate. Check the temperature to be sure the oil is still at 375°F and repeat with the remaining onion rings, frying them in as many batches as necessary. Sprinkle with the chives, and serve immediately with some ketchup on the side.

creamy cilantro-garlic dip

1 cup mayonnaise

1½ teaspoons minced garlic

¼ bunch cilantro, leaves and tender stems, coarsely chopped

2 tablespoons capers, rinsed and minced

¼ teaspoon salt

⅛ teaspoon freshly ground black pepper

cindy's backstreet kitchen mojo

12 small cloves garlic

¼ teaspoon sea salt

¼ cup freshly squeezed bitter orange juice, or ¼ cup sweet orange juice plus 2 tablespoons lemon or lime juice

1½ teaspoons toasted ground cumin seeds

½ cup extra virgin olive oil

¼ teaspoon freshly ground black pepper

3 very green unripe plantains

Ice water

Salt, for seasoning the chips

Peanut or vegetable oil, for frying

1 or 2 limes, cut into wedges

Plantain Chips with Cindy's Backstreet Kitchen Mojo and Creamy Cilantro-Garlic Dip

Serves 6 (makes about 3 or 4 dozen chips)

Unlike the regular bananas we are so used to eating here in the United States, plantains cannot be eaten raw. Though they are a fruit, they are most often treated like a starch. They are very, very versatile, like potatoes, and can be boiled, baked, stewed, sautéed, grilled, or, as in this recipe, deep-fried. They can be used at any stage of ripeness, too, from green to yellow to black-ripe: it all depends on the recipe. For this one, you want the very green unripe ones. Plantains grow in most tropical areas of the world, but they are most popular in the Latin American countries and in the Caribbean. You can find plantains at Latin American and Asian markets.

The secret to this recipe is to get the plantains sliced consistently thin. Not paper-thin, but about one-sixteenth to one-eighth of an inch thick. I highly recommend you use a mandoline for this job. My favorites are the Japanese mandolines with carbon steel blades, which you can get in most cookware stores.

A mojo (pronounced "mo-ho") is a salsalike sauce, very common in the Caribbean and in Central and South America, especially Cuba and Brazil. It is often made with the juice of Seville oranges, or bitter oranges, as they are also known.

Mojos *tend to be much thinner than Mexican-style salsas and very full-flavored, and they make a great dip for grilled or fried foods. They are not usually cooked or pureed, but I do make this one in a blender. Mojos are good for adding zip to dishes. The word* mojo *comes from the Portuguese* molho, *which means simply "sauce."*

To make the dip, combine all the dip ingredients in a small bowl and mix well. Chill and reserve until needed.

For the mojo, put the garlic and sea salt in a blender and pulse until finely chopped. Blend in the bitter orange juice and cumin, and process finely. With the blender running, slowly add the oil in a steady, thin stream, and continue processing until the *mojo* is emulsified. Season with pepper.

To prepare the plantains, cut off the tips and remove the peel. You may need to make a few lengthwise slits along the ridges of the peel to loosen it first. Have a container of ice water ready for soaking the sliced plantains. Add a few shakes of salt to the water. Slice the plantains lengthwise about $1/8$ to $1/16$ inch thick, and soak them in the ice water for 15 to 20 minutes. Drain the plantains. To fry the plantains, pour the oil to a depth of $1^1/_2$ inches into a heavy-bottomed frying pan and heat to $365°$F. Carefully lower a few slices of plantain at a time into the oil, taking care not to overcrowd the pan. Fry for about 1 minute until crisp, remove to paper towels to drain, and salt while hot. Allow the oil to return to temperature before frying the next batch.

Serve the plantain chips like potato chips, with separate ramekins of the dip and the *mojo*, and plenty of lime wedges for squeezing.

Papas Bravas

Serves 6

brava sauce

2 tablespoons ground dry *ñora* peppers or mild sweet chili powder

1 to 2 tablespoons smoky or sweet *pimentón* paprika or other paprika

3 cloves garlic, peeled and minced

1½ tablespoons sherry vinegar

Tiny pinch of toasted ground cumin

Tiny pinch of cayenne pepper

1 cup very ripe chopped peeled tomatoes

1 teaspoon sea salt

⅓ cup extra virgin olive oil

12 to 18 small potatoes (about 2 pounds)

Olive oil, for frying

Additional sea salt

Loosely translated, papas bravas means "spicy potatoes." In this dish, the potatoes are like french fries, and the smoky, sweet-hot, garlicky sauce that comes with them is the brava part. Papas bravas is a favorite in tapas bars all over Spain. It's usually served with toothpicks, which makes for a lot of sauce dripped all about—somewhat messy, but the sauce is so addictive, nobody cares. For a truly authentic sauce, use Spanish pimentón paprika, Spanish olive oil, and, if you can get them, ñora peppers. Ñoras are medium-hot dried red peppers, often used in stews and sauces. You can grind them up in an electric coffee grinder; just be sure to clean it up well afterward. If you end up with any leftover brava sauce, it's great on just about anything from fried eggs to pork chops to scallops.

The best potatoes to use for this dish are small new-season potatoes—white-skinned, Yukon Gold, Kennebec, fingerling. Just don't use red-skinned potatoes because they don't fry up well, and they tend to absorb oil. The potatoes need to be boiled or steamed before you fry them.

This dish goes well with Chorizo and Goat Cheese Half-Moons (page 73).

Combine all the sauce ingredients in a blender and blend until smooth. Reserve until needed. (The sauce can be made up to 24 hours ahead. Refrigerate it, but bring it back to room temperature before serving.)

You can peel or not peel the potatoes, as you wish. Either way, steam them or boil them in salted water till just fork-tender: 15 minutes will do it for small fresh potatoes. Drain them well and cut them in half lengthwise.

(continued)

Pour the oil to a depth of about ¹/₂ inch into a heavy saucepan large enough to hold all the potatoes comfortably. If necessary, get a second pan going, as you want to fry all the potatoes at once. Heat the oil to 375°F and fry the potatoes till crisp on the bottom; flip them over and repeat. Don't stir them around a lot.

As they finish, scoop the potatoes out with a slotted spoon, and toss them into a stainless steel bowl, sprinkling them with salt as you go. When they are all done, scoop them onto plates, smother liberally with the sauce, and serve immediately. *Papas bravas* should be hot enough to burn your tongue if you forget to blow on them first.

Grilled "Street" Corn

Serves 6

3 to 4 tablespoons homemade or high-quality mayonnaise

½ teaspoon minced garlic

½ teaspoon salt

½ teaspoon cayenne pepper

¾ cup grated Parmesan cheese

3 ears garden-fresh corn, husks left on

1 lime, cut into 6 wedges

It takes a lot of space to grow corn, so we can manage only three small patches of corn in the Mustards Grill garden. In the summer when the corn is in, we can sell out of a day's harvest in less than an hour. People get so excited, whatever we have blows out before lunch is over. Some of our guests have even been known to eat three whole ears of our grilled corn as their lunch. We grill it with the husk on. This way, the corn creates its own steam, which intensifies the flavor. It's the best!

For the skewers, you need something fairly substantial. The ones we use in the restaurant look like skinny pencils, but then we are skewering whole ears of corn. The skewers meant for caramel apples would work well, or you could dig out those corn holders hiding at the back of your kitchen drawer.

We call this "street" corn because it's the kind of corn Oaxacan street vendors sell. As a small plate, I'd plan on half an ear of corn per person . . . but go ahead and double or triple up your servings if you want to be more generous.

Stir the mayonnaise and garlic together in a small dish. Mix the salt and cayenne together in another small dish or in a spare salt shaker if you have one. Put the Parmesan on a small plate (you'll be rolling the corn in the cheese). Have this all ready for when the corn comes off the grill.

When you're ready to serve, grill the corn over a hot fire 12 to 15 minutes, rolling it around so it cooks evenly. If you have other food to grill for the meal, move the corn to the side of the grill when it's done, turning it now and then while it's offstage. Or you could put the corn on a platter and cover it with a kitchen towel. To serve, shuck the corn and break each ear in half. If the corn has cooled down too much, quickly run the cobs over the grill. Stick corn holders on the ends of each piece or push wooden skewers through each end. Brush with mayonnaise, dust with the salt and cayenne mixture, and roll in the Parmesan, being sure to get a nice coating on each little corn. Serve warm with lime wedges for individual squeezing.

quick mustard sauce

1 tablespoon Dijon mustard

1 tablespoon coarse-grained
    mustard

1 tablespoon prepared creamy
    horseradish

2 tablespoons half-and-half

1 to 2 tablespoons water

croquettes

¼ cup butter

½ cup flour, plus 1 cup for
    coating croquettes

1½ cups whole milk

1 cup (packed) grated aged
    Parmesan or Gruyère cheese

½ cup grated Jarlsberg cheese

1 ounce soft fresh goat cheese

1 tablespoon minced fresh
    tarragon or 2 tablespoons
    minced fresh chervil

2 tablespoons minced chives

Salt and freshly ground white
    pepper

Cayenne pepper

1 large egg

1 tablespoon water

1 to 1½ cups fine bread crumbs

Peanut or vegetable oil, for frying

Three-Cheese Croquettes with Quick Mustard Sauce

Note: If you let people dip, this would be a good hors d'oeuvre.

Serves 6

This recipe goes way back to the early '80s and the beginning of my small-plate addiction, but I still really love them. The base is nothing but a very thick béchamel sauce made with lots of cheese. The recipe calls for Parmesan or Gruyère cheese, goat cheese, and Jarlsberg cheese, but you can use your favorite cheeses, or even clean out the cheese drawer of your fridge. It's best to form the croquettes themselves ahead, and fry them up at the last minute. Make them small so they'll fry quickly.

If you have any leftover mustard sauce, it is great with grilled steak, smeared on bread for ham and cheese sandwiches, or served with pork chops. The Double-Basil Tomatoes (pages 172–173) would be really good in addition to or in place of the mustard sauce.

To make the mustard sauce, mix together the mustards, horse-radish, and half-and-half, then whisk in just enough water to make the sauce thin enough to drizzle. Reserve in the refrigerator until needed.

For the croquettes, melt the butter in a saucepan over medium heat, and add ½ cup of the flour. Cook and stir 2 to 3 minutes, until you get a nutty aroma. It is important to cook this roux long enough to avoid a raw-flour taste, but you don't want it to brown. Gradually add the milk, stirring all the while, and cook over low heat until the mixture is very thick. Stir well to avoid

herb salad

1 tablespoon rice vinegar

3 tablespoons extra virgin
  olive oil

Pinch of salt

Pinch of freshly ground black
  pepper

3 cups chervil sprigs, watercress,
  or mixed fresh basil and
  tarragon (small leaves only)

lumps. When thickened, add the cheeses, and stir until they have melted and the batter is smooth and uniform. Stir in the tarragon and chives, and season with salt, white pepper, and cayenne pepper. Remove from the heat and pat out on a large plate or pan; refrigerate 2 to 3 hours, until thoroughly chilled.

Use a soupspoon to form the croquettes. Dip it in ice water, scoop out a bit of batter, and roll the batter into a little lozenge shape. Repeat until you've used up all the batter. Chill again.

When you are ready to fry the croquettes, combine the egg and water in a small bowl to make an egg wash. Put the remaining 1 cup of flour in a shallow bowl and the bread crumbs in another. Roll the croquettes in the flour, and pat off the excess. Then dip them in the egg wash and roll them in the bread crumbs, again patting off the excess.

In a deep, heavy-bottomed saucepan, deep-fry the croquettes at 365°F to 375°F until golden brown and heated through. Take care not to crowd the pan: you want plenty of circulation for even cooking. As the croquettes finish, transfer them to a wire rack or paper towels to drain. Keep in a warm oven until needed. If you need to fry another batch, skim out any bits left in the pan, and make sure the oil is at the proper temperature before going ahead.

To make a vinaigrette, combine the vinegar, olive oil, salt, and pepper in a small bowl, and whisk until well emulsified. To serve, very lightly dress the herbs with the vinaigrette, and place portions of salad in the center of the plates to make little nests. Top with croquettes and drizzle with the mustard sauce.

I always use organic eggs,
from free-range hens
if possible, and preferably
from local farms.

Hard-Boiled Eggs with Best Ever Tapenade

Serves 6

To hard-boil eggs Cindy style, put them in a pot with enough cold water to cover by 1 inch and add 2 teaspoons of salt. Bring to a boil, reduce to a simmer, and cook exactly 7 minutes. This will give you yolks that are bright and a tiny bit soft. Peel the eggs under cold running water.

When it comes to eggs, I don't like to compromise. I always use organic eggs, from free-range hens if possible, and preferably from local farms. These eggs are the highest quality you can get, with orange-yellow yolks and lots of flavor.

I recently discovered these great black olives called Empeltre olives. They also go by the name Farga Aragón, for the region from which they come—Aragón, in northeastern Spain. They are a sweet, tender-fleshed variety worth searching out on your travels (or get them from a good mail-order source). They receive minimal processing, though they are cured longer because of their higher sugar content. They have a mild, sweet, nutty flavor. Nutty is the word you use when you can't think of anything else to describe a flavor, says my friend John at Pacific Gourmet, one of the best specialty foods purveyors in America; but in this case, nutty is absolutely accurate. The character of Empeltre olives is what makes this tapenade the "best ever." You can substitute other types of black olives but the results will not be as good. Be sure to rinse other olives really well, and even consider soaking them to reduce their saltiness. French or Italian olives would also work, but don't use Kalamatas. They are too briny.

This tapenade is also excellent served on, over, or with toasted bread, artichokes, cardoons, fritters, asparagus, potatoes, or fish—swordfish and tuna in particular. Or try tucking some of it into a sandwich or an omelette, or swirling a spoonful into a pasta or risotto.

(continued)

best ever tapenade

1½ cups Empeltre olives or other black olives, pitted

1½ teaspoons Dijon mustard

2 tablespoons extra virgin olive oil

¼ teaspoon freshly ground black pepper

Grated zest of ½ orange

1½ teaspoons coarsely chopped garlic

3 pieces soft sun-dried tomato, coarsely chopped

2½ teaspoons coarsely chopped Italian parsley leaves

2½ teaspoons capers, rinsed

9 large eggs

Combine all the tapenade ingredients in a food processor and pulse till they reach the smoothness you prefer. I find it's more interesting in the mouth to have a few bigger pieces—they give the tapenade a nice bite. Refrigerate until needed.

Hard-boil the eggs as described in the sidebar. Slice them in half and arrange them cut side up on a platter or an egg dish, if you have one. Put a spoonful or two of tapenade in the center of each half egg; serve while the eggs are still warm.

Potato-Leek Pancakes with Sour Cream and Chives

Serves 6

These crispy pancakes are so simple, and so very good. If you would like to dress them up a bit, they can be topped with thin slices of gravlax, smoked fish, or roasted peppers. (There is a great recipe for gravlax on page 132.) Figure on three small cakes per person.

2 russet potatoes (large)

1 leek, white and light green parts only, sliced into thin circles and rinsed

1 teaspoon salt

½ to ¾ teaspoon freshly ground black pepper, plus additional for serving

2 to 3 tablespoons butter; duck or goose fat; butter and olive oil combined; or vegetable oil

½ to ¾ cup sour cream or crème fraîche

½ bunch chives, finely chopped

Peel and grate the potatoes, and put them into cold water. Drain the potatoes and squeeze out the excess water. Pat the leeks dry. Mix the potatoes and leeks together, then mix in the salt and pepper. In a large cast-iron or nonstick pan or griddle over medium-high heat, melt enough of the butter to coat the pan. Working in batches, place small portions (about 2 tablespoonfuls) of the mix in the pan and press with the back of a spatula to flatten. Add more butter as needed to keep the pan greased. Cook till golden brown on the underside, then flip and cook the other side until golden brown, about 2 minutes each side.

To serve, place dollops of sour cream on the pancakes and top with the chives and sprinkle with pepper.

risotto

1 tablespoon olive oil

1 tablespoon butter

1 shallot, sliced

1 clove garlic, sliced

2 ounces stemmed chanterelle mushrooms, diced

½ cup arborio rice

½ cup white wine

1 cup vegetable or chicken stock

¼ teaspoon salt

⅛ teaspoon freshly ground white pepper

¼ cup grated Parmigiano Reggiano cheese

2 tablespoons grated pecorino or fontina cheese

3 ounces fresh buffalo mozzarella cheese (optional)

1 or 2 large eggs

1 tablespoon water

½ cup flour

1 to 1½ cups *panko* or other bread crumbs

Peanut or vegetable oil, for frying

heirloom tomato sauce

1¾ to 2 pounds firm, vine-ripened heirloom tomatoes, peeled, seeded, and diced

Juice of ½ lemon or 2 teaspoons rice vinegar

1 tablespoon chiffonade of fresh basil leaves, plus 1 tablespoon additional for garnish

3 tablespoons extra virgin olive oil

½ teaspoon salt

¼ teaspoon freshly ground black pepper

Chanterelle Arancini with Heirloom Tomato Sauce

Serves 6 to 8 (makes 12 small *arancini*)

Arancini are deep-fried rice balls, an appetizer that originated in Sicily, I'm told. They are usually made with plain risotto and might have a bit of filling inside, a small piece of meat or some vegetables or sometimes cheese. After you've made this dish once, you could try playing with the basic concept. In this version, I've cooked some chanterelle mushrooms in with the rice. For a nice melty surprise, stick a tiny chunk of mozzarella in the center of each ball of risotto as you roll them up.

For the best results, the risotto for this recipe should be made a day ahead. In fact, if you have some leftover risotto, this recipe is definitely for you. Just sauté the chanterelles as described below, allow them to cool, stir them into the leftover risotto, and carry on with the recipe.

The risotto balls will hold for several hours in the refrigerator after they have been formed and coated with panko. So you could make the arancini to this point and fry them later. If they seem moist or soggy when you pull them out of the fridge to cook them, just roll them in additional panko and shake off excess before cooking.

The tomato sauce for this dish does not require cooking and comes together in a flash. It's a whole lot better if made just before serving, though; so you can peel and dice the tomatoes ahead of time, but wait until just before serving to combine the ingredients. If your tomatoes are extremely juicy, drain them for twenty minutes or so before using them. The juice can be saved for vegetable stock or gazpacho, or a really excellent Bloody Mary.

I don't know how many varieties of heirloom tomatoes there are in the world, but I know there are some excellent ones available here in Northern California (some practically grow like weeds!). Among my favorites are Brandywine, Green Grape, zebra varieties, currant types (which come in tiny clusters), and Sweet 100. There are also variegated yellow, orange, and red tomatoes, yellow-orange fig or pear tomatoes, and German White. . . . They all add to the fun of making tomato vinaigrettes and sauces. For more information on heirlooms, I recommend William Woys Weaver's excellent book *Heirloom Vegetable Gardening*.

To make the risotto, heat the olive oil and butter in a sauté pan over medium low heat. Add the shallots and sweat until tender, making sure you don't brown them. Toss in the garlic and mushrooms and increase the heat. Cook, stirring, until all the moisture has evaporated and the mushrooms are beginning to caramelize. Add the rice and cook for 3 minutes, stirring, until all the grains are coated with oil. Pour in the white wine and cook until the pan is dry. Add a bit of the stock and cook, stirring, until it is absorbed. Continue adding stock a little at a time, stirring and cooking until all the moisture is absorbed after each addition. When the mixture starts to bubble and squeak, it's telling you to add more. Repeat until the rice grains are just al dente and all the moisture is absorbed. (The risotto needs to be quite dry for making the *arancini*.) Season with salt and pepper and stir in the Parmigiano and pecorino cheeses. Taste for salt, adding more if necessary. Allow to cool completely (ideally overnight), or the risotto will be difficult to handle.

If you are going for the mozzarella center, cut the mozzarella into 12 small cubes. Wet your hands, take a walnut-size portion of risotto, and flatten it into a circle in the palm of your hand. Place a cube of mozzarella in the center and fold the rice around it. If you're omitting the cheese, just roll the risotto into small balls. You could also make larger balls—egg-size, perhaps—with larger cubes of cheese at the center. Or you could simply form the risotto into flat cakes. I often make soupspoon-size ovals to get a higher ratio of crispy outsides to creamy insides. Whatever shape or size you decide on, finish forming the fritters by putting a little indentation in the top of each one to hold sauce—as if you were making thumbprint cookies to hold a bit of jam. Refrigerate again, to chill thoroughly, 1 to 1 1/2 hours.

When you're ready to go on to the next step, whisk together 1 egg and the water in a shallow bowl, and set out the flour and *panko*. Roll the risotto balls in the flour, patting them gently between your hands to remove the excess flour, then dip them in the egg wash and drain them well. Next, roll them in the *panko*, pressing gently to get good coverage and, again, patting

(continued)

them gently between your hands to knock off the excess. Mix up another batch of egg wash if necessary. Put the *arancini* back in the refrigerator to set, about 10 minutes.

***To fry the* arancini**, heat about 1 inch of oil to 375°F in a wide cast-iron or other heavy-bottomed pan. You need enough oil to submerge the *arancini* at least halfway. Carefully add just enough risotto balls to fill the pan without overcrowding. Cook, turning, until golden and crispy on all sides. As they finish, transfer them to paper towels or a wire rack to drain. Keep in a warm oven until needed. If you need to fry a second batch, skim out any bits and make sure the oil is at the right temperature before going ahead. If you prefer, you can deep-fry the *arancini*, in which case you'll need to heat up additional oil and use a slotted spoon, strainer, or spider to keep them submerged while they're cooking.

Make the tomato sauce shortly before you are ready to serve. Simply put all the ingredients in a bowl and stir to combine. To serve, spoon sauce into the dents in the *arancini*, and sprinkle the remaining basil about.

Hard-Boiled Eggs with Green Garlic Cream

Serves 6

6 large eggs

3 to 4 bulbs green garlic

1 tablespoon butter

½ to ¾ cup whipping cream

Salt

¼ teaspoon freshly ground black pepper, plus additional for garnish

This is a great, warm two-bite delight of spring. Green garlic begins showing up in farmers' markets around February here in Northern California. It looks like baby leeks or mature scallions and is much milder than regular garlic. Like leeks, spring garlic needs to be rinsed well. When green garlic is not available, you can substitute baby leeks or scallions, or a smaller amount of regular garlic. When it is very young you use the whole bulb, moist, tender skin and all.

I usually plan on a whole egg per person, but these little guys are rich, so if you have a lot on the menu, half an egg per

person would be plenty. The sauce is also great over poached eggs for a variation on the traditional eggs Benedict.

Hard-boil the eggs per the instructions on page 33.

Prepare the sauce while the eggs are cooking. Remove 1 or 2 outer layers of the green garlic heads and split them all length-wise (it's okay to use a bit of the stalk nearest the bulb). Rinse really well, as they can be sandy, and mince crosswise into fine pieces. Melt the butter over medium heat and sauté the garlic till tender, 1 to 2 minutes. Add the cream and season with the salt to taste and the $^1/_4$ teaspoon pepper. Increase the heat to medium-high and continue cooking 1 or 2 minutes, stirring, until the cream is reduced to a thick, silky, spoonable consistency.

When the eggs are done, remove them from the heat and run cold water over them until they are just cool enough to handle, but still warm. Shell and split them in half lengthwise, then arrange them on individual plates or on an egg platter, cut side up. Top each half with a dollop of the cream and sprinkle with additional freshly ground black pepper.

pictured on page 42

3 or 4 large artichokes

poaching liquid

3 quarts water

2 cups white wine

¼ cup freshly squeezed lemon juice

1 small onion, diced

1 or 2 bay leaves

5 peppercorns

3 coriander seeds

3 cloves garlic

2 tablespoons salt

tarragon-basil dipping sauce

1½ cups sour cream

½ cup mayonnaise

1½ teaspoons freshly squeezed lemon juice

¼ bunch fresh tarragon, leaves finely chopped

Salt and freshly ground black pepper

⅓ bunch basil, leaves only

1 small clove garlic

2 tablespoons olive oil

2 tablespoons olive oil

2 tablespoons butter

3 or 4 lemons, halved

Salt and freshly ground black pepper

Roasted Artichokes with Tarragon-Basil Dipping Sauce

Serves 6 to 8

The secret trick to this dish is to roast lemons along with the artichokes. As they roast together, the volatile oils in the lemon peel permeate the chokes, and the result is very tasty. After trying out this recipe, my niece Aimee wrote, "It was refreshing to have a different way to serve artichokes. We love them so much that sometimes they are our main course for dinner. I always thought . . . [artichokes] were just a vehicle for butter. I was wrong because they are fabulous this way too." People come back to the restaurant over and over again especially for these artichokes!

Use large artichokes for this, four to four and a half inches across, with meaty, creamy hearts, and count on half an artichoke per person. For a tiny treat, you could also make this with small, young loose chokes. These will need less trimming, as their leaves will not have developed spiny tips yet. Be sure to reduce the cooking time on the smaller artichokes.

If you have any leftover Tarragon-Basil Dipping Sauce, it's great on sandwiches, and spectacular on tuna salad. The Creamy Cilantro-Garlic Dip (page 22) also goes well with these artichokes.

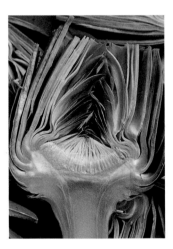

Cut off the top inch of each artichoke, and snip any remaining pointy ends off the leaves. Cut the stalks off about 1 inch from the bottom of the artichoke. Put all the poaching liquid ingredients in a large pot and bring to a boil. Add the artichokes, bring the water back to a boil, and immediately reduce to a simmer. Cook until the artichokes are tender at the heart, 30 to 45 minutes (gently poke them with a fork to test for doneness). Remove them from the water, and turn them upside down to drain and cool. When cool to the touch, cut them in half from top to bottom; scoop out and discard the feathery chokes. Preparation can be done to this point up to 24 hours ahead.

For the dipping sauce, mix the sour cream, mayonnaise, lemon juice, tarragon, salt, and pepper together in a medium-size bowl and set aside. Put the basil, garlic, and olive oil in a food processor or blender and puree until the mixture is very thick and creamy, similar in texture to a pesto. Combine the puree with the sour cream–mayonnaise mixture and mix thoroughly. Cover and refrigerate until needed.

About 20 minutes before serving, preheat the oven to 500°F. Heat the 2 tablespoons of olive oil and the butter in a large ovenproof sauté pan until hot. Add the lemons, cut side down, and the artichokes, cut side up, and cook 1 minute, moving the artichokes around the pan to get their outer leaves nicely coated with oil. Season with salt and pepper. Flip the artichokes over and cook until golden brown, 2 to 3 minutes. Place the pan in the oven to roast 8 to 10 minutes, until the artichokes are caramelized. Have your guests squeeze the roasted lemon over the artichokes, and serve hot with individual ramekins of the dipping sauce.

Roasted Artichokes (page 40)

Use large
artichokes
for this . . .

spice mix

spice mix

½ teaspoon coriander seeds

⅛ teaspoon black peppercorns

⅛ teaspoon dried thyme

⅛ teaspoon dried rosemary

1 bay leaf, crumbled

2 tablespoons sea salt

⅛ teaspoon cayenne pepper

apple balsamic vinaigrette

¼ cup apple balsamic vinegar

1½ teaspoons Dijon mustard

¼ to ½ teaspoon salt

Pinch of freshly ground black pepper

1½ teaspoons minced shallots

¾ teaspoon minced fresh thyme

¾ teaspoon minced garlic

¾ cup olive oil

¼ cup extra virgin olive oil

12 asparagus spears

Additional olive oil, for coating

Salt and freshly ground black pepper

18 ounces ahi tuna, cut into 12 cubes

2 tablespoons minced fresh parsley

Spiced Ahi Tuna Sticks, New Year's Eve

Serves 6 as a small plate, 12 as an hors d'oeuvre

This delicious combination of tuna and asparagus was on the menu at Mustards for our 2002 New Year's Eve celebration. It works both as a small plate and as an hors d'oeuvre. For hors d'oeuvres, cut off the asparagus tips and thread them onto skewers with the tuna (one piece of tuna and two asparagus tips per skewer). Served as a small plate, only the tuna goes on skewers, and the asparagus spears are left whole.

The spice mix in this recipe was developed especially for the tuna, but it works just as well on swordfish, mahi mahi, shark, ono, and other fish with a high fat content. Actually, it goes with just about any fish that's going on the grill. It's good on duck, squab, quail, and turkey, too. Or try it on chicken breast meat for a great Mediterranean-style satay. For a twist on your basic fried chicken, add a little of the spice mix to your coating.

If you can't find apple balsamic vinegar for the vinai-grette, you can use regular balsamic vinegar and add a splash of apple juice.

Short flat skewers are best for this dish. You'll need twelve for hors d'oeuvres, six if you're doing small plates.

Preheat the grill.

Soak the skewers in enough water to cover at least thirty minutes.

To make the spice mix, combine the coriander seeds and black peppercorns in a spice or coffee grinder and grind coarsely. Add the thyme, rosemary, bay leaf, salt, and pepper, and grind finely. Reserve until needed.

For the vinaigrette, combine the vinegar, mustard, salt, pepper, shallots, thyme, and garlic in a large bowl, and mix well. Drizzle in the olive oils in a slow steady stream, whisking as you go. Continue whisking until well emulsified. Reserve until needed.

To prepare the asparagus, snap off the tough ends (they will naturally break off where the tender part begins). If you are making hors d'oeuvres, cut the tips off the asparagus (save the rest for soup), coat with olive oil, sprinkle with salt and pepper, and marinate for 30 minutes to 1 hour. If you are going to serve this as a small plate, follow the same procedure but leave the spears whole.

If you're making this for an hors d'oeuvre, make the skewers with 1 piece of tuna sandwiched between 2 crosswise asparagus tips. For a small plate, thread only the tuna onto the skewers, 2 pieces per skewer. Dust with $1^1/_2$ to 2 teaspoons of the spice mix, then brush with some oil.

To finish for a passed hors d'oeuvre, grill the skewers so that the tuna is seared and caramelized on the outside but still rare inside and the asparagus tips are just barely cooked, 1 to $1^1/_2$ minutes per side. Drizzle with some of the vinaigrette, sprinkle lightly with additional spice mix and parsley, and serve.

To finish for the small-plate version, grill the asparagus spears till just al dente, then move them to the outside of the grill to keep them warm while you cook the tuna. Grill the tuna over high heat. Rotating a quarter turn halfway through cooking on each side will give you nice crosshatch grill marks. Cut the asparagus into thin diagonal strips, and dress it with the vinaigrette. Arrange piles of asparagus on each plate, and place the tuna on top of the asparagus nests. Lightly drizzle with vinaigrette and sprinkle with the remaining spice mix and the parsley.

1 jalapeño chile, stemmed,
    seeded, and minced

½ cup freshly squeezed lime
    juice

¾ teaspoon soy sauce

¼ bunch cilantro, leaves and
    tender stems only, minced

1 tablespoon sugar

Pinch of salt

Freshly ground black pepper

fritters

2 cups cake flour

½ tablespoon sugar

¾ teaspoon baking powder

1¾ teaspoons baking soda

1¾ teaspoons turmeric

1½ teaspoons salt

¾ teaspoon freshly ground black
    pepper

2 cups water

2 cups grated peeled sweet
    potatoes or yams

1 cup sweet corn kernels, freshly
    cut off the cob

½ pound fresh Dungeness or
    blue crabmeat (1 cup)

Peanut or vegetable oil, for frying

Lime wedges, for garnish

Dungeness Crab–Sweet Potato–Corn Fritters

Serves 6 generously

These fritters are a very loose interpretation of an Indonesian snack made with sweet potatoes, corn, and shrimp. I like to use Dungeness crabmeat in it, but blue crab is excellent, too. Whichever you use, just be sure it is as fresh as can be. Or you could try it with chopped shrimp or lobster in place of the crab. Two small ears of corn should do it for the corn. Figure about three to five fritters for each guest, as they are petite.

When you make the fritters, coat your spoon with a little oil before scooping them out, and the batter will slide off the spoon easily. Always work away from yourself when transferring the batter to the hot oil. The fritters will be a beautiful golden brown with streaks of orange, which are the strips of sweet potato.

To make the dip, put all the ingredients in a small bowl and mix together thoroughly. This can be done up to 2 hours before serving. Be sure to stir it well before serving.

For the fritter batter, combine the flour, sugar, baking powder, baking soda, turmeric, salt, and pepper in a large bowl. Whisk in the water and stir until smooth. Stir in the sweet potatoes, corn, and crab.

To make the fritters, heat 1 inch of oil to 375°F in a wide cast-iron or other heavy-bottomed pan. Carefully scoop 1 tablespoonful of batter at a time into the hot oil. Take care not to overcrowd the pan: the fritters should not be touching. Fry 3 to 4 minutes, turning them halfway through, until the fritters are golden brown on both sides. When they are done, remove them to a metal rack or to paper towels to drain. Keep them in a warm oven while you fry up the rest. Skim out any bits of batter, and allow the oil to come back to 375°F before cooking each new batch.

Serve with the Jalapeño Chile–Lime Dip (remember to give it a stir) and wedges of lime on the side.

Pablo's Boquerones

Serves 6

1/3 cup finely sliced plump sun-dried tomatoes

1/2 cup finely shaved or julienned fennel bulb

1 to 2 tablespoons torn fennel fronds

1 tablespoon aged Spanish sherry vinegar

Tiny pinch of salt (remember that the fish are salty)

Freshly ground black pepper

3 tablespoons Spanish extra virgin olive oil

18 to 30 *boquerones* (fillets of white anchovy)

1/3 cup tiny croutons (1/4-inch dice; optional)

1 shallot, minced, or cut into thin circles and separated

1 or 2 *piquillo* peppers, finely sliced, or 1/2 cup finely sliced roasted red bell pepper

1 tablespoon minced fresh thyme leaves

Boquerones are another simple but delicious food treat from Spain. They are white anchovies that have been cured in vinegar instead of salt, so they are more like a ceviche. Good delis and fish markets here in the States carry them or should be able to order them for you. Mail order is another possibility. We get them from our fish supplier. Like the seafood in a ceviche, boquerones are perishable and must be kept refrigerated.

In this dish, the boquerones are dressed up with sun-dried tomatoes and fennel. If you're serving them as a small plate, I would recommend five per person; as an hors d'oeuvre, three per person should do it. Serve with nice, crusty bread to mop up the delicious dressing.

Combine the sun-dried tomatoes and the fennel bulb and fronds in a small bowl; set it aside. To make a dressing, combine the vinegar, salt, and pepper in another small bowl, stir until the salt has dissolved, then gradually whisk in the oil. Set this aside, too.

When you are ready to serve, place 3 to 5 *boquerones* around each small plate. Lightly dress the sun-dried tomatoes and fennel with vinaigrette and sprinkle them over the anchovies so the anchovies still show. Over that go the croutons if you are using them, shallot, *piquillos*, and thyme. Finish with a drizzle of the remaining dressing and a few grindings of black pepper.

piquillo vinaigrette

¼ cup sherry vinegar

3 tablespoons dry sherry

¾ teaspoon salt

¼ teaspoon freshly ground black
    pepper

2 shallots, thinly sliced

2 cloves garlic, thinly sliced

1 cup extra virgin olive oil

1 cup julienned *piquillo* peppers;
    or red or yellow bell peppers,
    roasted, peeled, and seeded

18 large (16 to 20 count) prawns

¼ teaspoon salt

½ teaspoon freshly ground black
    pepper, plus additional for
    serving

9 paper-thin slices of Serrano
    ham or prosciutto

3 tablespoons olive oil

3 cups living watercress,
    trimmed of roots

Serrano Ham– Wrapped Prawns with Piquillo Vinaigrette and Living Watercress

Serves 6

To my mind, Serrano ham is the best of the best, better even than prosciutto. I was introduced to Serrano ham on my first trip to Spain, and it was a mind-blowing experience. Like prosciutto, Serrano ham is salt-cured, but there is something about the Spanish curing process that produces a ham that is leaner, firmer, and more flavorful. Or it may have more to do with the feed the hogs are given (acorns, I've been told), which results in a rich, nutty taste. At one time, Serrano ham could not be imported, but that has changed, and now you can get it at specialty markets here. As with prosciutto, there are many different producers, so you need to "taste around" before buying.

Living watercress is a product available here in Northern California. It's a bit lighter in color and less spicy than regular watercress, but still very flavorful, and its delicate stem is 100 percent edible. This cress is grown hydroponically, and it comes with the roots on. If you can't find living watercress, any variety of cress will do. I like ancho cress, with its clean, peppery taste. Curly cress is good too. Cress makes a great addition to just about any small plate or salad, both for the body it gives and for its flavor. It is also a good palate cleanser, something you could keep in mind when offering a series of small plates.

Be careful about adding salt, as both Serrano ham and prosciutto are usually quite salty.

Soak 6 bamboo skewers in water at least 30 minutes.

To make the vinaigrette, combine the vinegar, sherry, salt, pepper, shallots, and garlic, and mix until the salt has dissolved. Whisk in the olive oil and stir in the *piquillos*.

For the skewers, peel the prawns three-quarters of the way down, leaving the tail section intact. Remove the veins and season the prawns with the salt and pepper. Cut the slices of ham in half vertically and wrap a piece of ham around each prawn. Bending the prawns along their natural curve, thread 3 prawns onto each skewer, pushing the skewer in near the tail and out near the head section of each prawn and securing the ham in place at the same time. The skewers can be prepared several hours ahead and refrigerated until you are ready to cook them.

To cook, coat the skewered prawns well with the olive oil and grill over a medium-high wood or charcoal fire, 2 to 2¹/₂ minutes per side. The prawns will firm up and become pink when they're done. Toss the cress with just enough of the vinaigrette to coat all the leaves nicely. Divide the salad among 6 small plates and season with pepper. Arrange 3 prawns around each salad and dress with the remaining vinaigrette.

Thai-Style Fish Cakes
with Erasto's Nuoc Cham
and Sriracha Sauce
(page 54)

pictured on pages 52–53

erasto's nuoc cham

¼ cup rice vinegar

6 tablespoons freshly squeezed lime juice

½ cup fish sauce

½ cup water

¼ cup sugar

1 tablespoon minced peeled fresh ginger

1 tablespoon red chile–garlic sauce

¼ cup peeled and finely julienned daikon

¼ cup peeled and finely julienned carrot

1 to 2 tablespoons fresh spearmint leaves, julienned or, if small, left whole

fish cakes

1 pound salmon, halibut, cod, or snapper

4 ounces pencil-thin asparagus, *haricots verts*, or other green beans

1 stalk lemongrass

4 shallots, minced

1-inch piece fresh ginger, peeled and minced

3 to 4 tablespoons minced cilantro leaves

2 cloves garlic, minced

2 kaffir or other lime leaves, sliced, or 3 or 4 gratings of lemon or lime zest

1½ teaspoons sugar

1½ teaspoons fish sauce

Pinch of salt

Pinch of freshly ground black pepper

Thai-Style Fish Cakes with Erasto's Nuoc Cham and Sriracha Sauce

Serves 6 to 8

Just about every Vietnamese family and every Vietnamese restaurant has its own version of nuoc cham, *which is a fish sauce–based dipping sauce (*nuoc mam, *the fish sauce, being the one essential ingredient). I love the combination of the sweet and salty from Erasto's Nuoc Cham with the hot and spicy of the sriracha sauce in this dish. In Southeast Asia, sriracha sauce is as common as ketchup; here in the States, you'll always find it on the table at noodle shops and fast-food restaurants that feature Southeast Asian food, and it's as easy to find in our local markets as soy sauce. The Huy Fong brand with the rooster on the squeeze bottle is everywhere. They also make the chile-garlic paste we use in the* nuoc cham, *but you can use any hot red chile sauce you have. I'm especially fond of* sriracha *because it contains no shrimp paste—a wonderful thing for a person with a deadly shellfish allergy.*

Typically, Thai fish cakes are made with green beans, but Erasto works with whatever's fresh, tasty, and handy, so when it's asparagus season, in they go, and later in the summer he'll use green beans or haricots verts. If you have to use chunkier asparagus, as opposed to the pencil-thin asparagus called for, just make sure you halve the spears lengthwise before slicing them up. If they are really fat, you might even have to quarter them.

Peanut, olive, or vegetable oil,
  for coating
1 pound spinach, cut into a fine
  chiffonade
Sriracha sauce
2 or 3 Key limes if you can get
  them (or 1 or 2 Persian limes),
  completely peeled and
  segmented

To make the nuoc cham, combine all the ingredients and mix well. It's that simple. Cover and refrigerate till needed.

For the fish cakes, roughly cut the fish into $1/2$-inch pieces; cover and refrigerate until needed. Snap off the ends of the asparagus and discard. Cut the asparagus into $1/8$-inch-thick rounds. Get a small pot of water boiling, add the asparagus, and blanch 30 seconds to 1 minute. Be careful not to overcook, as you want a little firmness left in the asparagus. Drain and immediately plunge into ice water to stop the cooking process. When cold, drain and dry with paper towels. Peel off the outer layers of the lemongrass and cut off the bottom 3 inches of the bulb end. Mince this and put it in a large stainless steel or ceramic bowl, along with the shallots, ginger, cilantro, garlic, lime leaves, sugar, and fish sauce; mix thoroughly. Put this mixture in the fridge to chill 30 minutes, and take the fish out. Pulse small batches of the fish chunks in a food processor or chop it by hand. You want very fine pieces but not a puree. It's very important to do this in small batches so the fish is cut cleanly and is not turned into a paste, which would result in tough fish cakes. When the 30 minutes are up, remove the shallot-ginger mixture from the refrigerator and add the asparagus and fish to the bowl, along with a sprinkle of salt and pepper. Gently combine all, being careful not to overmix. Form 18 fish cakes, each about $1/2$ inch thick and $1 1/2$ inches across. The fish cakes can be held at this point: cover them well and refrigerate until needed.

To cook the fish cakes, brush both sides of the cakes with oil and grill for $1 1/2$ to 2 minutes per side until nicely caramelized. You can also panfry them in a nonstick skillet, 3 to 5 minutes each side, until golden brown and cooked through. Serve the patties on a bed of the spinach, topped with a dollop of the *sriracha* sauce. Set out a bowl of Erasto's Nuoc Cham and the lime segments on the side.

tortilla dough

2 cups all-purpose flour

1 teaspoon salt

½ teaspoon baking powder

½ cup chilled butter, cut into small pieces

½ cup cold water

6 to 8 ounces *queso Oaxaca*, or mozzarella or Monterey Jack cheese

12 to 24 squash blossoms (the more the better)

2 *pasilla* or other medium-hot chiles, roasted, peeled, and chopped

6 fresh epazote leaves, julienned (optional)

Cindy's Backstreet Tomatillo-Avocado Salsa (page 207)

Cilantro leaves, for garnish

Squash Blossom Quesadillas with Homemade Tortillas and Queso Oaxaca

Serves 6

I wrote about quesadillas at some length in my Fog City Diner Cookbook, but I decided to expand on the quesadilla theme a little here. For those of you who haven't tried them, a quesadilla could best be described as a hot flour tortilla sandwich. The filling can be almost anything, but less is best! No more than three ingredients, and one of them has to be cheese. In this recipe, we use squash blossoms, pasilla chiles, and a special Mexican string cheese called queso Oaxaca.

Homemade flour tortillas are not that hard to make, and they are really worth the effort. Just try them once and you'll see. When rolling out the dough, a marble surface would be ideal, but if you don't have that, make sure you roll on something smooth and clean. It's best to fill the quesadillas when the tortillas are fresh off the griddle. At that point, you can stack them between pieces of parchment or waxed paper, wrap up the whole stack, and refrigerate it till you are ready to serve.

Queso Oaxaca (the name just means "Oaxacan cheese") is mellow, rich, and creamy, like a whole-milk mozzarella, Monterey Jack, and string cheese all in one. Many different cheesemakers in Oaxaca produce this cheese, and each one is slightly different. Though there are other sources, we order ours from the Mozzarella Company in Dallas, which is run by my friend Paula Lambert. In my opinion, she makes the best-quality queso Oaxaca in the United States. If you can't find queso Oaxaca, get a moist, fresh whole-milk mozzarella or good-quality Monterey Jack. Avoid any overprocessed string cheese or nonfat mozzarellas.

Oh, and when shredding squash blossoms, watch out for ants. They love the nectar!

On one of my many trips to Mexico, we went to a farm where we were shown how to make *queso Oaxaca*. The cheesemaker kept a salted veal stomach on the roof of his shed, and would cut a small piece for each batch of cheese to "set" the curd. We asked him, Why on the roof? Did it need to be sun-dried? He said, No, it kept the dogs off it. Paula's cheeses are a lot more hygienic.

To make the tortilla dough, combine the flour, salt, and baking powder in a mixing bowl. Cut the butter into the flour with a pastry blender or 2 knives, as if you were making pie dough, until you have fairly uniform pea-size pieces. Add the water all at once, and mix until just combined. Do not overmix. Turn the dough out onto a lightly floured surface and roll into a 2-inch-diameter log. The dough can now be covered and refrigerated until needed, or you can go on to the next step.

When you are ready to roll out the tortillas, cut the dough log into 12 equal pieces and roll each out very thinly on a smooth, lightly floured surface. If you want perfectly round tortillas, use a 4-inch plate as a template: place it over each tortilla and trim away the excess dough. Stack the tortillas up, placing a sheet of waxed paper or sprinkling a bit of flour between each to keep them from sticking together.

To cook the tortillas, heat an ungreased griddle or cast-iron pan over medium heat. Cook each tortilla until the flour no longer looks raw and light brown spots appear. This could take as little as 30 seconds to 1 minute per side, depending on how hot the pan is and how thick the tortillas are. As they finish, stack the tortillas on a plate with a tea towel over them to keep them warm.

Prepare the fillings next, putting them on separate plates. If you are using *queso Oaxaca* or pullable mozzarella, pull the cheese apart and cut it into 2-inch lengths. Other kinds of cheese should be grated. Shred the squash blossoms into $1/4$-inch strips.

To assemble the quesadillas, sprinkle some of the cheese, squash blossoms, chiles, and epazote, if desired, evenly across

(continued)

1 tortilla, then top with a second tortilla. Press gently so the quesadilla holds together. Continue with the remaining tortillas. You should fill the quesadillas while the tortillas are still hot, but the quesadillas can then be held again after they are filled. Stack them between pieces of parchment or waxed paper, cover with plastic wrap, and refrigerate until needed. Or you can proceed with the final cooking.

To finish the tortillas, heat an ungreased griddle or flat-bottomed pan—the thicker the better—over medium heat. Using a wide spatula, slide the quesadillas onto the cooking surface and cook on 1 side until golden brown and crisp; turn and cook until the cheese is melted and the quesadillas are nicely browned on both sides.

As the quesadillas finish, slide them from the pan onto a cutting board and cut into the desired number of pieces (I usually cut into sixths or eighths). Transfer to serving plates, put a dollop of salsa off to the side, and sprinkle cilantro leaves around.

dipping sauce

1 tablespoon rice vinegar

2 tablespoons ketchup

2 to 3 tablespoons *ketjap manis*

filling

1 tablespoon regular sesame oil

3 medium shiitake mushrooms, stemmed and very thinly sliced

2 cups very finely shredded Napa cabbage

3 scallions, white and light green parts only, thinly sliced on the diagonal

3 to 4 inches of daikon, peeled and julienned

1 tablespoon minced peeled fresh ginger

2 cloves garlic, minced

1 red Fresno chile or other hot chile, stemmed, seeded, and julienned

½ cup coarsely chopped cilantro leaves and tender stems

1 tablespoon rice vinegar

2 tablespoons *ketjap manis* or dark soy sauce

12 to 18 pencil-thin or medium asparagus spears

1 large egg

1 tablespoon water

6 *lumpia* or egg-roll wrappers

Cornstarch, for dusting

Peanut or vegetable oil, for frying

Chinese-Style Mustard Sauce (page 228)

Asparagus and Shiitake Spring Rolls

Serves 6

The best wrappers to use for these deep-fried rolls are the very thin egg-roll wrappers used for making lumpia, *the Filipino-style spring rolls. You can find fresh or frozen* lumpia *or egg-roll wrappers at most Asian markets. These wrappers are about eight inches square, somewhat bigger than wonton skins. If you can find it, get the Menlo brand: it's my favorite because it crisps up so nice. Make sure you keep the egg-roll skins covered with plastic wrap or a damp towel while working with them, otherwise they will dry out. Ketjap manis is an Indonesian soy sauce—dark and a little sweet. You should be able to find it at the same store you find the* lumpia *wrappers, but if you can't, you can substitute a mixture of two parts tamari and one part molasses.*

It's very important that these spring rolls be served while still hot. You can make them up ahead of time, but don't fry them until the last minute.

To make the sauce, combine the rice vinegar, ketchup, and *ketjap manis* in a small bowl. Mix well and reserve until needed.

For the filling, heat the sesame oil over medium-high heat and quickly sauté the mushrooms until lightly caramelized on the edges. Remove from the heat and allow to cool. Combine the Napa cabbage, scallions, daikon, ginger, garlic, chile, cilantro, rice vinegar, and *ketjap manis* in a large mixing bowl. When the mushrooms are cool to the touch, stir them in as well. Set the filling aside until needed.

(continued)

To prepare the asparagus, snap off and discard the tough ends. Blanch the spears 30 seconds to 1 minute, then plunge into ice water until chilled. Drain and cut into 3-inch lengths, and if you're using medium-size asparagus, cut each piece in half lengthwise. Pencil-thin asparagus will be fine as is.

To assemble the spring rolls, mix the egg with the water in a small bowl to make an egg wash. Lay out a wrapper so it is oriented as a diamond in front of you and paint its surface with some egg wash. Place about 2 tablespoonfuls of the mushroom mixture in the center, leaving space on all sides for wrapping. Lay some of the asparagus on top sideways, alternating the direction of the tips so you have some tips at each end. Bring the bottom of the wrapper up over the filling, folding it almost in half. Brush the sides with additional egg wash and fold the sides in. Brush the top of the wrapper and finish by rolling from the bottom up to the top point, being sure to get a good seal. The roll should be about 6 inches long and 1 inch around. Place the finished rolls on a baking sheet that has been dusted with cornstarch, and cover with a towel until all are ready. The spring rolls can be held at this point for a couple of hours and fried later. Dust the tops with cornstarch, cover with plastic wrap, and refrigerate. If you have to stack them up, separate the layers with plastic wrap or parchment paper; they should not touch.

To fry the rolls, heat 3 inches of oil to 375°F in a deep, heavy-bottomed pan. Shake excess cornstarch off the spring rolls, then carefully lower them into the oil. Top them with a basket, strainer, or spider to keep them submerged. (Whichever device you use will get very hot, so use caution.) Cook for 2 to 3 minutes, until crisp and golden brown. Do not overcrowd the pan: if necessary, fry the spring rolls in 2 or 3 batches. As they finish, transfer them to a wire rack or to paper towels to drain.

Serve the spring rolls while still hot with little bowls of the dipping sauce and the mustard sauce. For a cocktail party, cut the spring rolls into bite-size chunks and arrange them on a platter. Drizzle with small amounts of the two sauces, and serve with cocktail napkins. It's too hard to dip if you are standing, chatting, and holding a cocktail.

pictured on page 63

Salt Cod Cakes with Aioli

Serves 6

In today's world of refrigerators and freezers and fresh seafood shipped by overnight express worldwide, salt cod seems like some oddball thing from the past. It's still very popular in Europe, but there's not a lot of call for salt cod in the States. This mainstay of the early explorers and New England settlers fell out of favor in the United States long ago. But here I am putting in a good word for this wonderful foodstuff. I love its salty, rich taste (better even than crab), and the versatility of it. It's great in fish cakes, stews, stuffings, and salads, to name just a few uses. If that testimonial doesn't inspire you, read Mark Kurlansky's great book Cod: A Biography of the Fish That Changed the World. *Then run out and buy some salt cod.*

Salt cod needs a good twenty-four-hour soak in clear water to reduce the saltiness. It is then poached in milk or water, or—my preference—a combination of water and milk that has been enhanced with vegetables and herbs. I think this adds an extra dimension to the flavor of the fish. Once the fish has been poached, you can flake it and mix it with the other ingredients to make the cod cakes. I use baked potatoes as a binder, but the trick here is to flake the potato flesh while it is still hot, otherwise it will get gooey. Cut the potatoes in half; using a towel for protection, pick up the hot potato halves and flake them with a fork.

You could make the salt cod patties up to a day ahead, and refrigerate them until needed. Just don't bread them more than a few hours before frying them, or the crust will get soggy. As an alternative to deep-frying, the cakes could be panfried in a mixture of equal amounts butter and olive oil. The aioli could be replaced by a good-quality mayonnaise if you are short on

(continued on page 64)

I love the salty, rich taste of the cod (better even than crab), and the versatility of it.

Salt Cod Cakes
with Aioli
(page 61)

1 pound salt cod fillets

poaching liquid

1 quart water

1 cup milk

½ small onion

½ jalapeño or Fresno chile, seeded if you wish

2 cloves garlic

1 sprig thyme

1 bay leaf

1 slice peeled fresh ginger

5 whole peppercorns

aioli

2 large egg yolks

1 tablespoon freshly squeezed lemon juice

4 cloves garlic, sliced

1 teaspoon cold water

¼ to ½ teaspoon salt

1 cup pure olive oil

¼ cup extra virgin olive oil

time, or if you're concerned about using raw eggs. Just stir in three or four cloves of smashed garlic for flavoring. For a winter sauce and garnish variation, try this with the Saffron Cream Sauce (page 282) and minced fresh parsley.

Soak the salt cod for 24 hours in at least 3 or 4 changes of water (more if you think of it—be liberal with the soaking). Rinse very well before you start the poaching step.

Combine all the poaching liquid ingredients in a large pot and bring to a boil. Reduce to a strong simmer and cook for 15 to 20 minutes, until flavorful and aromatic. If you wish, you can strain the liquid at this point, though this is not really necessary. Add the salt cod and simmer until it is tender but not mushy and flakes easily, 15 to 20 minutes. Scoop out the fish and allow it to cool, then flake the fish into a bowl, picking out any bones and skin. Set the fish aside.

For the aioli, lightly beat the egg yolks together with the lemon juice in a medium-size bowl. Mash the garlic to a smooth paste with a pinch of salt. Set aside one-fourth of the paste and add the rest to the egg-yolk mixture, along with the cold water and ¹/₄ teaspoon of salt, and stir. Gradually whisk in the oils, and continue whisking until the aioli is thick and creamy. Taste, then fold in the remaining garlic paste and/or add additional salt if needed. Refrigerate until needed. You could make the aioli in a blender or food processor, if you prefer.

To prepare the cod cakes, preheat the oven to 350°F. Prick the potatoes several times with a fork, and bake them for 50 to 60 minutes, until fork-tender in the center. You can continue with other parts of the preparation, but as soon as the potatoes are done, stop whatever you're doing and remove them from the oven. Cut them immediately, and press the ends together to open them so they don't steam up and get mushy. Flake them into a medium-size bowl while they're still hot, and set aside.

cod cakes

2 large Yukon Gold potatoes

1 tablespoon olive oil

½ small onion, minced

½ teaspoon minced garlic

¼ cup finely minced celery heart and leaves

½ jalapeño chile, seeded and minced

1 to 1½ teaspoons minced fresh tarragon

2 tablespoons minced fresh parsley

1 scallion, white and light green parts only, minced

1 or 2 shakes of cayenne pepper

⅛ teaspoon salt

¼ teaspoon freshly ground black pepper

1 large egg

1 tablespoon water

1 cup flour

1½ to 2 cups *panko* or fine bread crumbs

Peanut or vegetable oil, for frying

1 cup watercress, coarse stems trimmed

1 cup arugula

Radishes sliced very thinly on a mandoline

½ lemon or lime

Extra virgin olive oil, for drizzling

Salt and freshly ground black pepper

Cindy's Backstreet Tomatillo-Avocado Salsa (page 207)

Heat the olive oil in a small sauté pan over low heat. Add the onion and garlic and slowly sweat until just tender, 3 to 4 minutes, being careful not to caramelize them. Allow them to cool, then add them to the bowl of potatoes, along with the celery, minced jalapeño, tarragon, parsley, scallion, cayenne, salt, pepper, and ¼ cup of the aioli. Using a fork, mix thoroughly but gently. Add the flaked cod and give it a final gentle mixing, taking care not to break up the cod any further. Form the cod mixture into 6 balls, using about ¼ cup per ball. Chill well.

When you are ready to cook the cakes, mix the egg and water together to make an egg wash. Arrange a breading area, with the egg wash set between a small plate of flour and a small plate of panko. Using your hands, flatten the cod balls into cakes about 2 inches in diameter and ¾ inch thick. Dip the cakes into the flour, then the egg, then the *panko*, shaking off excess flour and *panko* as you go.

Pour the oil to a depth of 1 inch in a deep, heavy-bottomed saucepan and heat it to 375°F. Carefully add just enough cakes to fill the pan without overcrowding. Cook about 2 minutes on each side until golden and crispy, turning them once halfway through the cooking. As the cakes finish, transfer them to paper towels or a wire rack to drain. Keep in a warm oven until needed. Before cooking the next batch, skim out any bits left in the pan, and make sure the oil is at 375°F before going ahead. Continue until all the cod cakes have been fried.

For the salad, combine the watercress, arugula, and radishes in a bowl. Squeeze in some lemon juice, drizzle with olive oil, and toss lightly. Season with salt and pepper. To serve, arrange the salad on plates, place cod cakes on the salad, and top with a couple spoonfuls of the tomatillo-avocado salsa, and garnish with the remaining aioli. You can thin the aioli with a drizzle of water, if necessary.

champagne vinaigrette

1 tablespoon champagne vinegar

3 tablespoons extra virgin
olive oil

1 to 2 tablespoons finely
chopped fresh dill weed,
fennel fronds, or chives

Salt and freshly ground black
pepper

1 tablespoon sesame seeds

1 tablespoon yellow mustard
seeds

1 tablespoon brown mustard
seeds

12 ounces king salmon fillets

¼ cup Dijon mustard

1½ cups *mizuna*

Summer King Salmon Kebabs

Serves 6

When it comes to salmon, there's nothing in the world like the Pacific king salmon. Most of the salmon sold in markets these days are farm-raised, but the jury is still out on whether raising salmon in cages is really an environmentally sound deal. For me, it doesn't matter. I'd rather eat tofu than farm-raised fish, they taste that awful. Someday I hope they'll figure it all out so we can enjoy the best without depleting our natural resources. The season for king salmon varies from year to year, from state to state (its natural range is from Northern California to Alaska), and even from river to river. So don't think twice: if you see it for sale, buy it.

We do these on the grill at the restaurant, but this dish is also great pan-seared or griddled. In fact, if you get skinless fillets, you should pan-sear the kebabs anyway. If you don't have brown and yellow mustard seeds, just double up on whichever kind you do have. The seeds can be ground in a spice mill, in a coffee grinder, or in a mortar with a pestle. When salmon's not in season, you can use this spice mix on halibut or cod.

Mizuna is a Japanese mustard green. It has dark green, spiky leaves and is mildly peppery. If you can't find it, wild or regular arugula or frisée would work well in its place. Mizuna is great for the home gardener, as it grows quickly and plentifully and is pretty enough to make a beautiful edible border.

For the skewers, try to get those flat Japanese bamboo skewers that are about four to five inches long. If you will be using traditional skewers, double them up and break off the excess.

Soak 6 bamboo skewers in enough water to cover, at least 30 minutes.

To make the vinaigrette, combine the vinegar, olive oil, dill weed, salt, and pepper in a small bowl, and whisk until well emulsified. Reserve till needed.

Toast the sesame seeds in a dry pan, shaking them all the while, until aromatic and lightly golden, and put them in a small bowl. Toast the mustard seeds the same way, but watch out: mustard seeds will toast faster, and will also pop all over the place. You might want to cover the skillet when you toast them. Add the mustard seeds to the sesame seeds and allow them to cool. Stir them up, then set aside half the seeds for garnish. Finely grind the rest of the seeds, and spread the powder out on a plate or on waxed paper.

Remove any small bones from the salmon fillets, and cut them into 6 equal-sized rectangular pieces. Smear the fleshy sides of the salmon (not the skin sides) with mustard. Firmly press the salmon, mustard side down, into the ground seeds so that they adhere and make a nice coating. Now thread the fish onto the skewers, keeping the pieces as flat as possible to ensure good contact with the grill. If your fillets are skinless, coat both sides with mustard and seeds.

To grill the kebabs, give them $1^1/_2$ minutes per side for medium-rare. To pan-sear, coat a cast-iron skillet or pancake griddle with a little olive oil or use a pan spray, and put it over high heat. Sear the skewers, $1^1/_2$ minutes per side.

Very lightly dress the greens with the vinaigrette and portion them out onto 6 small plates, or pile them all up in the center of a large serving plate. Lay the kebabs out on top of the greens, drizzle with some additional vinaigrette, and sprinkle with the reserved whole seeds.

Buckwheat Blini with Caviar

Serves 6 (makes about 18)

blini

⅔ cup buckwheat flour

⅓ cup all-purpose flour

½ teaspoon baking powder

¼ teaspoon baking soda

2 teaspoons sugar

½ teaspoon salt

1 large egg

⅓ cup buttermilk

⅓ cup beer

4 tablespoons butter, melted

1 tablespoon minced shallot

1 tablespoon minced chives

6 tablespoons crème fraîche or sour cream

2 ounces caviar, or more, if you can afford it

Freshly ground black or white pepper

Traditional Russian blini are yeast-risen pancakes. There's no yeast in these nontraditional blini, however, which makes them much easier to make. I use baking soda and baking powder instead of yeast, and add a little beer to give the pancakes a yeasty taste.

These blini are meant to be served with caviar and crème fraîche (or sour cream), which is very traditional. But if Russian or Iranian beluga caviars will put too big a dent in your budget, there are alternatives. There are some very fine American caviars, for instance, and I have also served the blini with smoked salmon and smoked trout to my guests who don't like caviar. For those people who do not like "fishy" tastes, try using tobiko, Japanese flying fish roe. Tobiko is fun to eat because it gives a nice pop, just like caviar, and it even comes in different flavors—wasabi and ginger being my two favorites.

Put the buckwheat flour, all-purpose flour, baking powder, baking soda, sugar, and salt in a large bowl and stir with a fork to combine. Put the egg, buttermilk, and beer in another bowl and beat with a fork to mix well. Make a well in the middle of the dry ingredients. Put 2 tablespoons of the melted butter in the well, along with the egg-buttermilk mixture. Mix until just combined, and all the dry ingredients are moistened.

To cook the blini, heat a griddle or nonstick pan over medium-high heat and lightly coat it with some of the remaining melted butter. (If you prefer, you can use oil or a pan spray.) Drop heaping tablespoonfuls of batter onto the griddle, about ¹/₂ inch apart; the batter will spread a bit. Cook until the blini are brown

For variations on this recipe, you can make larger cakes, using about ¼ cup of batter each, and try one of the following:

- Make a blini BLT. Top the blini with crispy pancetta or other bacon, a leaf of arugula, Cherry Tomato Salsa (page 298), and Lime Crème Fraîche (page 199) or yogurt.

- These blini make great breakfast griddle cakes. Serve with maple syrup or jam and berries. A fruit compote and strong black coffee would round out the meal.

- For brunch, top each pancake with a poached egg, a slice of prosciutto or crispy country ham, and a dollop of the sauce from the Papas Bravas (page 24).

- Top the blini with mushrooms from the Morel Mushroom "Casseroles" (page 169)—a killer combination, but what a way to go!

on the bottom and bubbles start to form on the surface, 1½ to 2 minutes, then flip the blini over and cook for an additional minute. Transfer the cooked blini to a towel-lined plate in a 200°F oven to keep warm. Repeat until you've used up all the batter. Brush a little more butter on the pan if the blini start to stick. The blini take a bit longer to cook than traditional pancakes, maybe an extra 30 to 40 seconds.

To serve, transfer the blini to 6 individual plates, sprinkle with shallots and chives, then drizzle with some melted butter. Add a dollop of crème fraîche, and crown with some caviar. Finish with a sprinkling of freshly ground pepper.

pancakes

2 cups all-purpose flour

2 tablespoons peanut oil or
 olive oil

¾ cup boiling water

sauce

½ cup hoisin sauce

2 teaspoons grated peeled fresh
 ginger

3 tablespoons tamari

1 tablespoon black bean paste
 with chile

1 tablespoon soy sauce

filling

1 pound pork tenderloin

3 tablespoons (or more) peanut
 oil or olive oil

2 generous cups shredded green
 cabbage

1 red bell pepper, finely
 julienned

1 yellow bell pepper, finely
 julienned

3 stalks celery, strings removed,
 thinly sliced on the diagonal

1 bunch scallions, white and light
 green parts only, thinly sliced
 on the diagonal

1 bunch cilantro, 16 sprigs
 reserved for garnish,
 remaining leaves and tender
 stems chopped

Mu Shu Pork "Burritos" with Mandarin Pancakes

Serves 8

Here's our version of a classic northern Chinese dish. The filling is somewhat different from the original, which is always made with stir-fried pork and eggs, but the seasoning sauce is pretty close and the pancake wraps are absolutely authentic. When he was chef at Fog City Diner, Douglas Monslude worked a long time on getting this dish perfect, and it's guaranteed to wow everyone.

You can make this dish with chicken breast, turkey, or tofu in place of the pork. You may be able to find the hoisin sauce and black bean paste for the seasoning sauce at your local supermarket if it has a large ethnic food section; if not, go to an Asian market. If you have a bit more sauce than you need, leftovers will keep covered in the refrigerator. It makes a great marinade or basting sauce for grilled fish, poultry, or beef.

The pancakes take the most time, but they can be made the day before. Just wrap them carefully and refrigerate until needed. The sauce can be made ahead, as well.

To make the pancake dough, set your mixer up with the dough hook attachment. Combine the flour and oil in the bowl, add the boiling water, and mix until the dough comes together. Turn the dough out onto a smooth, dry surface and knead until smooth. Wrap the dough in plastic wrap while it's still hot and let it rest at room temperature 15 minutes.

After the dough has rested, roll it into a log and cut it into 16 pieces. If you use a pasta machine, set it on number 4 and run each dough circle through once. Reduce the machine to number

6, give each circle a quarter turn, and run it through the machine one more time. You'll end up with thin pancakes, about 6 inches in diameter. Alternatively, you could roll the dough out with a rolling pin till paper-thin. During the recipe testing, we discovered that the dough rolls out very easily with a rolling pin, as it is tender and moves well, so a pasta machine is not necessary. Stack the pancakes between pieces of parchment paper or waxed paper, wrap the stack in plastic wrap, and refrigerate until needed.

To cook the pancakes, heat a dry griddle over medium heat. I usually use a stove-top cast-iron griddle or an electric griddle and make a batch of as many as will fit without touching. Turn the pancakes back and forth until the dough is dry and no longer translucent, about 2 minutes. When they are finished they should be caramelized around the edges with a few brown specks. Wrap them in a cloth napkin or kitchen towel and set them aside.

Combine all the sauce ingredients in a bowl and mix well. Keep covered and refrigerated if you are making it ahead.

Trim the pork of all sinew and fat. Working from the thin end of the tenderloin, cut the meat diagonally into thin slices (you'll get oval pieces about 1½ inches long.) Stack the slices, 4 or 5 of them at a time, and cut crosswise into ¼-inch strips or a bit less. Keep refrigerated until needed (you could do this up to a day in advance).

About 20 minutes before you're ready to serve, wrap the pancakes in a damp towel and warm them in a 375°F oven 10 to 15 minutes, checking now and then to see that the towel is still moist. Meanwhile, prepare the filling.

For the filling, heat the oil in a very large pan over medium-high heat. When the pan is hot, stir-fry the pork in batches, adding oil as needed to coat the bottom of the pan, so the pork does not get steamy but is almost crisp. Remove the meat from the pan and reserve. Now toss the cabbage, peppers, and celery

When mixed, the dough should feel slightly oily to the touch. Ideally, kneading should be done on a marble or stainless steel countertop. If you have neither, any other smooth, dry, nonporous surface will do. Don't work on a porous surface, such as wood, because it will soak up the oil from the dough.

(continued)

into the pan and stir-fry just until hot, 30 seconds to 1 minute. Don't overcook the vegetables: they should still be crunchy. Add just enough of the sauce to moisten the vegetables, and toss until well mixed. Put the reserved pork back into the pan and cook until the pork is heated through again. Add a little more sauce if needed. Toss in the scallions and chopped cilantro at the very end.

Place the pancakes on a flat surface. Fill each with some of the mu shu filling and fold it into a cone, tucking the small end under. Place 2 mu shu "burritos" on each plate, and garnish with the reserved cilantro sprigs.

Chorizo and Goat Cheese Half-Moons

Serves 6

2 to 3 ounces of your favorite soft fresh goat cheese

12 to 18 paper-thin slices of chorizo or other sausage (about 3 ounces)

1 large egg

1 tablespoon water

Panko

Peanut or vegetable oil, for frying

You can use any spicy dry sausage with a 2- to 2¹/₂-inch diameter for this. We like to use a special chorizo that comes from the city of Soria, in Spain. What makes this chorizo unique is that it is made with chunks of cured pork loin at the center. Whatever sausage you select, be sure to have your deli person slice it paper-thin. Salami is a possibility.

Plan on two or three half-moons per person, depending on how many other small plates you plan to serve. By the way, you should really include the Papas Bravas (page 24) on your menu when you serve this. Trust me: the combination is spectacular!

Put 1 teaspoon of goat cheese on each slice of sausage. Fold over to create half-moon shapes, and press to seal. Cover and refrigerate at least 1 hour, or as long as overnight.

About 30 minutes before you're ready to cook the half-moons, mix the egg and water together in one bowl and pour out some *panko* in another. Dip each half-moon in the egg wash, then roll it in the *panko*, pressing to get an even coating and gently shaking off the excess. Chill 30 minutes, or the coating will get soggy.

To fry the half-moons, pour oil to a depth of ¹/₂ inch into a cast-iron or other heavy-bottomed pan and heat it to 375°F. Carefully add enough half-moons to fill but not overcrowd the pan. You want them to have room to move without touching. Cook until golden brown and crispy, about 1 minute on each side, then remove to drain on absorbent paper. Skim out any leftover bits and let the oil return to 375°F before frying the next batch. Serve immediately with toothpicks.

These perfect ribs are great for Chinese New Year or Super Bowl Sunday, or any other festive occasion.

Ken Hom's
Pork Riblets
(page 76)

pictured on page 75

mongolian marinade

½ cup hoisin sauce

1½ teaspoons sugar

2¼ teaspoons tamari

2¼ teaspoons sherry vinegar

2¼ teaspoons rice vinegar

1 to 2 scallions, white and light
green parts only, minced

½ teaspoon Tabasco sauce

¾ teaspoon black bean chili
sauce or hot garlic sauce

¾ teaspoon grated peeled fresh
ginger

2¼ teaspoons minced garlic

¼ to ½ teaspoon freshly ground
white pepper

2 tablespoons minced cilantro
leaves and tender stems

1½ teaspoons sesame oil

1 to 1½ slabs spareribs, cut
crosswise into 1½-inch strips
(2½ to 3 pounds)

garnishes

Toasted sesame seeds

Thinly sliced scallions

Sliced Fresno chiles

Additional cilantro leaves

Ken Hom's Pork Riblets

Serves 6

I met Ken Hom when he lived in Berkeley in the early '80s. He led a trip to Hong Kong, where he taught Chinese cooking and all about Chinese ingredients. It was one of the best "foodie" trips I've ever been on. This is a variation on a recipe he taught in the class, and one of the greatest ways to use my favorite marinade, the Mongolian Marinade.

These perfect ribs are great for Chinese New Year or Super Bowl Sunday, or any other festive occasion. At Mustards Grill, we first smoke these ribs for about two hours, then brush on more marinade and braise them in the oven until tender. The marinade is so flavorful that it is not absolutely necessary to smoke the ribs. You can simply cook them on a wood or charcoal grill, or you can braise them in the oven, then run them under the broiler for a few minutes to brown them nicely. If you have extra marinade, save it to serve alongside the cooked ribs. Just before serving, bring the marinade to a boil and serve it hot.

It would be easiest to get your butcher to cut the spareribs for you. You could do it yourself with a clean hacksaw blade, but be careful. The slab of ribs should be cut crosswise into 1¹/₂-inch strips. Allow an extra day for the meat to marinate.

The Mongolian Marinade (at least a close facsimile of it) was originally printed in my Mustards Grill Napa Valley Cookbook. There are about ten thousand really tasty things you could do with any extra marinade. Let me suggest just a few. Try brushing it on beef, pork, or chicken satays as they are cooking, or on grilled eggplant or portobello mushrooms as they're finishing. It would also make a wonderful marinade for Mini Duck Burgers (page 226), lamb chops, or leg of lamb before grilling or roasting; or how about using a warm drizzle over tofu, or a splash as a stir-fry seasoning? It would also be excellent on wild duck, turkey, or venison. Any meat would enjoy this marinade.

For the marinade, whisk together all the marinade ingredients in a stainless steel or ceramic bowl.

Put the ribs in a sealable plastic bag or a suitable container. Pour the marinade over, making sure all surfaces get coated well. Marinate in the refrigerator for 24 hours, shaking the bag or turning the ribs occasionally.

To cook the ribs, place them in a smoker and smoke for 2 to 3 hours over low heat. Remove from the smoker to a roasting pan and brush with some of the marinade. Roast, covered, for 45 minutes to 1 hour in a 450°F oven, until the meat is pulling away from the bone. Check several times as they are roasting and add a small amount of water if they are getting too caramelized.

You can serve the ribs now while they are still hot and sticky, or let them cool and reheat later under the broiler or on a barbecue grill. To serve, cut the strips of ribs into individual riblets, and sprinkle liberally with sesame seeds, scallions, Fresno chiles, and cilantro.

sweet-and-sour sauce

½ cup rice vinegar

½ cup sugar

3 scallions, white and lightest green parts only, thinly sliced on the diagonal

2 tablespoons chile paste

3 cloves garlic, minced

1 shallot, minced

filling

2 cups finely shaved green cabbage

1 cup bean sprouts or other sprouts

1 cup thinly shredded carrots

1 cup finely sliced snow peas or sugar snap peas

1 tablespoon cornstarch

1 tablespoon cool water

3 to 4 tablespoons peanut oil

8 shiitake mushrooms, stemmed and thinly sliced

1½ tablespoons finely grated peeled fresh ginger

1½ tablespoons minced garlic

2 cups minced smoked duck meat

¾ tablespoon salt

½ tablespoon freshly ground white pepper

1 tablespoon sugar

1½ tablespoons Shaoxing rice wine or dry sherry

1½ tablespoons dark soy sauce

1½ teaspoons sesame oil

Smoked Duck Spring Rolls with Sweet-and-Sour Sauce

Serves 6

We use our Tea-Smoked Duck from the Mustards Grill Napa Valley Cookbook *to make these spring rolls, but the dish will work with any smoked duck. Remove any noncrispy skin, bone, and tough cartilage before mincing and measuring the meat. I have also had success with ground duck meat, though of course it does not have the smoky flavor. You can use roast chicken or turkey, as well, but if you live near a Chinatown where those great roast ducks are sold, that's the way to go! For information on the wrappers for making spring rolls, see page 59.*

To make the sauce, combine the vinegar and sugar in a small saucepan and bring to a boil. Remove from the heat and immediately stir in the remaining ingredients. Mix well and reserve.

For the filling, combine the cabbage, sprouts, carrots, and snow peas in a large bowl and place this near the cooktop. Stir the cornstarch and cool water together in a small bowl, and set this next to the vegetables. Heat a large wok or sauté pan over high heat and add enough of the peanut oil to coat the pan nicely. When the oil is hot but not yet smoking, add the shiitakes and sauté them until tender, then scrape them out into the bowl with the vegetables. Pour the remaining oil into the pan, reduce the heat to medium-high, add the ginger and garlic, and sauté until just tender. Toss in the duck meat and cook 2 minutes more, stirring everything about. Add the salt, pepper, sugar, rice wine, soy sauce, and sesame oil, and mix well. Give the cornstarch mixture a stir, and add it to the pan. Cook, stirring,

1 large egg

1 tablespoon water

6 egg-roll or *lumpia* wrappers

Cornstarch, for dusting

Peanut or canola oil, for frying

until the mixture becomes thick and rich. Pour it over the vegetables and mix gently but well.

To assemble the spring rolls, mix the egg with the water in a small bowl to make an egg wash, and set it on the work surface, along with the vegetable-duck mixture and the egg-roll wrappers. Keep the wrappers covered with a clean damp towel as you are working. Lay out one egg-roll wrapper like a diamond in front of you, and brush the edges with the egg wash. Place about 2$\frac{1}{2}$ tablespoons of the filling in the center of the bottom half of the wrap. Fold the bottom up over the filling, tuck in the left and right sides like an envelope, and finish by rolling from the bottom up to the top point. Make sure the edges are well sealed, painting with additional egg wash if needed. The spring rolls can be held at this point and fried later. Dust the tops with cornstarch, cover with plastic wrap, and refrigerate. If you have to stack them up, separate the layers with plastic wrap or parchment paper.

In a large, heavy-bottomed pan, heat 2 inches of the oil to 375°F. Carefully slip the egg rolls into the pan and fry until crisp and golden brown all around. Transfer the egg rolls to a metal rack or a few layers of paper towels to drain. Cut each in half on an angle and serve with Sweet-and-Sour Sauce for dipping.

Colombian-Style Pork Empanadas

Serves 6 to 8 (makes 24 to 32, depending on size)

Just about every country in the world has its own kind of baked filled pastry. The Chinese have bao, the English have Cornish pasties, Italy has calzones, Russia has pierogis, and the Spanish-influenced countries have empanadas. Most empanadas have savory meat, cheese, or fish fillings, but there are sweet fruit-filled empanadas, too.

The pastry for empanadas can be like a bread dough, or it can resemble a pie crust. The dough in this recipe is very flaky and easy to work with. It can be made ahead and kept refrigerated up to 24 hours, or you can even freeze it and pull it out to use months later (it will keep at least two months). I usually make the dough with butter, because it's handier. When I feel like treating myself I use lard, which is more traditional, makes a flakier pastry, and is extra-delicious. This recipe uses a combination of the two. I really don't feel good about using vegetable shortening, however, because of the current research on how bad trans fats are for us.

Making empanadas takes a bit of work, but the results are well worth the effort. Since the empanadas freeze so well, you could always double the recipe and stash some in the freezer for another day. Or get crazy: double the dough recipe, make the Gaucho Empanadas too (page 84), and have an empanada fiesta. If you end up with extra filling, it would be great worked into a paella, used as a stuffing for roasted chiles, or in omelettes or enchiladas.

(continued)

empanada dough

2 cups flour

½ teaspoon salt

½ cup chilled butter, cut into small pieces

4 tablespoons lard, frozen and cut into small pieces

1 large egg

1 large egg yolk

4 tablespoons ice water

filling

8 ounces boneless pork shoulder or Boston butt

1 tablespoon olive or vegetable oil

½ onion, minced

½ *pasilla* chile or green bell pepper, stemmed, seeded, and minced

1½ teaspoons minced garlic

1 tomato, peeled and chopped

1½ teaspoons chopped pimiento-stuffed green olives

1½ teaspoons capers, rinsed and finely chopped

1½ teaspoons raisins, chopped

¼ to ½ teaspoon salt

¼ teaspoon freshly ground black pepper

¼ cup dry sherry

1 small hard-boiled egg, chopped

To make the dough, combine the flour, salt, butter, and lard in a mixer bowl. Using the paddle attachment of an electric mixer or (if by hand) a pastry blender, cut the butter and lard into the dry ingredients until the mixture resembles coarse meal. In a separate bowl, combine the egg, egg yolk, and water; beat lightly. Pour this into the flour mixture and combine quickly, being very careful not to overmix. Stop just before the dough actually comes together completely, and finish it with a few pats by hand. Form the dough into a ball, wrap it in plastic wrap, and flatten it to a 1-inch-thick disk. Chill for at least 1 hour (and up to overnight).

To make the filling, trim the meat of any fat, gristle, or tough sinew. Finely chop it by hand, or you could run it through on the coarse blade of a meat grinder. If you choose to do that, make sure the grinder and the meat are both very cold before you start. Heat the oil in a large skillet over medium-high heat. When hot, add the onion and chile; cook 2 or 3 minutes, until soft. Add the garlic and cook a minute more. Next, stir in the pork and continue cooking till it is no longer pink, 3 to 5 minutes. Add the tomato, olives, capers, raisins, ¼ teaspoon salt, pepper, and sherry. Continue cooking until the liquid has almost completely evaporated. Taste and add more salt, if needed. Allow the mixture to cool completely, then add the egg and mix well. Set the filling aside.

About 10 minutes before you are ready to fill the empanadas, remove the dough from the fridge. Frozen dough should be allowed to defrost overnight in the refrigerator first. In either case, the dough should be cold when you work with it. Roll out the dough on a lightly floured surface to a ¼-inch thickness. Cut out circles using a 4-inch round pastry cutter. You can chill the scraps for 10 minutes, then gently combine them and roll them out again. Don't use the scraps again, though, as the dough will get tough. When I tested this, I was able to get 21 rounds.

To fill the empanadas, place 1½ tablespoons of filling just off center on each dough circle, leaving room around the edges for sealing. Fold into half-moons and crimp the edges with your fingers. The empanadas can be baked right away, or you can freeze them and finish them later. To freeze, place them on a baking sheet and put them in the freezer. When frozen solid, put them in freezer bags and return them to the freezer. Use them up within 4 weeks, if you can.

To bake the empanadas, preheat the oven to 400°F. Bake on an ungreased baking sheet for 25 to 30 minutes, until golden brown. Frozen empanadas will take an extra 10 to 15 minutes; they should go straight from the freezer to the hot oven.

1 recipe Empanada Dough
(page 82)

filling

1½ tablespoons olive or
vegetable oil

8 ounces hanger steak, cut into
thin shreds

8 ounces onions, sliced into thin
wedges

1½ teaspoons chopped garlic

1½ teaspoons chopped fresh
oregano

1 large tomato, diced

1 teaspoon toasted ground
cumin seeds

1 tablespoon sweet *pimentón*
paprika

1 large hard-boiled egg, chopped

7 green olives, chopped

1 teaspoon chopped fresh
parsley

¼ to ½ teaspoon salt

¼ teaspoon freshly ground black
pepper

Gaucho Empanadas

Serves 6 to 8 (makes 24 to 32, depending on size)

*There are many different kinds of beef empanadas in the
countries of South America. In some, golden raisins and
almonds are added to the meat. This one has hard-boiled eggs
and olives. At first I thought I wouldn't like the combination,
but these are truly delicious. If you can find it, use Spanish
sweet smoked paprika, also called* pimentón *paprika, for this
recipe. It really adds a wonderful smokiness to the dish. Use
the empanada dough from the Colombian-Style Pork
Empanadas (page 80). Like the pork empanadas, these freeze
well, and they can be made ahead and baked later. They are
best baked just before serving.*

Make the empanada dough as directed on page 82, and place in
the refrigerator to chill.

To make the filling, heat the oil in a large skillet over medium-
high heat. Add the steak and cook, stirring, until it's nicely
browned, 5 to 8 minutes. Scoop the meat out into a bowl. Using
the same skillet, reduce the heat to medium-low and toss in the
onions. Stir, and let the onions sweat for 5 minutes, until tender.
Add the garlic and cook, stirring, a minute more, just till the
garlic loses its rawness. Return the beef to the pan and add the
oregano, tomato, cumin, and paprika. Cook for 3 to 5 minutes,
stirring, until the sauce has just thickened. Let this mixture
cool, then add the egg, olives, parsley, ¼ teaspoon salt, and
pepper, and mix. The olives are somewhat salty, so taste, and
add salt only if needed.

To make the empanadas, roll out the dough on a lightly floured
surface to a ¼-inch thickness. Cut out 4-inch rounds with a

pastry cutter. Put about $1^1/_2$ tablespoons of filling just off center on each dough circle, leaving room around the edges for sealing. Fold into half-moons and crimp the edges with your fingers. The empanadas can be refrigerated now and baked just before serving. They can also be frozen at this point. (Place them on baking sheets and put them in the freezer. When they are frozen solid, place them into freezer bags.)

To bake the empanadas, preheat the oven to 400°F. Bake on an ungreased baking sheet for 25 to 30 minutes, until golden brown. (Frozen empanadas will take 35 to 45 minutes.)

pictured on pages 88–89

6 to 12 single-bone lamb rack or
rib chops, frenched

1 recipe Mongolian Marinade
(page 76)

6 tablespoons Chinese-Style
Mustard Sauce (page 228)

1 cup loosely packed cilantro
sprigs

2 tablespoons toasted sesame
seeds

Mongolian Barbecued Lamb Chops

Serves 6

*In Beijing, I once saw beautiful charcoal grills that were six to
eight feet long but very narrow—about the width of a lamb
chop. There was a fine metal grate over the coals, which made
it perfect for grilling small food. That was the inspiration for
this dish.*

*I served these at a charity event several years ago, and
people are still talking about them. Not only are they tasty, but
they are also fun to eat. The chops are served like an hors
d'oeuvre on a stick, except that here, the lamb chop's bone is
the stick. You should use only rib chops cut from the rack for
this, and not the T-bone chops, and have your butcher
"french" the chops for you. In a pinch, you can do this yourself: just scrape away all the fat and gristle to expose the last
couple inches of bone on each chop. I prefer the taste of
domestic lamb, which is a bit stronger than Australian or New
Zealand lamb, but either will do. With domestic lamb chops,
plan on one chop per person, or two at the most: with imported
lamb, figure on two to three per person. Allow an extra day for
marinating.*

*Eggplant is a great vegetarian alternative to the lamb
chops. Chicken and pork tenderloin would both work well, too.*

Place the lamb chops in a sealable plastic bag or shallow container and pour the marinade over them, making sure that all
surfaces are liberally coated. Marinate in the refrigerator for 24
hours, turning them occasionally.

To cook, grill over high heat to caramelize the outside, about 2 minutes at most on each side for medium-rare, longer if you like the meat well done, less if your grill is extremely hot.

To serve, lay the chops out on a long platter, with the bone ends sticking out so that your guests can easily grab them. Drizzle with mustard sauce, and sprinkle with cilantro and toasted sesame seeds.

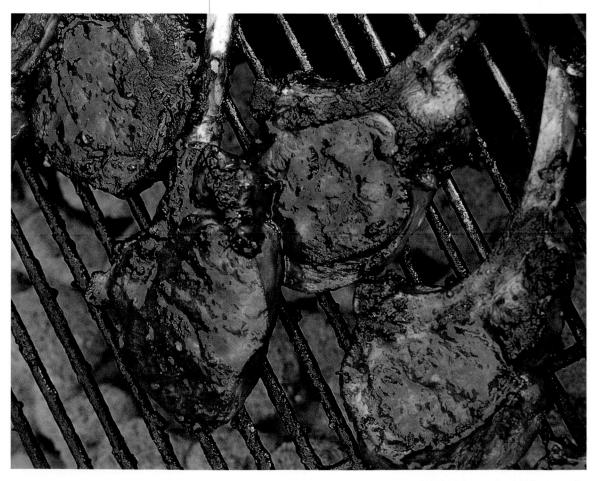

Mongolian Barbecued Lamb Chops (page 86)

marinade

2 tablespoons Dijon mustard

2 tablespoons balsamic vinegar

1 tablespoon rice vinegar

6 tablespoons hoisin sauce

½ teaspoon minced garlic

½ teaspoon minced peeled fresh ginger

2 teaspoons minced shallots

12 to 16 ounces boneless, skinless chicken thighs (or breasts, if you must)

lemon olive oil vinaigrette

Juice and zest of 1 lemon

1 tablespoon Dijon mustard

1 teaspoon minced shallot

Pinch of sea salt

Freshly ground black pepper

6 to 8 tablespoons lemon olive oil

½ cup baby arugula

1 cup baby red mustard greens

½ cup shaved Napa cabbage

6 big or 12 small butter lettuce leaves, for cups

½ cup toasted macadamia nuts, chopped

¼ cup shredded, toasted coconut

6 to 12 thin slices fresh pineapple

Chicken "Satay" in a Lettuce Cup with Lemon Olive Oil Vinaigrette

Serves 6

Strictly speaking, this is not a satay, because the chicken doesn't come on a stick. Marinated morsels of chicken are threaded onto skewers and grilled like an ordinary satay, but then the meat is taken off the skewers and served in a lettuce cup on a bed of greens dressed with a double-lemon vinaigrette.

I tend to get excessive when I'm in my kitchens because I have all sorts of unusual ingredients handy . . . like lemon olive oil, which is made by pressing lemons together with the first pressing of olives. You can find both Italian and American brands of lemon olive oil in specialty foods shops, and it's really worth the effort to hunt it down. But if you don't want to bother, you can make a fine substitute by grating some lemon zest into an extra virgin olive oil.

As for the greens, you are looking for a flavorful, peppery combination. If you can't find those suggested, try watercress with basil or cilantro, or arugula with cilantro. Regular American mustard greens would probably work fine in place of the red mustard greens. Pick leaves that are young and tender, and finely julienne them before mixing them with your other greens.

Depending on the amount of chicken you have, soak 6 to 12 bamboo skewers in enough water to cover for at least 30 minutes.

Combine the marinade ingredients and whisk until well emulsified.

LETTUCE CUPS

Here and on the following pages are a trio of dishes served in lettuce cups. I would not exactly recommend they be served together, though, because they are each quite different. One is Japanese-inspired, one has Vietnamese seasonings, and the third—well, maybe you could call it Hawaiian. One is made with beef, one with pork, and one with chicken. The idea of serving food in lettuce leaves is a neat one; you get to eat your bowl.

For the lettuce cups, usually one outside leaf or two slightly smaller interior leaves of Bibb or butter lettuce will work per serving. If you can't find nice butter or Boston lettuce, try cutting cups out of iceberg lettuce as the Chinese do for minced squab dishes.

Cut the chicken into bite-size pieces and coat liberally with the marinade, reserving some for basting. Marinate at least 2 hours.

To make the vinaigrette, combine the lemon juice, zest, mustard, shallot, salt, and pepper in a bowl, and mix well. Add the oil in a slow, steady stream, whisking continuously, and whisk till well emulsified. You will need less or more oil depending on how juicy your lemon is. (A basic rule of thumb for all vinaigrettes is 1 part citrus juice or vinegar to 3 parts oil.) Set aside until needed.

Thread pieces of marinated chicken onto the skewers so that they are right next to each other but not all scrunched up. Try to keep the chicken as flat as possible so that all surfaces of the meat can get good grill contact. Grill over a hot fire, rotating a quarter turn halfway through cooking on each side to create nice grill marks. This should only take 1 1/2 to 2 minutes per side.

While the chicken is grilling, combine the greens and dress them with enough of the vinaigrette to coat. Arrange the lettuce cups on plates and fill them with some of the greens. Slide the grilled chicken off the skewers and place some on top of the greens in each lettuce cup. To lend a nice shimmer to the meat, moisten it with leftover vinaigrette, if you have any, or lemon olive oil, if you don't. Sprinkle with the nuts and coconut and top with a slice of pineapple.

Mustards' Vietnamese-Style Pork Lettuce Wraps (page 94)

pictured on pages 92–93

dipping sauce

1 tablespoon sugar

3 tablespoons freshly squeezed
  lime juice

½ cup fish sauce

2 or 3 small hot red chiles,
  Fresno or Thai bird, seeded
  and julienned

3 scallions, white and light green
  parts only, finely sliced on the
  diagonal

1 pound pork tenderloin

marinade

2 cloves garlic, minced

1 tablespoon fish sauce

1½ teaspoons freshly squeezed
  lime juice

1 tablespoon sugar

3 or 4 kaffir lime leaves, finely
  julienned, or grated zest of
  1 lime

6 inches lemongrass, from the
  base, finely minced

1 tablespoon finely grated
  peeled fresh ginger

½ small hot chile, such as a
  habanero, Thai bird, or Fresno,
  seeded if you wish and minced

3 ounces dried rice noodles

2 cups peeled and finely julienned carrots

½ cup small fresh mint leaves

½ cup small cilantro leaves

½ cup small fresh basil leaves

12 butter lettuce leaves, for cups

Mustards' Vietnamese-Style Pork Lettuce Wraps

Serves 6

I could eat about a hundred of these . . . well, maybe not a hundred, but I do love pork and this is so fantastic—crunchy, cold, hot, and refreshing, all at once. If you don't like pork, you could use boneless, skinless chicken breasts, or chicken thighs (thigh meat actually has much more flavor than breast meat). The meat can be grilled, broiled, or griddled. Oyster mushrooms would be an excellent substitute for vegetarians.

Plan on two wraps per person unless you are not serving much else, in which case your guests could easily sneak in three apiece. If you are having a large party, do 1½ per person—most people will only have one, and some might have two. One pound of pork tenderloin should clean up to three-quarters of a pound, which should be enough for twelve nice quarter-inch-wide slices. I usually buy a whole pork tenderloin and marinate it all. I can always find someone to eat the extras!

Our favorite brand of fish sauce has three crabs on the label. As for the rice noodles, we use Chao Ching dried rice noodles (the sailing boat brand). Dried rice noodles look like white spaghetti, but they are usually rolled up into bundles, and they don't need cooking. All you have to do is soak them in hot water, and they become soft and slippery and are ready to use. At the restaurant we soak the bundles in boiling-hot water for 10 minutes. At home, I use very hot tap water and let them soak a little longer. For this dish, you should need only one 3-ounce bundle of these noodles.

Get 6 bamboo skewers soaking in water and soak for at least 30 minutes.

To make the dipping sauce, combine all the ingredients, and mix until the sugar dissolves. Chill until needed.

Cut the tenderloin on the diagonal into $1/4$-inch-thick slices.

Combine all the marinade ingredients and mix thoroughly. Place the pork in a sealable plastic bag or a shallow dish and pour the marinade over, making sure that all the surfaces are coated well. Marinate in the refrigerator at least 20 minutes and up to overnight.

Soak the rice noodles in plenty of hot water to cover, 10 to 15 minutes.

When you are ready to cook, thread 2 pieces of pork onto each skewer. You want them flat so the meat will touch the grill surface and thus cook and caramelize evenly. Just before grilling the pork, mix together the rice noodles, carrots, and herbs and set that to the side. Then grill the pork over a medium-hot fire for 2 to 3 minutes per side. Do not overcook! If you broil or griddle the meat, be sure to use a hot setting.

To serve, fill each lettuce cup with some of the noodle salad, topped with a slice of pork and a spoonful of sauce. Roll the lettuce up tightly and eat over your napkin. Serve any extra sauce on the side for dipping. Or set all the ingredients out on a nice platter and let your guests make their own wraps.

Miso-Glazed Beef
in Lettuce Cups
(page 98)

pictured on page 97

Miso-Glazed Beef in Lettuce Cups

marinade

2½ tablespoons sake

2½ tablespoons mirin

1½ teaspoons sugar

⅓ cup *shiro* miso

12 ounces beef tenderloin or tenderloin tips

⅛ teaspoon salt

⅛ teaspoon freshly ground black pepper

8 ounces asparagus or green beans

¾ cup watercress leaves

12 *shiso* leaves, torn if large

1 6-inch piece daikon

vinaigrette

2 tablespoons rice vinegar

1 teaspoon sugar

1½ teaspoons dark soy sauce

¼ cup peanut or vegetable oil

⅛ teaspoon sesame oil

Tiny pinch of salt

12 butter lettuce leaves, for cups

Serves 6

Miso is a paste made from fermented soybeans and a little wheat, barley, or rice. There are many different varieties of this staple Japanese cooking ingredient. In this dish we use shiro miso, or white miso, the lightest and sweetest of them all. You can find miso at Asian markets, in with the refrigerated foods, or with the produce. It comes in plastic tubs, jars, or vacuum-packed bags. You won't need a whole container for this recipe, but miso keeps very well, so you'll have plenty of time to experiment with it. Shiro miso is especially good in salad dressings and soups.

Shiso is a very graceful plant with large, jagged-edged leaves. The leaf is most often used as a garnish in Japanese cooking, but is also chopped up and rolled into sushi or stirred into rice. Shiso is a member of the mint family, but it has its own distinctive flavor. You can find packages of the green shiso leaves at many Asian markets. It is also known as perilla and as beefsteak plant. There is a red variety of shiso, too, but that's not what you want for this dish. Its main use is in making Japanese pickled plums. If you can't find shiso, you can substitute iceberg or butter lettuce.

To make the marinade, combine the sake, mirin, and sugar in a small pot and bring to a boil. Remove from the heat, add the miso, and stir until it is well mixed in. Cut the meat into 6 cubes or rectangles. Season with salt and pepper, and coat it well with the marinade. Marinate 2 to 4 hours in the refrigerator.

To prepare the asparagus for the salad, snap off the ends of the spears where they break naturally. Cook the asparagus by blanching or grilling it until just barely done: 1 or 2 minutes for blanching, 2 to 4 minutes on the grill, depending on how fat the spears. Cut into bite-size pieces. Mix the watercress, asparagus, and *shiso* together in a medium-size bowl and set aside. Peel the daikon, then shred it into long thin strips with the peeler. Put the daikon in a separate bowl and set it aside, too.

To make the vinaigrette, combine the vinegar and sugar in a small pot. Heat and stir just until the sugar has dissolved. Put this in a blender along with the soy sauce, peanut oil, sesame oil, and salt; blend until well emulsified. Set aside until needed.

Over a hot fire, grill the meat about 2 minutes per side for rare, a little longer if you prefer. Baste with the marinade as you go, and rotate the meat a quarter turn halfway through cooking on each side to get nice crosshatch grill marks.

To serve, cut the beef into bite-size slices. Whisk the vinaigrette if it has separated, and dress the asparagus mixture with just enough of it to moisten. Use a light hand with the vinaigrette, or the vegetables will wilt really fast. Place a *shiso* leaf in each butter lettuce cup, then top with a small amount of the asparagus mixture, some daikon and some sliced beef. Sprinkle any remaining vegetables about or place in a pile in the center of a platter for guests to help themselves. Finish with a little drizzle of vinaigrette over the cups and serve the remaining vinaigrette on the side for dipping or spooning.

10 to 12 ounces beef tenderloin tails, flank steak, or hanger steak

marinade

2 tablespoons finely minced lemongrass

1 clove garlic, minced

1 teaspoon grated peeled fresh ginger

2 tablespoons Dijon mustard

1 tablespoon rice vinegar

1 tablespoon olive oil

½ teaspoon freshly ground black pepper

tomato-lemongrass salsa

½ bunch cilantro

3 tablespoons finely minced lemongrass

2 tablespoons rice vinegar

2 cloves garlic, minced

2 red serrano chiles, seeded and minced

1 yellow tomato, peeled, seeded, squeezed, and minced

3 tablespoons extra virgin olive oil

½ teaspoon salt

¼ teaspoon freshly ground black pepper

Chopped fresh chives

Grilled Beef "Sticks" with Tomato-Lemongrass Salsa

Serves 6

If you've never worked with lemongrass before, here's your chance to get acquainted with this unique flavor-enhancer from Southeast Asia. You can find lemongrass in the produce department of any Asian market. It looks like a foot-long reed or dried-up stalk of grass. You'll need two or three stalks for this dish, as there is lemongrass in both the salsa and the marinade. To prepare lemongrass, peel off one or two outer layers to reveal the pale yellow bulb, and trim off the very bottom of the bulb. The bottom four to six inches of the bulb is the part you want for the marinade and salsa. The rest of the stalk and fronds can be used in fish or chicken stocks. Use a good sharp knife to mince up the bulb, as lemongrass is very coarse and fibrous. When you cut it, the lemony aroma will hit you right away, and you'll know why this stuff is so popular. You'll need five tablespoons of minced lemongrass altogether for this recipe.

You can use six-inch skewers for the sticks, with three or four pieces of meat on each. For a cocktail party, you could cut the meat into smaller pieces and use shorter skewers or toothpicks, with one bite-size piece on each. Be sure to give the skewers a half-hour soak in enough water to cover them. You can make up the skewers ahead of time, and let them drain on a small rack placed over a baking sheet. Use the extra marinade for basting. If you don't want to get your hands messy, you could also thread the meat on the skewers first before you marinate it, and then marinate the meat, skewers and all.

Trim any fat off the beef. If you are using flank or hanger steak, pin the meat with a handheld Jaccard tenderizing machine (see the Glossary). Cut the meat across the grain into $1/4$-inch-thick slices. (If you don't have the tenderizing machine and are using flank or hanger steak, you can get by with slicing the meat thinner.) You want to end up with pieces that are about 2 inches wide. If you want to make up the skewers before marinating the meat, do that now.

Mix all the marinade ingredients thoroughly. Place the beef in a plastic bag or a shallow dish and pour the marinade over, making sure that all surfaces are coated well. Seal the bag or dish, and marinate in the refrigerator at least 3 hours but no more than 6, shaking or turning occasionally.

Just before grilling the beef, make the salsa. Reserving some whole cilantro leaves for a garnish, mince the rest of the leaves and tender stems and put them in a small bowl. Add the lemongrass, rice vinegar, garlic, serranos, tomato, olive oil, salt, and pepper; mix gently but thoroughly. Set this aside.

If you haven't made up the skewers yet, loosely thread the beef onto the skewers, dividing it equally among them. Keep the meat as flat as you can, so that as much of it as possible touches the surface of the grill. Grill the meat over a medium-hot fire to the desired doneness, $1^1/_2$ minutes per side for medium-rare.

To serve, spoon out a small pool of salsa in the center of each small plate, top it with a skewer, and sprinkle with the remaining cilantro and some chives. Or you could arrange the dish on a single oval platter: for this, run a strip of salsa down the center of the platter and lay the skewers across it, then sprinkle with cilantro and chives.

My Very First Beef Satay

Serves 6

8 to 12 ounces flank, skirt, or
  hanger steak

12 medium-size shiitake
  mushrooms (optional)

marinade

3 tablespoons tamari, or
  1 tablespoon plus
  1½ teaspoons each of light
  and dark soy sauce

1 tablespoon sugar

2 tablespoons dry sherry or
  Shaoxing rice wine

1 tablespoon minced peeled
  fresh ginger

1 clove garlic, minced

1½ teaspoons sesame oil

½ recipe Chinese-Style Mustard
  Sauce (page 228)

1 to 1½ tablespoons toasted
  sesame seeds

Cilantro leaves

This recipe goes way back to Chicago in 1976, and a cooking class I was taking from a local "celebrity chef" of those days. That's when I first learned about this classic street food from Southeast Asia. Satays are skewers of marinated meat, fish, or shrimp cooked over charcoal, and wherever you go in that part of the world, you can buy these tasty treats at street stalls or from sidewalk vendors.

This one is wonderful served plain, fresh off the grill, or sprinkled with toasted sesame seeds and served with the Chinese-Style Mustard Sauce from page 228. To dress it up, marinate some shiitake mushrooms and alternate the mushrooms with the beef on each skewer.

You can thread the meat on long skewers (one per person), but short three- or four-inch skewers work better. Each one will be like a lollipop: much easier to eat, and less danger of stabbing yourself with the skewer point.

Soak the bamboo skewers in enough water to cover them at least 30 minutes. Use 6 long skewers or 12 short ones, whichever you prefer.

Trim the meat of excess fat, then pin it with a handheld Jaccard tenderizing machine (see Glossary) or poke it all over with a fork. Cut the meat across the grain into 12 slices, each about ¼ inch thick, and put it in a sealable plastic bag or a shallow dish. If you're going to do the mushrooms, cut off the stems and put the mushroom caps in another plastic bag or shallow dish. Combine all the marinade ingredients and mix well. Pour the marinade over the meat (and optional mushrooms), making sure that all surfaces are coated well. Marinate in the refrigerator 2 hours, shaking or turning the bag(s) occasionally.

Thread the marinated steak onto skewers, 2 pieces each for long skewers, 1 piece for the short ones. Keep the meat as flat as you can for more even cooking. If you're doing mushrooms, thread them onto the skewers in the same manner (make it meat, mushroom, meat, mushroom for the long skewers). Grill over a hot charcoal or wood fire until the meat is crisply caramelized on the edges and nicely browned, but still rare. This should take 1 to 2 minutes per side, depending on the heat of your fire.

To serve, place a small bowl of the mustard sauce in the center of a platter and arrange the satays around it. Sprinkle the satays with sesame seeds and a bit of cilantro.

Black Pepper and Garlic Chicken Wings

Serves 6

These are so-o-o delicious, and so-o-o easy to make! They are also very sticky, so be sure to have plenty of moist finger towels on hand when you serve them.

The easiest way to cook these wings is to roast them. Just put them on a cake rack in a low-sided roasting dish and pop them in a hot oven. You could grill them instead over a medium-low to medium fire, but I find they get crisper in the oven. Remember to allow at least twelve hours to marinate the wings. It may seem like there's too much garlic and pepper in the recipe, but be brave—use it all. The mushroom soy sauce is easily found in Chinese markets, or you could use regular soy.

marinade

½ cup mushroom soy sauce

2 tablespoons brown sugar or palm sugar

1 tablespoon honey

2 tablespoons minced garlic

2 tablespoons freshly ground black pepper

3 pounds chicken wings

Minced garlic, chives, or scallions, for garnish

Combine all the marinade ingredients in a bowl and mix well.

To prepare the wings, trim off and discard the tips, and cut each wing at the joint so you end up with one tiny drumstick and one flat section per wing. Place the wings in a sealable plastic bag or a large flat plastic container and pour the marinade over the wings, making sure that all surfaces are coated well. Close the bag tightly, and marinate in the refrigerator for 12 to 24 hours, shaking or turning the wings often.

To cook the wings, preheat the oven to 450°F. Arrange the wings on a rack in a shallow roasting pan. Roast for 12 to 18 minutes, until the skin is dark brown and crispy and the meat has begun to shrink away from the ends of the bones. The juices should run clear when the wings are pierced with a knife point. Sprinkle with the garnishes and serve them up!

dressed, not naked

One of my food pet peeves is undressed salads.

chapter 2: Dressed, Not Naked

In this chapter you will find refreshing light dishes to help balance out your menu. Featured are cool salads using a variety of greens and fruit or seafood, along with several suggestions for doing grilled vegetables. Each recipe comes with its own dressing or sauce. One of my food pet peeves is undressed salads. Make sure you dress your salads before you plate them. Most of these sauces and vinaigrettes can be done ahead, and then you just need to dress the dish at the last minute, when you're ready to serve. My kind of party dish!

If you're going to fire up the grill to prepare other parts of your meal, try doing your vegetables on the grill, too. It's quick and easy, and the results are sure to please. Depending on seasonal availability, you could do the Grilled Baby Leeks and Spring Onions or the Grilled Radicchio and Scallions recipes. Asparagus is great whether you grill it or sear it in a hot skillet on the stove (see the recipe called Seared or Grilled Asparagus, which gives two options for dressing the asparagus, an aioli flavored with white truffle oil and a brown butter vinaigrette).

The Avocado-Papaya Salad is on the menu at Cindy's Backstreet Kitchen—not just because I'm addicted to it, which I am, but because everybody raves about it. Sometime in your life you should make it, and see what all the fuss is about.

Tuna Tartare
with Cucumber Salad
and Avocado

Serves 6

12 ounces sushi-grade ahi or
   albacore tuna

wasabi paste
2 tablespoons wasabi powder
¼ to ½ cup water

cucumber salad
1 English cucumber, unpeeled,
   sliced paper-thin
2 teaspoons kosher salt
2 jalapeño chiles, stemmed,
   seeded, and julienned
3 red Fresno chiles, stemmed,
   seeded, and julienned
½ medium-size red onion, thinly
   sliced
2 tablespoons rice vinegar
2 tablespoons extra virgin
   olive oil

san bai su drizzle
¼ cup tamari
¼ cup rice vinegar
¼ cup mirin

12 slices avocado
2 tablespoons toasted sesame
   seeds

This cool, elegant, Japanese-inspired appetizer is great in the summer, especially if you have cucumbers, sweet red onions, and chiles fresh from your garden (or from your favorite farmers' market). For an hors d'oeuvre party you could serve the tuna on crackers, such as the Crispy Sesame Crackers in the Mustards Grill Napa Valley Cookbook. And of course you could feature it as presented below in any small-plates meal.

It takes a bit of time for the cucumber to "weep," and the wasabi paste needs to sit for at least 30 minutes before being used, but everything can be done ahead of time. Then final assembly will take just a few minutes.

Wasabi is a Japanese horseradish. For this dish, we mix wasabi powder with water to make the wasabi paste. You could buy a tube of ready-mixed wasabi paste instead, though you should check out the label to see if it has been loaded up with additives. Wasabi powder and paste are both easy to find at Asian markets. If you're really lucky, you might find fresh wasabi roots, and could try grating your own paste. Fresh wasabi roots are much smaller than Western horseradish roots, dark brown on the outside, and bright light green inside.

Cut the tuna into tiny dice, $^1/_4$ inch or smaller. Put it in a bowl, and set the bowl over ice in order to keep the fish well chilled. Refrigerate until needed, up to 2 hours maximum.

(continued)

Because the tuna is going to be served raw, it's very important to buy the very best quality. If you're buying ahi, it should be deep red, not a cherry red or candy-apple look that is achieved by gassing the fish with carbon monoxide. You definitely don't want that. Pass it up if the blood line is brown rather than red, or if the flesh has soft spots or dimples. Albacore tuna is lighter in color, but equally delicious. For both, look for clear, firm flesh with a clean, fresh smell. Tell your fish purveyor you're serving the tuna raw, and you want sushi- or grill-grade tuna.

In a small bowl, combine the wasabi powder with just enough of the water to make a drizzleable paste. Mix well, cover, and set aside. Let it sit for at least 30 minutes before using. If it thickens too much add a few drops of cold water to thin.

Spread the cucumber slices over a baking sheet and sprinkle them with the kosher salt. Let them sit for 30 minutes to draw out the excess moisture. Combine the chiles, onion, rice vinegar, and olive oil in a mixing bowl large enough to hold the cucumbers, and keep refrigerated until needed. After 30 minutes, pat the cucumbers dry with paper towels and toss them into the bowl with the chiles and onions.

Mix the ingredients for the San Bai Su Drizzle together in a small bowl. Chill 6 medium-small plates in the fridge.

To serve, drizzle the chilled plates with some of the wasabi paste, then gently measure out ¹/₃-cup portions of tuna and turn them out onto the center of each plate. Place three mounds of cucumber salad about, and drizzle with San Bai Su. Cross 2 slices of avocado on top of each portion of tuna, and sprinkle the sesame seeds over all.

pictured on page 115

Hearts of Romaine, Watercress, and Avocado Salad with Erasto's Red Jalapeño–Lime Vinaigrette

Serves 6

The color contrast in this salad—from the light green of the hearts of romaine and the dark green watercress to the tiny pieces of red jalapeño—really says Christmas to me. At the restaurants we use a product called living watercress, which is milder than most commercially grown watercress; but if you like things a bit more peppery, as I do, stick with regular watercress. The stems of living watercress are edible, but with regular cress, coarse stems need to be removed. If you can't find perfectly ripe avocados, papaya or mango slices would be nice instead.

red jalapeño–lime vinaigrette

2 tablespoons sugar

¼ cup freshly squeezed lime juice

2 red jalapeño or Fresno chiles, stemmed, seeded, and minced

¼ teaspoon salt

¼ teaspoon freshly ground black pepper

3 shallots, minced

¼ teaspoon toasted ground cumin seeds

1½ cups extra virgin olive oil

3 hearts of romaine

2 cups watercress

1½ avocados, pitted and peeled

3 tablespoons toasted pumpkin seeds

To make the vinaigrette, combine the sugar and lime juice, and mix until the sugar dissolves. Add the jalapeño, salt, pepper, shallots, and cumin; whisk until the salt dissolves. In a slow, steady stream, whisk in the olive oil till the dressing is well emulsified. Keep refrigerated.

When you're ready to serve, cut the romaine hearts into quarters lengthwise and put them in a large bowl. If you're using living watercress, trim off the roots. For regular watercress, trim off the coarse stems. Set the watercress aside.

To serve, gently toss the romaine with enough dressing to coat. Cross 2 wedges of romaine on each plate. Using the same bowl, toss the watercress with a little more of the dressing, and sprinkle some watercress over the romaine. Cut each half avocado into 6 lengthwise slices. Arrange 3 slices of avocado over each salad, then finish with a sprinkling of pumpkin seeds and a drizzle of additional dressing.

The color
contrast in this
salad...really
says Christmas
to me.

Hearts of Romaine,
Watercress, and Avocado
Salad with Erasto's
Red Jalapeño–Lime
Vinaigrette (page 113)

Avocado-Papaya Salad with Papaya Seed Dressing

Serves 6

1 or 2 papayas (about 1 pound)

papaya seed dressing

2 tablespoons papaya seeds

3 tablespoons freshly squeezed
   lime juice

3 tablespoons rice vinegar

1 tablespoon plus 2 teaspoons
   honey

⅔ cup olive oil

2 small cloves garlic

½ teaspoon toasted ground
   cumin seeds

1 teaspoon sweet paprika

¼ teaspoon salt

Freshly ground black pepper

2 cups baby mâche, or endive,
   lamb's lettuce, butter lettuce,
   or Bibb lettuce

2 cups baby arugula

2 or 3 avocados, peeled, pitted,
   and sliced

1½ tablespoons toasted
   hazelnuts, coarsely chopped

Freshly ground black pepper

1 lime, cut into 6 wedges

My mom was always making avocado-grapefruit salads, so whenever we serve this salad, it reminds me of her. In fact, this recipe comes from a very old cookbook my mom gave me years ago. Our version receives raves at Cindy's Backstreet Kitchen. The fantastic color has a lot to do with it, with the orange-red of the papaya and the soft green of the avocados. It's a favorite among the staff as well.

For this dish, you want ripe papayas, with tender but not mushy flesh. The skin should be bright yellow with a few mottled spots, and the fruit should be sweet-smelling and aromatic. The papaya has small black seeds that look a little like capers or caviar. These seeds have a little heat in them, and they can be used for a garnish or to add a little zip to salad dressings.

If you have mangoes that are ripe, they are wonderful here as well. If you would like to try something other than hazelnuts, pecans, almonds, macadamias, or pistachios would all be really nice, but I don't think walnuts would work.

Split the papayas in half lengthwise. Scoop out the seeds, and set aside 2 tablespoons of seeds for the dressing, picking off any membranes attached to the seeds. Peel the papayas and cut crosswise into ¼-inch-thick slices.

To make the dressing, combine all the dressing ingredients in a blender and blend until smooth.

To serve, dress the mâche and arugula with half the dressing, and pile this in the center of 6 salad plates. Alternate slices of avocado and papaya across the greens and drizzle with the remaining dressing. Sprinkle on the nuts and some freshly ground black pepper, and place lime wedges on the side. Or if you prefer, you could compose the plate with the fruit on the bottom and the greens on top. Either way, it's yummy.

pictured on page 120

Baby Octopus Salad with Malagueta Chile Relish

Serves 6

Because my allergy to crustaceans has limited what I can eat in the shellfish family, I have developed a love for the ones that are safe for me to eat, such as cuttlefish, squid, and especially octopus. In this dish, the combination of flavorful baby octopus meat and spicy-hot chile sauce over crisp greens and herbs is just perfect.

Baby octopus is very tender, but the younger and smaller the better, so try to stick with ones that are about one to two inches in length. You can usually find frozen baby octopus in ethnic markets, particularly Spanish, Japanese, and Italian ones. You might even find fresh octopus there, too. When picking out fresh octopus, go for the ones that are translucent gray, moist, slimy, and bright-eyed. They should smell clean and slightly of the sea. Both Pacific and Atlantic octopus will work for this recipe. Don't forget, the tentacles are the best part to eat.

A malagueta is a Brazilian chile that is used both green (unripe) and red. They are tiny and round, like capers, and when ripe they are super-hot. They are used a lot in sauces in Brazil, and are also served as a side dish or condiment with meat and black beans. Fresh malaguetas are hard to find, but if you have a good South American market nearby, you should at least be able to find them in jars, packed in vinegar or in cachaça, a Brazilian liquor made from sugarcane. Malaguetas are a little fruity, as are habaneros, so habaneros would be a good substitute if you can't find malaguetas. Or use serranos in a pinch.

malagueta relish

6 *malagueta* chiles or 1 or 2 habaneros or serranos, seeded and minced

2 tablespoons aged red or white wine vinegar

¼ cup peanut or olive oil

1 small sweet onion, minced

1 teaspoon finely grated peeled fresh ginger (about ¼ inch piece)

¼ teaspoon sea salt

1 pound baby octopus

Juice of 1 lime

½ large red onion, minced

¼ cup minced fresh Italian parsley, leaves and tender stems only

2 tablespoons minced cilantro leaves

2 tablespoons minced *pasilla* chile

2 tablespoons minced red bell pepper

⅓ generous cup olive oil

½ teaspoon salt

¼ teaspoon freshly ground black pepper

6 nice butter lettuce leaves, for bowls or cups

6 slices avocado

1 lime, cut into 6 wedges

For the relish, combine the chiles and the vinegar and let marinate for at least 1 hour (or as long as 24 hours, if you wish). If you are using cured chiles, skip this step and instead rinse these already-marinated chiles slightly, then proceed with the rest of the recipe. When you are ready to put the relish together, heat the oil over medium-low heat in a sauté pan and sweat the onions and ginger 2 to 4 minutes, till they are translucent and tender. Scrape them out onto a plate and let cool. Once cooled, combine them with the marinated chiles and season with salt. Reserve until needed.

If you buy fresh octopus, you'll need to clean it yourself. Turn the head inside out and scrape off the viscera and other organs. Trim away the small bone at the bottom of the head and remove the beak. Check the tentacles for sand, and rinse the entire octopus well. (Frozen octopus is usually cleaned already, in which case you can skip this step.)

Bring a big pot of salted water to a boil; reduce to a slow simmer and add the octopus. Cook 45 minutes to 1 hour, until tender but still chewy when you bit into it (test it by cutting off a small piece to taste). When finished, drain and rinse the octopus, and allow it to cool slightly. Cut the head and tentacles into nice bite-size pieces.

Put the lime juice, onion, parsley, cilantro, *pasilla*, bell pepper, and olive oil in a large bowl and mix well. Add the octopus, stir everything around well, and season with the salt and pepper.

To serve, scoop spoonfuls of the octopus salad into the lettuce leaves, and top each with some of the relish and a slice of avocado. Serve with lime wedges on the side.

Baby Octopus Salad
with Malagueta Chile Relish
(page 118)

pictured on page 125

Shrimp, Crab, and Octopus–Stuffed Avocado with Cilantro-Caper Mayonnaise

Serves 6

16 ounces shrimp, cooked in their shells

24 ounces cooked octopus (about 2 cups) (see page 119)

8 ounces fresh crabmeat (about 1 cup)

cilantro-caper mayonnaise

1 cup mayonnaise

2 tablespoons minced cilantro leaves

1½ to 2 tablespoons capers, rinsed and minced

1 clove garlic, minced

¼ teaspoon salt

⅛ teaspoon freshly ground black pepper

lime vinaigrette

Juice of 1 lime

Pinch of salt

Pinch of freshly ground black pepper

3 tablespoons olive oil

3 avocados

3 cups shredded iceberg lettuce

2 pints cherry tomatoes, halved

1 or 2 limes, cut into wedges

You can usually find cooked octopus in supermarkets that have a good seafood department. If you can't find octopus, you could substitute an additional four ounces of shrimp or crab in the stuffing. For smaller portions, cut the avocado into quarters lengthwise. Place a mounded tablespoonful of the seafood stuffing in the hollow where the pit was and top with some of the Cilantro-Caper Mayonnaise. If you end up with any extra mayonnaise, it is excellent on almost any grilled vegetables.

Avocado flesh has a bad habit of turning brown when exposed to air. You can prevent this by coating the cut surfaces with lemon or lime juice, but it also works to dunk the sliced avocado in ice water, remove it, and set it on a paper towel until you need it.

Peel and devein the shrimp, and coarsely chop them up. Put them in a medium-size bowl. Slice the octopus into ¼-inch-thick rounds, and add to the bowl along with the crab. Cover and refrigerate until needed.

For the Cilantro-Caper Mayonnaise, combine all the ingredients in a small bowl and mix well. Keep chilled until needed.

To make the vinaigrette, combine the lime juice, salt, and pepper, then whisk in the olive oil in a steady stream. Continue whisking till well emulsified.

Cut the avocados in half lengthwise and remove the pits. Using a big spoon, scoop out the avocado halves as neatly as you can, being careful to keep them intact. Dunk them quickly in ice water to keep them from turning brown, and drain on paper towels.

To serve, dress the lettuce with just enough of the vinaigrette to coat lightly. Divide the lettuce among 6 bowls and top each bed of lettuce with an avocado half. Combine the seafood with the tomatoes and just enough mayonnaise to coat lightly, and mix gently. Scoop some of this salad into each avocado half. Place a small dollop of the remaining mayonnaise on top and drizzle a bit of vinaigrette about. Serve with wedges of lime on the side.

Avocado flesh has a bad habit of turning brown when exposed to air. You can prevent this by coating the cut surfaces with lemon or lime juice.

Shrimp, Crab, and Octopus-Stuffed Avocado
with Cilantro-Caper Mayonnaise (page 122)

Grilled Baby Leeks and Spring Onions with Garlicky Romesco Sauce

Serves 6

This recipe was inspired by a one-of-a-kind festival that's held each year in Catalonia to celebrate the calçot, *a long, skinny white onion that's something like a cross between a leek and a spring onion. The specialty of the festival is slow-grilled* calçots *served with plenty of romesco sauce, one of Spain's great sauces. You can't get* calçots *here, but it doesn't matter—spring onions and leeks will do just fine. If you can't find baby leeks, use all spring onions or scallions.*

In my library of cookbooks, there are probably twenty or thirty different recipes for romesco sauce, many of which I have worked with in variations over the years. All romesco sauces contain, in varying proportions, chiles, tomatoes, garlic, bread (as a thickener), and olive oil. They also contain ground almonds, which give the sauce a great texture and make it unique. The recipe below, which is my current favorite, goes heavy on the garlic. You could make a simpler version of it by substituting three to four cloves of fresh garlic for the head of roasted garlic. But if you want to go for broke, you'll need to roast a head of garlic first (see the directions below).

Use a fruity extra virgin olive oil from Spain, if you can. I've made this sauce with dried New Mexico chiles from the local grocery store and with choricero and guindilla chiles from The Spanish Table (see page 362). In a pinch, I once made a nice variation with roasted, peeled red bell peppers and pimientos. Dried ñora peppers from Spain would be the very best.

Romesco sauce is really best made a day ahead. Any leftovers would be good with steamed vegetables, poached or grilled poultry, rabbit, pork, shellfish or finfish . . . you name it.

garlicky *romesco* sauce

1 head garlic

1 cup plus 1 tablespoon fruity
    olive oil

2 dried *choricero* or *guindilla*
    chiles (or dried ancho or
    New Mexico chiles)

½ cup almonds

1 slice rustic white bread

1 tomato, peeled and seeded

2 tablespoons red wine vinegar

2 tablespoons water

½ teaspoon salt

⅛ teaspoon cayenne pepper or
    crushed dried red pepper

12 baby leeks

6 small spring onions or scallions

Additional olive oil, for coating

To roast the garlic, preheat the oven to 300°F. Break the head of garlic apart and trim off the root ends of the cloves. Put the unpeeled cloves in an ovenproof dish. Sprinkle with ½ cup of the olive oil and roast 45 minutes to 1 hour, until the garlic cloves are golden and soft.

Increase the oven heat to 375°F to prepare the chiles and almonds. Put the chiles and almonds on separate baking sheets and place them in the oven to toast. In 2 to 3 minutes, the chiles should to begin to release their aromas and start softening up, at which point remove them from the oven. Leave the almonds in for about 7 minutes, until golden brown, then remove and set aside. Put the chiles in a bowl or pot with just enough warm water to cover and soak for 10 to 15 minutes, until tender. Drain, reserving the soaking liquid.

Heat 1 tablespoon of the oil in a small skillet over medium-high heat. When the oil is hot, add the bread and fry until golden brown on both sides. Set this aside.

To make the romesco sauce, squeeze the cloves of garlic, popping the pulp out into a food processor. Add the bread, chiles, almonds, tomato, vinegar, water, salt, and cayenne, and blend until everything is well mixed and coarsely chopped. Continue blending while slowly adding the remaining ½ cup of olive oil in a steady stream. You don't want the sauce too creamy, so stop before you reach that point. You want a robust, rustic sauce that's a bit chunky and will adhere to whatever you dip into it. Thin with a little of the reserved chile soaking liquid only if necessary. Store in the refrigerator until needed. The sauce tastes better at room temperature, but it's good cold as well.

(continued)

Trim off the root ends of the leeks, then make 4 lengthwise cuts in each, being careful not to cut all the way through at the base. You want the leeks to fan out, but not fall apart. Rinse them well, as they can be very sandy. Trim the root ends of the spring onions and rinse well. Coat the leeks and spring onions with olive oil and place them over a low fire. Grill them slowly until they are very soft and tender on the inside and a bit charred on the outside, 5 to 6 minutes for the spring onions, 10 to 15 minutes for the leeks. Turn them as you grill them, and check for doneness with a knife, piercing them at their thickest point. Serve them warm from the grill with plenty of *romesco* sauce for dipping.

Grilled Radicchio and Scallions with Black Olives

Serves 6

Radicchio might be an acquired taste, but it's one of my favorites. I especially love radicchio when it is slowly grilled over a low fire. To tone down any bitterness, soak the radicchio in ice water first, then be sure you cook it long enough to tenderize it and let its natural sweetness develop—if it gets a bit charred, that's a plus.

I usually use the firm round Chioggia or Verona radicchio. These are two of the most common ones sold. Or you could try the Treviso radicchio, which has long narrow leaves and looks sort of like a red-and-white Belgian endive. It's a little milder than the other two. Whichever kind you use, the trick in preparing them is to trim off just a tiny amount of the base, leaving the core intact to hold the wedge together on the grill.

This is a good side dish to prepare when other parts of the meal are also coming off the grill. It's also good with grilled bread spread with Best-Ever Tapenade (page 34).

2 or 3 heads radicchio

6 scallions

Juice of 1 lime

5 tablespoons extra virgin
olive oil

¼ teaspoon salt

⅛ teaspoon freshly ground black
pepper

dressing

2 tablespoons balsamic vinegar

¼ teaspoon salt

⅛ teaspoon freshly ground black
pepper

6 tablespoons extra virgin
olive oil

3 or 4 dozen marinated or salt-
cured black olives

3 tablespoons shaved aged goat
cheese or dry-aged Monterey
Jack, Parmesan, or pecorino
cheese

2 tablespoons minced fresh
parsley or fresh basil

Cut each head of radicchio in half, from the core to the outside, to make sure there's enough core to hold the wedges together. Cut each half into 3 wedges, again making sure each wedge has a bit of the core for support. Soak the radicchio in ice water for 20 to 30 minutes, then drain it well. Place the radicchio in a flat container. Trim the roots off the scallions and remove 1 or 2 of the outer layers. Toss the scallions in with the radicchio. To make a marinade, combine the lime juice, olive oil, salt, and pepper in a small bowl, whisking gently but well. Thoroughly coat the radicchio and scallions with this, and let them marinate at least 30 minutes but no more than 2 hours.

To make the dressing, put the balsamic vinegar, salt, and pepper in a small bowl, and whisk to combine. Whisk in the oil. Set this aside. Later you will be adding chopped grilled scallions to this base to complete the dressing.

When you're ready to grill, put the scallions on first, and cook them until fork-tender, about 5 minutes. When they're done, chop them finely and toss them into the balsamic vinegar dressing. Grill the radicchio over a medium-hot fire, turning the wedges often, until caramelized at the edges, 8 to 10 minutes. The radicchio should be tender, but not so soft as to fall apart, and there should be a little bite to it.

To serve, place 2 or 3 wedges of radicchio on each small plate, and drizzle with the balsamic-scallion dressing. Garnish with the olives, cheese, and parsley or basil.

New French Café Gravlax
(page 132)

pictured on pages 130–131

There are endless ways to serve gravlax. I thought I'd include some of my favorites in case you wanted to get crazy and do a variety of presentations.

- In the summer it's nice to serve gravlax with tiny corn cakes or muffins and a drizzle of Lime Crème Fraîche (page 199) or sour cream.

- Here's a good winter option. Arrange a layer of thinly sliced gravlax on small plates and sprinkle with tarragon or chervil, freshly ground black pepper, and sea salt. Put a mound of grapefruit and/or orange sections and avocado slices in the center, then top all with some minced shallots and a drizzle of extra virgin olive oil.

- Drape tiny slivers of gravlax over deviled eggs or stir some into scrambled eggs.

- Or how about slices of gravlax topped with some

New French Café Gravlax

Serves 8 to 10

When I left Chicago in 1978, my idea was to go home to Minnesota, spend time with my dad, and take French lessons. My plan was to go to France and spend a year there cooking. But it never happened. Instead, I ended up moving first to San Francisco and then to Napa to open a bunch of restaurants. For the nine months I was home, I had a blast. In addition to the French lessons and fishing with my dad, I worked in a hip French café in the "arty" part of town. It was run by Pam Sherman and Lynn Alpert, two vibrant women with great aesthetics, who were smart enough to give their staff enough rope to try stuff out but not enough to hang themselves. I don't think the café still exists, but I remember it fondly. That's where I learned about gravlax.

Making gravlax requires no cooking and very little work—the salmon is cured with salt, sugar, and dill in the refrigerator. The curing process takes three days, though, during which you only need to turn the fish and pour off any liquids that have accumulated. Then you slice and eat. There are probably ten thousand ways to enjoy gravlax. For the simplest presentation of all, serve the gravlax with croutons, breadsticks, flatbread, or plain or rye crackers. For this recipe, you need only two to three ounces per person at most. You could offer a mustard sauce, and dress the plate up with a little fresh dill. You can use almost any sturdy bread for the croutons. Try a bâtard, sourdough, baguette, or rye bread. See the sidebar for other serving suggestions.

This recipe is for two pounds of salmon. Adjust it for however much fish you have. Go for uniformly thick fillets of salmon cut from the center. Don't use the tail end of the fish because it will cure too quickly.

sharp, peppery greens such as wild baby arugula or watercress, sprinkled with scallions or very finely sliced shallot, freshly ground black pepper, and a little chervil or tarragon? Finish this one with a drizzle of crème fraîche or thinned sour cream, extra virgin olive oil, and a couple pinches of sea salt.

gravlax

¼ cup kosher salt

½ cup sugar

2 teaspoons freshly ground white pepper

2 pounds wild king salmon fillets, skin on

½ to ¾ bunch fresh dill weed, coarse stems removed

sherry vinaigrette

¼ cup sherry vinegar

¼ teaspoon sea salt

Several grindings of black pepper

¼ cup sesame oil

½ cup extra virgin olive oil

2 cups arugula, watercress, or baby Japanese mustard greens

2 tablespoons chopped fresh dill weed

¼ cup finely minced fresh chives

2 shallots, sliced

1 cup tiny croutons (¼-inch dice or smaller)

¼ cup toasted sesame seeds

For the gravlax, combine the salt, sugar, and pepper in a small bowl and mix well. Place the salmon, skin side up, on a long cutting board. With a sharp knife held so that the blade is almost flat against the fish, make 3 or 4 shallow half-moon-shaped slits horizontally across the fish. The cuts should just graze the skin but not go deeply into the flesh. An index finger stuck under the flaps of mostly skin should go in to about the second knuckle. Take half of the salt-sugar mixture and rub it into the cuts and across the whole surface. Now tuck half of the dill into the cuts and lay a few extra pieces over the whole fish. Turn the fish over and coat it with the remaining salt-sugar mixture, and sprinkle on what's left of the dill.

Wrap the salmon very tightly in plastic wrap and place it between two plates. Put a 1- to 2-pound weight, such as a can or a bag or two of beans, on the top plate. Refrigerate for 3 days, turning the fish once a day and pouring off any juices. If you want the gravlax less salty and firm and a bit more medium-rare, cure it for just 2 days.

When the salmon is firm to the touch, scrape off the salt, sugar, and dill, starting from the tail end and working up. For slicing, I prefer the look of a wide horizontal slice to a straight-down cut. Using a very long, thin slicing knife, run the blade across the surface of the fish to get the very thinnest slices you can. You should be able to see the knife through the flesh. If you come to a point where you can no longer cut nice thin slices, dice the remainder for chowder, salad, pizza topping, or best yet, a cook's snack.

To make the vinaigrette, whisk together the vinegar, salt, and pepper until the salt has dissolved. Then gradually whisk in the oils, and continue whisking until the dressing is well emulsified.

When you're ready to serve, mix together the arugula, dill, chives, shallots, and just enough of the vinaigrette to coat. Place a slice or two of gravlax on each small plate, mound a bit of greens over each serving, and sprinkle with croutons and toasted sesame seeds.

Seared or Grilled Asparagus with Two Sauces

Serves 6

If you check through the recipes in this book, it will be pretty obvious to you that asparagus is one of my favorite things, as it turns up in everything from baked Brie to Thai fish cakes. Several years ago, I even started growing my own asparagus. It took a good three years for the bed to establish itself, but then, look out! For a few short weeks every spring, it's asparagus in some form for breakfast, lunch, and dinner! Of course, you don't have to grow your own asparagus to take part in the craziness. Just remember that the season is short, so when asparagus shows up in your market, don't hesitate.

There are probably a million ways to cook asparagus, but sometimes simplest is best, as in this recipe: asparagus spears cooked over a wood fire or on a coal-fired grill, a cast-iron grill pan, or an electric griddle, and dressed either with Brown Butter Vinaigrette or with White Truffle Oil Aioli (both are really good: see pages 136–137 for the recipes). If you opt for grilling, a grilling basket would be very helpful for keeping the asparagus under control.

1½ pounds pencil-thin asparagus

3 tablespoons olive oil

¼ teaspoon salt

⅛ teaspoon freshly ground black pepper

Brown Butter Vinaigrette or White Truffle Oil Aioli (recipes follow)

Snap off the ends of the asparagus where they break naturally. Coat the spears with the olive oil, and sprinkle with the salt and pepper. Let marinate at room temperature for 30 minutes to 2 hours. Grill or pan-sear the asparagus 2 to 4 minutes, till bright green and just tender, turning the spears as they cook.

To serve, arrange the asparagus as you like, and drizzle with warmed Brown Butter Vinaigrette or White Truffle Oil Aioli.

brown butter vinaigrette

brown butter vinaigrette

1 teaspoon minced shallots

1 teaspoon minced garlic

1 teaspoon Dijon mustard

3 tablespoons balsamic vinegar

¼ teaspoon salt

Pinch of freshly ground black pepper

4 tablespoons butter

1 tablespoon freshly squeezed lemon juice

5 tablespoons extra virgin olive oil

3 teaspoons capers (optional)

2 tablespoons olive oil (optional)

1 teaspoon minced fresh parsley leaves, rinsed and squeezed dry

To make the vinaigrette, combine the shallots, garlic, mustard, vinegar, salt, and pepper in a small bowl, and set it aside. In a wide-bottomed sauté pan, cook the butter over high heat, stirring constantly, until it turns a nutty caramel-brown. Mix in the lemon juice and remove from the heat. Slowly whisk the butter into the shallot mixture, then whisk in the extra virgin olive oil. Continue whisking until well emulsified. Keep the vinaigrette at room temperature, and warm it up before serving.

If you opt for the garnish of crispy capers, rinse the capers, then heat the olive oil in a small sauté pan over medium-high heat and fry the capers until they are crisp and have opened up. Scoop the capers out with a slotted spoon and drain on a paper towel.

To serve, warm up the vinaigrette, and pour it over the asparagus. Finish with a sprinkling of parsley and capers, if desired.

white truffle oil aioli

white truffle oil aioli

2 large egg yolks

1 tablespoon champagne vinegar

2 cloves garlic

1 or 2 pinches crushed dried red pepper

½ teaspoon salt

⅛ teaspoon freshly ground black pepper

2 tablespoons (lightly packed) chopped fresh tarragon leaves and tender stems

½ cup olive oil

¼ cup extra virgin olive oil

1 to 2 tablespoons white truffle–infused oil

1 cup tiny croutons (¼-inch dice; optional)

Truffle oil, the darling of a lot of fancy restaurants, can be quite tasty if not overused. In this case, just a tablespoon or two makes a big difference in a simple aioli—that and a little chopped tarragon. Most truffle oils are made by infusing olive oil with truffles, but the skinny is that there is no "pure" one sold, and none made with white truffle essence, as this essence is very volatile and won't hold. Instead, they contain some "nature-identical" products that taste like white truffle but are made with a chemical base. Some of the black truffle oils are actually made with real black truffles, but they are probably goosed as well.

For the aioli, put the egg yolks, vinegar, garlic, crushed red pepper, salt, and pepper in a food processor and blend until the mixture thickens and turns light lemon-yellow in color. With the machine running, add the tarragon, then slowly drizzle in the olive oils and the truffle oil until all are well incorporated. Taste for seasoning. Thin with water, if desired, to a drizzleable consistency.

To serve, arrange the asparagus on plates, drizzle with some aioli; sprinkle with tiny croutons, if desired.

8 ounces soft fresh goat cheese, at room temperature

½ cup minced celery leaves

2 tablespoons minced fresh tarragon

2 to 3 tablespoons minced fennel fronds or fresh dill weed

½ teaspoon freshly ground black pepper

Juice and finely grated zest of ½ lemon

1 cup chopped toasted walnuts

walnut oil vinaigrette

½ vanilla bean

Juice and grated zest of 1 lemon

Sea salt

Freshly ground black pepper

¼ cup walnut oil

¼ cup olive oil

6 thin slices of baguette or levain-style bread, cut diagonally

Olive oil, for brushing

3 cups mixed watercress (coarse stems removed), arugula, and butter lettuce

Herbed Goat Cheese and Walnut Log with Garden Greens

Serves 6

This is a light, bright dish that you can make any time of the year if you select the herbs and greens according to seasonal availability. In the spring, I'd use celery leaves, dill, and tarragon for the cheese log and a mix of watercress leaves, arugula, and butter lettuce for the salad. In the summer, it could be basil and garlic chives for the log, with frisée and arugula for the greens. In the winter, try parsley and chervil, with two or three varieties of radicchio as the greens mix. The version below is a spring rendition.

For the greens, I like to use a vinaigrette made with walnut oil, to pick up on the flavors of the walnuts on the cheese log. Walnut oil is highly flavorful and very aromatic, but it becomes rancid quickly, so buy it in small bottles and keep it refrigerated. Try different brands to discover your favorite: I think the oils made with roasted nuts are best. Several are produced in California that are just as good as the ones from France. Walnut oil is too strong to be used alone in a vinaigrette; it needs to be combined with a mild olive oil. The exact proportions of walnut oil to olive oil are negotiable.

Long, angular croutons look the best, so when cutting the bread, try for a pretty dramatic diagonal on the cut. And as for the vanilla, after scraping the beans into the dressing ingredients, don't just throw out the pod. Toss the scraped pod into a small bowl of sugar for vanilla sugar, or put it in a little jar of brandy for vanilla brandy. You could also keep it in your freezer and use it the next time you poach any kind of stone fruit.

For the cheese log, combine the goat cheese, celery leaves, tarragon, fennel, pepper, and lemon juice and zest; mix well. Roll the mixture into a 1¹/₂-inch-diameter log, wrap in plastic, and chill until firm, at least 1 hour. Once chilled, roll the log in the nuts, pressing so they adhere to the cheese. Wrap again in plastic and chill until needed.

To make the vinaigrette, split the vanilla bean open and scrape the seeds into a small bowl. Add the lemon juice, lemon zest, salt, and pepper, and stir until the salt has dissolved. Gradually whisk in the oils, and continue whisking until well emulsified. Set aside until needed.

Preheat the oven to 375°F. Brush the bread with olive oil. Place the bread on a baking sheet, and bake until toasted and golden brown.

To serve, cut the cheese log into ¹/₂-inch-thick rounds. Briefly whisk the dressing once more, and toss the greens with just enough of it to moisten. Pile some greens in the center of each small plate and top with a slice of cheese, then drizzle over a little of the remaining dressing. Sprinkle any additional walnuts about and place a crouton off to the side on each plate.

bowls and spoons

If you've read my other books, you know how much I love making soups and stews.

chapter 3: Bowls and Spoons

If you've read my other books, you know how much I love making soups and stews. They're easy to do, easy to eat, and leftovers are great for a midnight snack or quick meal. Some soups actually taste better if they've been made ahead, so they are great for entertaining (the Onion-Tomato-Bread "Soup," for example, or the broth for the Ahi and Shiitake Mushroom Wontons). Some are fairly light (Corn Soup or Garlic Soup, for example) and would make good precursors to a two- or three-dish small-plates meal. Others, like the Halibut "Stew" or the Morel Mushroom "Casseroles," are more substantial, and you could build the rest of your meal around them.

Not everything that comes in a bowl or cup is a soup. The Salmon, Halibut, and Scallop Ceviche and Pablo's Cóctel de Camarones are crosses between salads and bowls, very refreshing for spring and summer.

When prepping soups, think of how you will serve them. If the recipe has diced vegetables, it's important to cut them small enough so they'll be easy to scoop up with a spoon. If people are going to "drink" the soup, you should puree it, and finely mince the garnish. I once did a party where I served soup in very small handmade bowls. Unfortunately, the teaspoons I put out didn't fit into the bowls (oops!—demitasse spoons would have been handy). Luckily, the soup could be sipped.

Be really creative, and have fun with how you serve these soups. Try shot glasses, large silver or wooden spoons, sake cups, martini glasses, espresso or demitasse cups, or tiny bowls.

filling

4 ounces ahi tuna

4 ounces shiitake mushrooms

2 teaspoons toasted sesame oil

2 teaspoons peanut oil

1 teaspoon chopped garlic

1½ teaspoons grated peeled
     fresh ginger

1 or 2 kaffir or other lime leaves,
     finely julienned, or the grated
     zest of ½ lime

¼ to ½ teaspoon salt

⅛ teaspoon freshly ground black
     pepper

broth

3 tablespoons rice vinegar

2 tablespoons sugar

2 cups chicken or vegetable
     stock

2 shallots, sliced into very thin
     rings

1 or 2 scallions, white and light
     green parts only, cut thinly on
     the diagonal

2 cloves garlic, finely minced

2 tablespoons finely julienned
     peeled fresh ginger

2 tablespoons peeled and finely
     julienned carrots

1 tablespoon chili paste

1½ teaspoons tamari or dark soy
     sauce

1½ teaspoons toasted sesame oil

⅛ to ¼ teaspoon salt

Ahi and Shiitake Mushroom Wontons in Broth

Serves 6

The basic ingredient in a traditional wonton filling is minced pork or minced shrimp, or a pork-and-shrimp combination. So the filling in this recipe is a bit of a departure. The wrapping we use for the dumplings is very traditional, though, as we work with fresh wonton skins. These wrappers can be found in the refrigerator case of most markets in our area, usually in the produce department. They come in three- to four-inch squares or rounds. Either will work: it just depends on whether you'd rather end up with half-moon or triangle shapes.

You want to cook the wontons all in one go, so if you don't have a big ol' pasta pot, get two smaller pots of water boiling. You want plenty of room for movement around each of the wontons. And as with cooking any pasta, the more water, the better.

You can make the broth up to one day ahead of time and reheat it when you're ready to serve. And the broth is equally good with the Duck and Mustard Green Wontons (page 148).

For the filling, cut the tuna into ¹/₄-inch dice, and set it aside. Cut the mushrooms into ¹/₄-inch dice and set them aside separately. To make the filling, heat the sesame oil and peanut oil in a large sauté pan over medium-high heat. Add the mushrooms and cook, stirring, until lightly caramelized, about 2 minutes. Add the garlic and ginger and stir everything around well. Add the tuna, lime leaves, salt, and pepper; cook a minute more, stirring to make sure everything gets well mixed. Scrape the

Cornstarch, for dusting

18 wonton skins

3 to 4 quarts water

2 tablespoons salt

1 tablespoon tiny fresh basil leaves, or chiffonade of larger leaves

1 tablespoon tiny fresh mint leaves, or chiffonade of larger leaves

1 tablespoon cilantro leaves

mixture out onto a small baking sheet or shallow dish and place in the refrigerator to chill.

In the meantime, make the broth. Combine the vinegar and sugar in a small saucepan. Bring to a boil, reduce to a simmer, and cook just till the sugar has dissolved. Add the remaining broth ingredients, bring back to a simmer, and cook a minute more. Remove from the heat and reserve. Reheat the broth just before serving.

To make the wontons, dust a baking sheet with cornstarch. Lay out 2 or 3 wonton skins at a time on a clean dry surface, and brush them around the edges with water. Spoon a tablespoonful or so of filling onto the center of each wrapper, leaving space around the sides for sealing, and fold over to form a triangle. Crimp the edges with your fingers. Place the wontons on the baking sheet and repeat with the remaining wrappers. Cover and refrigerate till needed.

Shortly before you're ready to serve, put the water and salt in a large pot and bring it to a boil. Meanwhile, place 6 bowls in a warm oven and start reheating the broth. When the water has reached a boil, carefully add the wontons. Cook till they begin to float, which will take from 2 to 4 minutes, depending on the thickness of your wonton skins.

To serve, place 3 wontons in each of the warmed bowls, ladle some hot broth over them, and finish with a sprinkling of basil, mint, and cilantro.

vietnamese-style sauce

6 tablespoons freshly squeezed lime juice

4 tablespoons fish sauce (*nuoc mam*)

2 shallots, minced

2 tablespoons chopped fresh cilantro, mint, or Thai basil leaves

2 tablespoons sugar

¼ to ½ teaspoon cayenne pepper

filling

3 tablespoons peanut oil or light olive oil

1½ cups minced raw duck meat

1 tablespoon grated peeled fresh ginger

3 scallions, white and light green parts only, minced

1 tablespoon minced garlic

5 cups (firmly packed) chiffonade of baby mustard greens or beet greens

1 tablespoon tamari

1 tablespoon hoisin sauce

3 to 4 quarts water

2 tablespoons salt

30 wonton skins

garnishes

Thinly sliced scallions

Cilantro or mint leaves

Shredded carrot

Duck and Mustard Green Wontons with Vietnamese-Style Sauce

Serves 6

Here's another variation on the wonton theme—a filling made with sautéed minced duck and mustard greens. We are able to order ground duck meat for the restaurant, but this might be a trickier proposition for home cooks. If your butcher won't grind duck meat for you, you can mince it yourself. Breast meat is easier to manage than leg meat, which has a lot of silver skin and connective tissue that needs to be removed.

For the greens, you can use any kind of baby mustard greens. Our gardens are often overflowing with mustard greens of all kinds, including some of the Asian varieties. They practically grow like weeds in our climate. Japanese red mustard is great in these wontons, so get that if you can. It has a nice mineral flavor and a pepperiness that blends well with the rich duck.

For a different twist on the recipe, fry the wontons in peanut or canola oil till golden and crisp before serving them with the Vietnamese-style sauce. The wontons—either fried or boiled—are also excellent served in the broth from the Ahi and Shiitake Mushroom Wontons (page 146).

If you have the option, get fresh wonton skins, which can be found in the refrigerator case of most markets. They work much better than the frozen ones.

To make the sauce, combine the lime juice, fish sauce, shallots, cilantro, sugar, and cayenne; mix well. Reserve till needed.

For the filling, heat the oil in a large sauté pan over medium-high heat. Add the duck and stir-fry 2 to 3 minutes, until just cooked through. Toss in the ginger, scallions, and garlic; stir-fry another minute or so. Add the greens and cook until they have released their liquid. Pour in the tamari and hoisin and continue cooking until most of the liquid has evaporated. If this hasn't happened within 2 to 3 minutes, scoop out the solids and reduce the liquid until the pan is almost dry, then recombine. Place the mixture in the refrigerator to chill.

Once the filling is well chilled, you can make the wontons. Set the water and salt on to boil. Get a little bowl of water ready for wonton sealing and start stuffing. You'll want about a tablespoon of the duck mixture in each of the skins. Moisten the edges with just a little water, fold over to form a triangle, and pinch to seal. Cook 1 to 2 minutes in boiling water, until the dough is just tender and the filling is hot. Drain.

To serve, toss the scallions, cilantro, and carrots together. Place some of this garnish in the bottom of each bowl (Asian rice bowls are most attractive), and top with 5 wontons each. Pour some of the Vietnamese-style sauce over, and pass the remaining sauce around or keep it handy if anyone would like extra.

Halibut "Stew" with Saffron Broth

Serves 6

Actually, the fish in this recipe is grilled, not stewed, and the key to this dish is the broth, which is flavored with saffron, fennel, and sweet onions. It's probably easiest to use clam juice for the broth, as you can easily find bottled clam juice in markets. Fish stock is great, but unless you do a lot of fishing, it's not easy to come by. If you're using clam juice, be sure to get one without monosodium glutamate (MSG). If your tomatoes are really juicy, you may need less clam juice than called for, or use the smaller amount of wine. The broth can be made a day ahead and kept refrigerated until needed. Reheat it and add the fish just before serving.

Almost any kind of cooked seafood can be substituted for the halibut in this dish, or you can use a combination of fish and shellfish. Steamed mussels, grilled jumbo shrimp, or lobster or Dungeness crab, roughly chopped and cracked, would all work.

Thick-cut French bread or sourdough bread, brushed with olive oil and grilled, is a great accompaniment.

broth

½ sweet onion (Georgia, Vidalia, Maui, or white)

½ bulb fennel

1 to 1½ tablespoons olive oil

2 cloves garlic, minced to a paste

3 strands of saffron

½ to ⅔ cup white wine

2 juicy vine-ripened tomatoes, peeled and minced

2 cups clam juice, fish stock, or water

1 bay leaf

Salt and freshly ground black pepper

12 ounces halibut or sea bass

Olive oil, for brushing

Salt and freshly ground black pepper

garnish options

Finely chopped green olives

Minced parsley leaves

Torn or pinched fennel fronds

Aioli (page 64) or Garlicky Romesco Sauce (page 127)

For the broth, cut the onion and fennel bulb into ¼-inch dice, reserving some of the fennel fronds for garnish, if desired. Heat the olive oil in a saucepan over medium heat and sauté the onion and fennel 5 minutes or so, until they are just barely tender. Add the garlic and cook 1 minute more. Add the saffron and stir to toast 1 minute, then add the wine and reduce by half. Add the tomatoes, clam juice, bay leaf, salt, and pepper, and simmer for 20 minutes.

Shortly before serving, brush the fish with olive oil and sprinkle with salt and pepper. Grill the fish to the desired doneness, 2 to 3 minutes per side. The fish can also be seared in a skillet with the tiniest bit of oil. Ladle the broth out into warmed bowls, then flake nice-size pieces of the fish into each. Garnish as you like and serve steamy-hot.

Garlic Soup

Serves 6

1 whole head garlic

2 tablespoons extra virgin olive oil

1 leek, white and light green parts only, well rinsed and finely sliced

2 sprigs fresh thyme

2 small potatoes, cut into ½-inch dice

2½ to 3 cups chicken stock or water

Sea salt

Freshly ground black pepper

¼ cup cream (optional)

garnish options

Minced garlic chives and chive blossoms

Toasted almond slices

Finely grated hard-boiled egg

Minced parsley leaves with a drizzle of truffle oil

Sprigs of thyme

This basic soup dresses up or down very well. Blended with the optional cream, it is very elegant. Unblended, without cream, it's very rustic. For a great first course, fill coffee-cup-size bowls halfway with soup, and top each serving with a small poached egg and two or three croutons. For a Spanish tapas meal, add a teaspoon of pimentón *paprika while cooking the leeks and garlic and omit the cream. Then garnish with small quail eggs, poached or fried, and a crouton made with a nice fruity Spanish olive oil.*

My favorite type of garlic is Spanish red garlic, followed by Italian red garlic. Both of these are sweeter than the standard white garlic. However, if you are careful not to caramelize the garlic, whichever kind you use will become sweet and mild, and not at all overpowering.

Break up the head of garlic by pressing down on it with the heel of your hand or the broad side of a knife. Separate the cloves and cut off the root ends, then peel and slice the garlic. In a small saucepan, heat the oil over medium-low heat, add the leek and thyme, and sweat slowly until soft, 5 to 10 minutes or longer—the slower, the better. Add the garlic, increase the heat to medium, and cook, stirring often, till softened. Take care not to let the garlic brown.

Add the potatoes and stock and simmer until the potatoes are soft, 10 to 15 minutes. Remove the thyme and season to taste with salt and pepper. You may serve as is or, for a more elegant finish, put the soup in a blender, add the cream, and process until smooth. Reheat the soup if it has cooled too much. Sprinkle each serving with one of the garnish options, if desired.

6 half-inch-thick slices rustic
    country bread

Olive oil or butter, for coating

broth

2⅔ cups freshly squeezed
    tangerine juice or orange juice

⅓ cup white wine

1 tablespoon freshly squeezed
    lime juice

4 to 6 tablespoons olive oil

24 mussels, cleaned and rinsed

24 clams, cleaned and rinsed

¾ cup ¼-inch dice andouille
    sausage

1 teaspoon minced garlic

1 tablespoon minced shallot

2 to 3 tablespoons butter

1 teaspoon salt

¾ to 1 teaspoon freshly ground
    black pepper

1 tablespoon minced fresh basil
    leaves

½ tablespoon minced fresh
    parsley leaves

Mussels and Clams with Andouille Sausage in Tangerine Broth

Serves 6

This is one of our more popular small bowls at Mustards. It's made with a citrus broth that is a perfect match for the clams, mussels, and smoky sausage. Andouille is a highly seasoned, garlicky smoked pork sausage that is an essential ingredient in many Cajun and Creole dishes. We use Hobbs's applewood-smoked andouille sausage, but any high-quality smoked sausage, linguiça, or garlic sausage would also be tasty. We make this often in the winter, when tangerines are at their best.

For the grilled bread, we use a rustic levain or sourdough-style loaf. For another fabulous variation, skip the bread and try this dish with a pasta that has been cooked al dente. Farfalle or any short tube pasta such as penne would be my recommendation.

To make the toast, lightly brush the bread slices on each side with olive oil or butter, and toast over a grill or on a baking sheet in a 375°F oven until crispy and golden on the outside but still a little soft in the center.

For the broth, combine the tangerine juice, white wine, and lime juice and keep chilled until ready to use.

Heat 2 large sauté pans or 1 large roasting pan set over 2 burners using high heat (you want a lot of surface area). Add the olive oil and allow it to heat up. Toss in the shellfish and sausage and cook, shaking and stirring, for 1 to 2 minutes. Add the garlic and shallot and cook 30 seconds or so. Add about 2 cups of the tangerine juice mix and cook, stirring, until the shellfish have opened and the sauce has reduced by about half. Remove and discard any shellfish that have not opened. If the pan seems to be getting too dry, add more tangerine broth. Reduce the temperature and add the butter, salt, pepper, basil, and parsley; stir and toss around until everything is well coated.

Dish up in deep soup bowls, pouring pan juices equally over each bowl. Tuck a slab of grilled bread in at the side of the bowls to soak up the juice.

Salmon, Halibut, and Scallop Ceviche with Coconut

Serves 6

There's no real cooking involved when you make a ceviche, but you do need to plan ahead, as the seafood needs to marinate at least three hours but not more than eight hours. The fish "cooks" in the lime juice marinade: too long, and it will actually be overdone and mushy. Use only the freshest fish for this recipe. When it's in season, we use Pacific king salmon; it's so-o-o good! Amounts don't have to be exact, but you'll need about 10 ounces each of salmon and halibut.

For an interesting show, serve the ceviche in chunks of fresh coconut. To crack a coconut, place it on top of several layers of newspaper on a strong, stable surface—and then give it a good whack with a mallet, or some more refined hits with a pick and a hammer. You want to end up with three or four large pieces. Have some paper towels handy for the liquid that is in the center of the coconut, or catch it in a cup if you can. Some people like to drink the juice, some don't. Some people eat the coconut meat, others don't. Either way, the pieces of coconut make for a great presentation. Coconut milk is an extract of the coconut meat itself and not of the juice; you can buy cans of coconut milk at most regular supermarkets.

To keep the avocados fresh and bright, cut them in half and remove the pits, then dunk them quickly in ice water. Peel and slice them when you're ready to serve. Plantain Chips (page 22) or tortilla chips would be an excellent accompaniment to this dish.

(continued)

4 ounces scallops

8 to 12 ounces salmon

8 to 12 ounces halibut

1 cup freshly squeezed lime juice

1 teaspoon sea salt

¼ teaspoon freshly ground white
pepper

½ teaspoon finely chopped
seeded serrano chile

1 red onion, minced

1 (14-ounce) can unsweetened
coconut milk

2 coconuts

1 or 2 avocados, sliced

Cilantro sprigs

Extra virgin olive oil, for garnish

Slice the scallops into $^1/_4$-inch-thick circles and place in a non-reactive bowl big enough to hold all the seafood. Cut the salmon and halibut into 3 or 4 lengthwise strips about 1 inch wide, then cut these strips crosswise into $^1/_4$-inch slices to match the scallops. Add the fish to the scallops. Pour $^3/_4$ cup of the lime juice into the bowl and mix gently but well, making sure all the seafood gets coated with some juice. Cover and put in the refrigerator to marinate 2 hours.

Put the seafood in a colander to drain, and clean out the bowl while it's draining. Return the seafood to the clean bowl, along with the salt, pepper, chile, onion, coconut milk, and remaining $^1/_4$ cup lime juice. Mix gently but well, then cover and refrigerate at least 1 hour, but no longer than 6 hours.

When you're ready to serve, crack each of the coconuts into 3 cup-shaped pieces. Check the ceviche for seasoning and fill each of the coconut bowls with some of it. Garnish with avocado slices, a sprig of cilantro, and a drizzle of olive oil. If the coconut shells are too much trouble, just serve the ceviche in small bowls or in sea scallop shells, if you have them.

Pablo's Cóctel de Camarones

Serves 6

cocktail sauce

1 tablespoon grated peeled fresh ginger

3 tablespoons grated peeled fresh horseradish

¼ cup freshly squeezed lime juice

¼ cup minced peeled daikon or other radish

1 cup tomato juice

¾ cup ketchup

¼ teaspoon salt

¼ teaspoon freshly ground black pepper

1 tablespoon minced cilantro leaves

1 shallot, minced

1 jalapeño chile or ½ *pasilla* chile, seeded and minced

1 tablespoon minced fresh parsley

1 clove garlic, minced

1 shake Worcestershire sauce

2 shakes Tabasco sauce

1 tablespoon good-quality tequila

(continued)

This dish features huge prawns that have been poached in an aromatic and somewhat spicy broth, and a cocktail sauce that will knock your socks off. There are several unexpected ingredients in our cocktail sauce: ginger, jalapeño, and daikon, for example, and they all help lift this sauce to a higher realm. But what really gives it extra zing is that we make it with fresh horseradish. If you can't get fresh horseradish, you can use freshly prepared store-bought horseradish, but get the kind that is kept in the refrigerated section of your market. Refrigerated preparations are made in small batches and are much better than those that have been stabilized and left sitting on the shelf at ambient temperatures for unknown lengths of time. Any extra sauce would be great on fried oysters, oysters on the half shell, lobster salad, or a variation of this cocktail made with cooked, diced octopus and small shucked oysters.

In the restaurant we poach the camarones in a basket-strainer that is just smaller than the pot with the bouillon, so we can easily lift them all out when they are done. I always poach prawns with the shells on, as it increases flavor. After poaching, the bouillon can be strained and used again to make a soup. If you are not going to use the bouillon right away, though, it should be cooled and frozen.

For the cocktail sauce, mix the ginger, horseradish, and lime juice together in a good-size bowl. (The lime juice will keep the ginger and horseradish light-colored.) Then add the remaining

(continued)

bouillon

4 quarts water

1 onion, chopped into 1-inch chunks

1 carrot, peeled and chopped into 1-inch chunks

3 stalks celery, chopped into 1-inch chunks

1 tablespoon paprika

1 teaspoon cayenne pepper

2 bay leaves

¼ bunch fresh thyme

½ bunch fresh parsley, stems only

Freshly ground black pepper

2 lemons, halved

½ cup white wine

18 large prawns (21 to 25 count)

6 medium-size romaine leaves, chopped

1½ avocados, sliced

6 sprigs cilantro

Extra virgin olive oil

ingredients for the cocktail sauce and mix well. Cover and keep chilled until needed.

To make the bouillon, put the water, onion, carrot, celery, paprika, cayenne, bay leaves, thyme, and parsley in a large pot. Grind in a little black pepper, squeeze in the juice of the lemons, and add the wine. Cover and bring to a boil.

Once the bouillon reaches a boil, reduce it to a simmer and add the prawns. Poach until they are just cooked through. This should take between 3 and 5 minutes, depending on the size of the prawns and the heat of your poaching liquid. Spread the cooked prawns out on a baking sheet and put them in the fridge. You want them to cool quickly, so they don't get mushy. Once cool, peel 6 of the prawns ³/₄ of the way down, leaving their tails intact. Peel the remaining prawns completely. Devein all the prawns; set aside the 6 with tails attached for garnishing, and coarsely chop the rest.

To serve, place some of the chopped romaine in the bottom of a stemmed glass such as a parfait or martini glass. Add some cocktail sauce and chopped prawns on top of the romaine, then some avocado slices. Garnish with the whole prawns, cilantro sprigs, and drizzle a few drops of extra virgin olive oil around. Serve with extra cocktail sauce on the side.

Onion-Tomato-Bread "Soup"

Serves 6 to 8

¼ onion, peeled and cut into
¼-inch wedges

4 tablespoons extra virgin
olive oil

2 cups diced vine-ripened
tomatoes, peeled if you wish

1 tablespoon Spanish sherry
vinegar

2 tablespoons minced scallions,
white and light green parts
only

1 clove garlic, minced to a paste

Juice of ½ lemon

1 tablespoon chopped fresh basil
leaves

1 tablespoon chopped fresh
tarragon leaves

½ teaspoon salt

¼ teaspoon freshly ground black
pepper

Pinch of cayenne pepper

1 cup ½-inch-square croutons
made from a good rustic
French bread

¼ cup crumbled soft fresh goat
cheese or feta cheese

Toasted pumpkin seeds or
hazelnuts (optional)

You can make this as soupy or as thick as you like, depending on when you put the croutons in. If you prefer a soupier version with a little crunch, add the croutons just before serving; if you are looking for something more saladlike, add the croutons earlier to give them time to absorb more of the juices. Be sure to use a sturdy rustic loaf of bread for the croutons. To make this cool soup more interesting, use two different colors of tomatoes.

Some thoughts on serving: serve in teacups (this is a great way to use your grandma's collection) or in espresso cups. With espresso cups, you will get eight servings.

Preheat the oven to 300°F. Put the onion in a small baking dish and drizzle it with 1 tablespoon of the oil. Stir it around to be sure it's well coated, then cover with aluminum foil. Bake till steamy-tender, 20 to 30 minutes, then remove the foil and continue baking until the onion caramelizes, 10 to 15 minutes.

Put the tomatoes and sherry vinegar in a large bowl and mix well. Run half the tomatoes through a food mill or whirl them in a blender until smooth. Strain to remove the seeds and any tough bits. Return the pureed tomatoes to the bowl and add the onion, scallions, garlic, lemon juice, basil, tarragon, salt, pepper, and cayenne. Whisk in the remaining 3 tablespoons olive oil at the end. If you want the thicker version of the soup, fold in the croutons 15 to 20 minutes before serving; otherwise, add them at the last minute.

Garnish with the cheese and with pumpkin seeds or hazelnuts, if desired.

Baked Goat Cheese and Tomato Fondue

Serves 6

6 thin slices sturdy bread

2 pounds heirloom tomatoes
or 2 (16-ounce) cans diced
tomatoes

2 tablespoons extra virgin
olive oil

2 large shallots, sliced

4 cloves garlic, sliced

¼ teaspoon salt

⅛ teaspoon freshly ground black
pepper

1 fresh bay leaf, if possible,
or 1 sprig fresh basil

2 tablespoons white wine

2 tablespoons sliced dates,
prunes, or dried apricots

1 (9-ounce) jar Cabecou cheese,
at room temperature

Okay, let's say it's January, and you've completely forgotten how wonderful fresh heirloom tomatoes taste: you could still make this dish with canned diced tomatoes and the results would be pretty decent. But sometime in your life, make this with ripe, warm-from-the-garden tomatoes and treat yourself to something spectacular!

Cabecou is an aged goat cheese that is formed in disks. It comes in jars, packed in olive oil. Save the olive oil to use in vinaigrettes. We use Laura Chenel's Cabecou.

Drain the tomatoes if they are too juicy. And don't let the sauce cook too much: you just want to warm the tomatoes. You don't want them to break down and become saucelike.

You can make one large serving of this or six individual ones. Terra-cotta baking dishes would be ideal, but any oven-proof dishes will work. If you have one, I recommend using a convection oven for the baking; just watch your time, as the fondue will cook faster.

If you want smaller croutons, cut the slices of bread in half. Grill, toast, or oven-toast them so they are nice and crispy. Set them aside.

For the fondue, peel and seed the tomatoes. If they are extremely juicy, set them in a colander to drain 20 minutes or so, then chop them into ¹/₂-inch pieces. (Canned tomatoes should be drained, too.) Heat the olive oil in a heavy wide pan

(continued)

over medium heat. Add the shallots and garlic and cook slowly until very tender, 8 to 10 minutes. Increase the heat and add the tomatoes, salt, pepper, and bay leaf; cook another 30 seconds or so. Add the wine and cook until it has evaporated. Add the dried fruit and take the pan off the heat. The dish can be held at this point and finished later.

To finish the dish, preheat the oven to 500°F. Cut the disks of cheese in half horizontally, making 6 small rounds. Spoon the tomatoes into a baking dish and top with the cheese. Bake until the top of the cheese is golden and the tomato sauce is heated through and looks rich and thick. Depending on your oven, this should take 6 to 8 minutes.

Set the baking dish on a napkin-lined plate (to keep it from sliding around) with the "croutons" alongside, so your guests can make their own toasts. It is best to spread some cheese first, then spoon some tomatoes on top. Make sure you warn everyone about the hot dish.

Alternatively, cut the bread into bite-size cubes, toast till crispy, and have your guests skewer them with fondue forks and coat them with the cheese and tomato fondue.

Wild Mushroom Stew

Serves 6

One of my favorite things to do is to wander around at farmers' markets. You can usually find many more varieties of mushrooms there than you will at most supermarkets. You can also find kits for growing your own mushrooms, which is a fun thing to do. Hunting for mushrooms in the wild can be deadly, even if you have an expert with you. I have a friend who ended up in the hospital because, even after sixty years of experience hunting for wild mushrooms, she picked the wrong one. So don't be crazy! When you want to make this stew, go to your local farmers' market first.

This is super with any fresh mushroom. Morels, porcini, chanterelles, hedgehogs, trumpets—they're all great, and it just depends on what's in season. You can also use a mixture of reconstituted dried wild mushrooms and domestic mushrooms. Reconstitute one and a half to two ounces of dried mushrooms, then add enough domestic mushrooms to equal three cups. It's not absolutely necessary, but the stew will be more interesting if you make it with three different types of mushrooms.

To clean mushrooms, use a brush with semifirm bristles, or a pastry brush for more delicate types. There is nothing worse than sand in the mouth, so if your mushrooms seem really dirty, rinse them with cold water as briefly as you can, and dry immediately with paper towels. Trim off any tough stems, and cut the mushrooms in half if they are big.

The stew is served over roasted potatoes, but put out plenty of crusty hot bread, too, so your guests can mop up every last bit of the densely flavorful sauce. Roast the potatoes while you prepare the stew, and everything will come together

(continued)

6 small Yukon Gold potatoes

Olive oil, for coating

Salt and freshly ground black pepper

18 pearl onions

18 cloves garlic

sauce

3 tablespoons olive oil

1 tablespoon porcini powder or other powdered dried mushroom

2 tablespoons sherry, preferably Pedro Ximénez

⅔ cup diced peeled tomatoes

1 to 1¼ cups vegetable or mushroom stock

½ cup cream

3 cups mixed whole wild mushrooms, or cut in halves or quarters if very large

2 tablespoons finely shredded fresh basil, tarragon, parsley, or chives

at the same time. For a variation, try serving the stew over noodles or polenta instead of the potatoes. And another little tip: it's great with poached eggs, too.

Preheat the oven to 375°F. Cut the potatoes in half, roll them in a little olive oil, and sprinkle with salt and pepper. Roast 20 minutes.

Cut off the root ends of the onions and garlic cloves and blanch in boiling salted water about 1 minute to tenderize them. Shock in ice water and pop them out of their skins. Finely mince 2 of the cloves of garlic, and set the rest aside along with the onions.

To make the sauce, heat 1 tablespoon of the oil in a medium saucepan over medium heat; add the minced garlic and cook 1 minute, but don't let the garlic brown. Stir in the mushroom powder and cook about 30 seconds, till aromatic. Add the sherry and reduce by half, then add the tomatoes. Toss and simmer 3 to 5 minutes, until the tomato juices have evaporated. Add the stock and cook, stirring now and then, until reduced by half. Add the cream and heat till just hot through, then remove from the heat.

In a large sauté pan, heat the remaining 2 tablespoons of the oil over high heat, and add the mushrooms. Let them sweat for a bit, then increase the heat to cook off the juices and caramelize the mushrooms. Add the reserved onions and garlic, stir, and cook until caramelized. Add the reserved sauce and reduce to a nice thick consistency. Season with salt and pepper to finish.

To serve, place the potatoes on small plates or in small bowls (traditional Spanish *cazuelas,* if you have them) and top with mushroom stew. Sprinkle with herbs and serve with lots of hot crusty bread.

Morel Mushroom "Casseroles" with Pedro Ximénez Sherry and Thyme

Serves 6

2 pounds fresh morel mushrooms, stemmed, or 2 ounces dried morels and 1¾ pounds fresh cultivated mushrooms, stemmed

2 tablespoons butter or olive oil

½ small sweet white onion, cut into thin crescents

1 tablespoon minced fresh thyme

3 cloves garlic

½ cup Pedro Ximénez sherry or other cream sherry

¼ to ½ teaspoon sea salt

¼ teaspoon freshly ground black pepper

¼ to ½ cup whipping cream

¾ cup shredded pecorino cheese, Pepato if possible

I invented this dish for a friend who loves to take in the smells of foods before eating them. It's served in individual lidded dishes so that each person gets the whole hit of the earthy aroma of this soup as they take the lid off their own little "casserole." I found these dishes in San Francisco's Japantown. If you live near a Chinatown, you might find them there, too. It's okay to make the soup ahead and bake it just before serving. This is a very rich soup, so keep the rest of the meal simple and light.

If you use dried morels, you can combine them with any fresh mushrooms, such as buttons, porcinis, or shiitakes. For the topping, we use a pecorino cheese called Pepato. Pepato is flavored with black peppercorns: this gives it a little extra bite, which works well with this dish. We get it from Bellwether Farms, a local cheese producer.

If you're using dried morels, soak them in hot water till soft. When softened, remove them from the water, reserving the water, and gently squeeze out the excess liquid. Slowly pour the soaking water into a clean bowl, stopping before any bits of sand get into the bowl. Use this liquid in addition to the sherry and cream. Cut all the mushrooms neatly into halves or quarters.

(continued)

Heat a large sauté pan over medium-high and add the butter. When hot, add the onion and cook, stirring, several minutes, till soft. Add the mushrooms, thyme, and garlic; cook 3 to 5 minutes, stirring occasionally, until the mushrooms have absorbed any liquid and are slightly caramelized. Add the sherry, salt, and pepper; cook over medium-high heat till reduced and very syrupy. Add the reserved mushroom water, if you have any, and $1/4$ cup of the cream. Reduce until the sauce is thick enough to coat the back of a spoon. Adjust the seasoning, if necessary, and add more cream if the mixture seems too dry. Pour into 6 individual ovenproof bowls and reserve till just before you're ready to serve. If you want to hold the dish for an extended length of time, refrigerate and increase the final baking time accordingly.

To finish the dish, preheat the oven to 475°F. Sprinkle with the cheese, cover, and bake 8 to 10 minutes, until heated through and bubbling. If you don't have lidded casseroles, cover the dishes with aluminum foil. To ensure doneness, remove 1 of the casseroles and carefully check the temperature at the center. If it doesn't seem hot, gently press everything back down and return to the oven for a few more minutes, till very hot. Serve with crusty warm bread for sopping up every bit of sauce.

corn soup

4 ears white corn

2 tablespoons butter or olive oil

½ leek, cut lengthwise and then into thin half-moons; or 1 small sweet onion, cut into thin slivers

½ *pasilla* chile, seeded and finely minced

½ teaspoon salt

¼ teaspoon freshly ground black pepper

3½ to 4 cups chicken, corn, or vegetable stock

¼ cup whipping cream

double-basil tomatoes

2 tablespoons extra virgin olive oil

4 tomatoes, peeled and diced

2 cloves garlic, sliced

2 sprigs each purple and green basil, plus small leaves for garnish

¼ teaspoon salt

⅛ teaspoon freshly ground black pepper

squash blossom garnish

1 (10¼-ounce) package squash blossoms

2 tablespoons butter or oil

2 cloves garlic, minced

¼ teaspoon (generous) salt

⅛ teaspoon freshly ground black pepper

1 tablespoon minced fresh epazote or oregano leaves

Corn Soup Two Ways

Serves 6

Pablo made this soup for one of the Supper Club dinners we do at Cindy's Backstreet Kitchen, and everyone asked for it to be on the menu always. It's quick and simple, and everyone loves it. If you make the soup and the garnishes ahead, it's easy as pie at service time. For added flavor, I often make a corn stock for the soup using the cobs. If you want to go this way, begin by making the stock (see the directions below).

Either serve the soup with the basil-flavored tomatoes only, or go for the combination of squash blossoms and huitlacoche. You can buy ten-ounce packages of squash blossoms in the market, and that is what I worked with in this recipe. This amount will give you enough for a garnish for six mini portions of soup as well as six Squash Blossom Quesadillas (page 56), should you choose to make some at the same time (just an idea).

Huitlacoche is a dark gray fungus that grows only on corn. Corn farmers consider it a blight, but gourmets consider it a delicacy (it is sometimes identified as the Mexican truffle). You can now get it fresh, canned, or frozen at Latin American markets (it may be spelled cuitlacoche on the label). We prefer fresh or frozen, but use whatever you can find. It's becoming more and more common, but is still fairly expensive. If you can get your hands on some, you're in for a treat!

Pablo's huitlacoche garnish is also great swirled into cream and used over pasta, or stirred at the end into a Parmesan risotto, or tucked into a quesadilla.

Cut or grate the kernels off the corn cobs into a bowl and reserve. If you are going to make a corn stock, simmer the corn cobs in 1 quart of water 30 to 45 minutes. To make the soup, heat the butter in a heavy-bottomed pot over medium heat. Add the leek and chile and cook 2 to 3 minutes, stirring often, until soft. Do not let them brown. Season with the salt and pepper, then add the corn and the stock and cook 5 to 8 minutes more. The soup can be chilled at this point, and reheated just before serving. To finish the soup, reheat it if necessary, add the cream, bring it just to a boil, and reduce the heat. Serve hot, either with the tomato garnish or with the squash blossoms and *huitlacoche*.

To make the tomatoes, heat the oil over high heat; add the tomatoes and garlic and cook until the tomato juices have evaporated. Add the sprigs of basil, and season with the salt and pepper.

For the squash blossom garnish, clean and roughly chop up the blossoms. Heat the butter in a sauté pan over medium-high heat, add the garlic, and cook 30 seconds or so, then add the salt and pepper. Add the blossoms and epazote and cook just till wilted. It can be used immediately or refrigerated for later use, in which case it can go straight into the soup without reheating.

To make the huitlacoche *garnish*, heat the oil in a sauté pan over medium-high heat. Add the mushrooms and *huitlacoche* and cook 3 to 5 minutes, stirring in the epazote, salt, and pepper as they cook. Add the onion, chile, and garlic; sweat 2 to 3 minutes, stirring occasionally, till soft. You can make this ahead and chill until needed. Reheat before serving.

For the tomato garnish option, reheat the soup if it has been refrigerated, and ladle it into 6 individual bowls. Spoon the tomato mixture on top of the soup and sprinkle small basil leaves about.

If you're doing the squash blossoms, stir them into the soup when the cream goes in. Reheat the *huitlacoche* garnish, if necessary. Ladle the soup into 6 individual bowls, and top each serving with a generous spoonful of Pablo's *huitlacoche* garnish.

pablo's *huitlacoche* garnish

2 tablespoons olive oil

1 cup ¼-inch dice shiitake mushrooms

½ cup chopped *huitlacoche*

1 tablespoon minced fresh epazote or oregano leaves

¼ to ½ teaspoon salt

¼ teaspoon freshly ground black pepper

2 to 3 tablespoons minced onion

½ jalapeño chile, minced

1 or 2 cloves garlic, minced

on a raft

chapter 4: On a Raft

In old diner lingo, if something came "on a raft," it meant the food was served up on toast. We've stretched the raft concept a bit in this chapter to include buns (for a selection of burgers) and tortillas (for an assortment of tostadas), plus oyster shells, and a potato raft, too. (This last dish, Grilled Beef on Potato Rafts with Salpicón, looks especially nice served on a long oval platter, with the rafts all lined up alongside each other. One night I made these for my boyfriend, Marshall, and he was really impressed. I should sell that recipe to a matchmaking company, it worked so well.)

Serving food on rafts cuts down on dishwashing, my least favorite part of cooking. Eating can get messy, though, so put out plenty of napkins! Use these recipes as guidelines and have fun creating rafts of your own.

In old diner lingo, if something came "on a raft," it meant the food was served up on toast. . . . Serving food on rafts cuts down on dishwashing, my least favorite part of cooking.

Bix Steak Tartare

18 thin slices rye or sourdough bread

Olive oil, for coating

12 ounces beef tenderloin

6 quail eggs, 3 chicken eggs, or 3 tablespoons homemade mayonnaise or aioli

3 tablespoons finely minced cornichons

½ bunch parsley, leaves only, finely minced, then rinsed and squeezed dry in a towel

3 tablespoons minced green peppercorns

3 tablespoons capers, rinsed and minced

3 to 4 tablespoons minced anchovy fillets

Worcestershire sauce

Dijon mustard

Pickapeppa or Tabasco sauce

Salt and freshly ground black pepper

Many years ago, I opened a restaurant in an alleyway in San Francisco's financial district. It was called Bix, and it was an elegant supper club, a cool place, and cool people went there—still do. Gérard Depardieu once kissed my hand there! Gordon Drysdale was the chef and Doug "Bix" Biederbeck, my partner in this venture, worked the front of the house. Doug was the one who had a clear vision of what the restaurant should be: a speakeasy with updated, hip, tasty food, like Bix Steak Tartare, for example. It's still on the menu, and I believe it's as good as any steak tartare you could get anywhere, including Paris.

In recent times people have become squeamish about raw eggs and meat. I use very fresh meat from a reputable butcher and mince it myself—so I know it's freshly done. You can also purchase bottled mayonnaise or pasteurized eggs.

This is pretty much a do-it-yourself affair. I like to set out all the garnishes and condiments so people can mix and season to their own tastes. Have Maldon flake salt available, if you can. This salt comes from England, and it's my very favorite sea salt. The salt crystals are lacy, papery flakes that dissolve very quickly. In cold dishes, they add a tiny bit of crunch without overwhelming you with saltiness. You can use mayonnaise or aioli as a substitute for the egg yolks. Oh, and a vodka martini, shaken, not stirred, is the ideal mood setter.

To make the croutons, preheat the oven to 375°F. Coat each side of the bread with oil and bake until crisp, 7 to 11 minutes.

To prepare the beef, remove any tough sinewy pieces, and trim off a bit of the fat but not all of it. Finely mince the beef using a sharp cleaver. I have done this with a food processor, too, which is almost as good. Just be sure it has a sharp blade, and do it in small batches, pulsing it on and off. Do not grind the meat in a meat grinder, as this will result in an unpleasant texture.

Mound the beef in the center of a serving plate, and make an indentation in the top of the mound with the back of a spoon. Separate the eggs, and carefully place the yolks in the indentation (save the whites for some other use). If you're using mayonnaise or aioli, spoon it into the indentation instead. Arrange the croutons on one side of the plate, and on the other, arrange the cornichons, parsley, peppercorns, capers, and anchovies in individual piles. Set out the Worcestershire sauce, Dijon mustard, hot sauce, salt, and pepper. Let your guests mix the condiments into the beef as they like.

If you're using quail eggs, here's a neat serving option. Make 6 burger-shaped patties of the diced meat and place them on individual plates. Using a knife, make crosshatch marks on the surface of the patties, then make a small indentation in the center of each patty. Separate the eggs, and place a yolk in each little hollow. Arrange the garnishes and toasts around each patty. You can do this with yolks from chicken eggs, too, but then you'll need to break the yolks and stir them up before spooning some into the center of each patty.

Put freshly chopped parsley in a kitchen towel and twist it shut; run it under cold water and then squeeze dry. This releases the extra chlorophyll and makes the parsley taste sweeter and less grassy. I don't do this with any other fresh herb, but almost always with parsley.

Set out a tray of freshly shucked oysters and let them grill up the oysters themselves.

Grilled Oysters—Easy as Pie (page 184)

pictured on page 183

Grilled Oysters—Easy as Pie

Serves 6

Here's a great trick for keeping your guests busy while you pull the rest of the meal together. Set out a tray of freshly shucked oysters and let them grill up the oysters themselves. They can help themselves to the mix-and-match sauces and eat the oysters hot off the grill. Offer a choice of a spicy-hot barbecue sauce and a citrus-soy sauce, or some people may opt for seasoning their oysters as they do in Mexico, with a squeeze of lime juice, a couple of shakes of Tabasco sauce, and a sprinkle of salt and pepper.

For the most part, we get our oysters from a local concern, the Hog Island Oyster Company. Wherever you are, you'll need to find a good supplier nearby (or consider ordering by mail if you live inland). There are many varieties of oysters available now. Have fun—try different kinds. Just keep in mind a couple of general rules: the larger oysters are better for cooking and the smaller ones are better for eating raw. And if a raw oyster doesn't smell good, throw it out! If you are not into shucking oysters, just give them a good scrub beforehand. Put the whole oysters on the grill to cook, and they'll automatically pop open when they're done. Discard any that do not open when cooked.

cindy's barbecue sauce

½ cup barbecue sauce (your favorite brand)

½ cup freshly squeezed lemon juice

1 tablespoon Worcestershire sauce

1 teaspoon freshly ground black pepper

Tiny pinch of cayenne pepper

soy-lime sauce

4 tablespoons tamari

2 tablespoons freshly squeezed lime juice

18 to 24 fresh oysters

Tabasco sauce

Lime wedges

Fine sea salt

Additional freshly ground black pepper

For the barbecue sauce, combine all the ingredients in a small saucepan. Bring this mixture just to a boil, remove from the heat, and reserve in the pan. You will need to reheat this sauce before serving and, when you do, try to time it so it is hot just as the oysters are coming off the grill.

For the Soy-Lime Sauce, combine the tamari and the lime juice in a squirt bottle and shake well.

Carefully shuck the oysters, leaving each oyster and as much of its juices as possible in the cupped bottom shell. To grill, place the oysters over a hot fire and cook until the juice in the shells gets bubbly and the edges of the oysters are just beginning to curl, 30 seconds to 1 minute. Take care not to overcook them: you want a bit of the natural juices left around the oysters when you pull them off the grill.

Reheat the barbecue sauce if necessary and set it out, along with the squeeze bottle of Soy-Lime Sauce (give it a good shake) and the Tabasco sauce, lime wedges, salt, and pepper. Dressing the oysters is a do-it-yourself thing that should be done while the oysters are still hot—or while they're still on the grill, just before you pull them off.

Braised Portobello and
Porcini Mushrooms with
Spiced Flatbread
(page 188)

You may burn one
or two before you
get the hang of it.

pictured on page 186

flatbreads

1 cup flour

½ cup masa harina

½ teaspoon finely ground toasted cumin seeds

½ teaspoon salt

½ teaspoon finely ground black pepper

½ cup plus about 2 tablespoons water, as needed

mushrooms

1 ounce dried porcini mushrooms

3 tablespoons olive oil

1 tablespoon butter

4 large portobello mushrooms, stemmed and cut into bite-size pieces

1 or 2 cloves garlic, smashed

¼ teaspoon sea salt

⅛ teaspoon freshly ground black pepper

1 heaping tablespoon finely chopped fresh basil or marjoram leaves

Juice of ½ lemon

½ cup mascarpone cheese or *fromage blanc*

¼ to ½ cup finely shredded Parmesan cheese

Garlicky Romesco Sauce (page 127; optional)

Braised Portobello and Porcini Mushrooms with Spiced Flatbread

Serves 6

These flatbreads are very crispy and crackerlike. They're as light as air, yet sturdy enough to support a generous topping of braised mushrooms, or whatever else you have in mind. When making the flatbread dough, be sure to grind the cumin seeds and black peppercorns very finely, otherwise the dough might tear when you roll it out. A perforated baking sheet is preferred for baking, because it will give you better heat circulation and a more evenly cooked flatbread, but a flat baking sheet or a pizza stone would also work. Keep a close eye on the breads as they're baking: they'll seem to be taking forever, and then all of a sudden they're done. You may burn one or two before you get the hang of it. The flatbreads will keep several days: wrap them well in plastic wrap, otherwise they'll get soggy.

The mushrooms can be prepared a couple of hours ahead; then the dish will be a snap to finish.

To make the dough, combine the flour, masa harina, cumin seeds, salt, and pepper in a large bowl and mix well. Work in the water a little at a time, using only as much as you need to make the dough come together. It should be moist to the touch but not sticky. Cover the bowl with plastic wrap or a damp towel and let the dough rest at room temperature 30 minutes. If you want to hold it longer, refrigerate it.

- Instead of the mushrooms, sprinkle the flatbreads with one or two cheeses of your desire, plus whatever happens to be in the fridge, such as some caramelized or roasted onions and/or garlic, and some sun-dried tomatoes or roasted tomato slices. Bake as described and serve.

- You can substitute semolina flour for the masa harina in the flatbread. Semolina, which is a wheat flour, will result in a more "Mediterranean" flavor as opposed to the "Latin" taste of the flatbreads made with masa harina.

When you are ready to bake the flatbreads, preheat the oven to 425°F. Place a perforated baking sheet or a baking stone in the oven and let it heat through while you roll out the dough. Lightly dust a work surface with flour. Divide the dough into 8 equal pieces and roll each into a paper-thin round, stacking the finished rounds with parchment paper between to keep them from sticking. The rounds should be about 7 to 8 inches in diameter. If you have a large enough baking stone, or 2 perforated pans, you can bake 2 breads at once. But the baking goes quickly—$1\frac{1}{2}$ to 2 minutes for each—so it's not that important. Bake until golden brown and crispy, turning the bread several times.

To prepare the porcinis, place them in a small pot and pour in just enough very hot water to cover them. Soak 20 to 30 minutes, until soft. When soft, scoop out the porcinis and pat them dry with a kitchen towel or paper towel. Cut any large mushrooms into bite-size pieces. Slowly pour the soaking water through a fine mesh strainer into a container. Discard the sediment and reserve the soaking liquid. To finish, heat the oil and butter in a large sauté pan over medium-high heat. When the butter turns frothy, add the porcinis and portobellos. Sauté for several minutes, until the mushrooms have begun to caramelize. Add the garlic and cook 30 seconds to 1 minute more, until it is aromatic but not yet beginning to caramelize. Add the mushroom soaking liquid and the salt, pepper, basil, and lemon juice; simmer until reduced enough so that the juices just coat the mushrooms. They should be almost dry.

Just before serving, preheat the oven to 425°F. Smear the flatbreads gently with the mascarpone or *fromage blanc*, sprinkle with the mushrooms and the Parmesan, and bake 3 to 5 minutes, until the mushrooms are heated through and the cheese is hot and light brown. If desired, a drizzle of *romesco* sauce would be a fabulous final touch. Serve immediately.

pictured on pages 192–193

Grilled Beef on Potato Rafts with Salpicón

Serves 6

"Stacked" food makes me cringe most of the time—it's an over-done, outdated setup that makes food hard to eat, and after one bite, the precarious tower of food usually looks very unattractive. But this dish is gently constructed, and "stacking" seems to work here. The base is a sturdy slab of grilled potato that's followed by a layer of somewhat spicy grilled beef and topped by the great salpicón. And voilà! A balanced meal in two bites.

So what is a salpicón? Most often it's a salad or marinated vegetable slaw that includes finely sliced sweet onion or scal-lions, sweet bell pepper in a variety of colors, chiles usually, and sometimes finely shredded cabbage. It is often served with crabmeat, shrimp, or beef, and I did find one reference to quinoa. It must have come to the New World from Spain, though this would have to have been after we sent them pep-pers. I've found recipes in Spanish cookbooks, Mexican cookbooks, and South American cookbooks.

If you prefer a less spicy marinade, remove the seeds from the serrano chiles before mincing them. If you can't find hanger steak, you could substitute flank steak. Allow at least two hours, and up to one day, for the meat to marinate. When buying the potatoes, keep in mind that you want six half-inch-thick slices, each about two bites long. Yukon Gold potatoes work well. You could even try sweet potatoes.

Another great presentation for this dish is to serve it in butter lettuce leaves rather than on the potato rafts. For this, cut the meat and potatoes into tiny dice or julienne them, scoop

marinade

2 cloves garlic, minced

2 serrano chiles, minced

2 to 3 tablespoons Worcestershire sauce

Zest and juice of 1 lime

2 to 3 tablespoons olive or vegetable oil

6 to 8 ounces hanger steak or flank steak

Salt and freshly ground black pepper

salpicón dressing

4 tablespoons sherry vinegar

1½ teaspoons Dijon mustard

2 shallots, minced

1½ teaspoons ground toasted cumin seeds

¼ teaspoon salt

⅛ teaspoon freshly ground black pepper

½ cup pure olive oil

¼ cup extra virgin olive oil

6 half-inch-thick slices potato

Olive oil, for coating

Salt and freshly ground black pepper

1 cup finely shredded cabbage

6 sprigs cilantro

½ roasted *pasilla* chile, peeled and cut into strips

½ large roasted red bell pepper, peeled and cut into strips

6 slices avocado

12 to 18 small pieces shaved Asiago cheese

some of each into the lettuce cups, and top with a small amount of the salpicón.

Put all the marinade ingredients in a sealable plastic bag large enough to hold the meat. Mix well and set it aside. Pin the steak with a handheld Jaccard tenderizing machine, if desired (see page 360). Season the meat with salt and pepper and place it in the bag of marinade, making sure that all surfaces get nicely coated. Seal the bag, squishing all the air out as you go, and put it in the fridge at least 2 hours and up to 24 hours before grilling. Be sure not to leave the meat in the marinade any longer than 24 hours, or the marinade will "cook" the meat and you will not be able to prepare it rare.

For the dressing, combine the vinegar, mustard, shallots, cumin, salt, and pepper in a medium-size bowl and stir until the salt has dissolved. Add the olive oils in a slow steady stream, whisking as you go. Continue whisking until well emulsified. Reserve until needed.

Steam the potatoes until fork-tender, about 6 or 7 minutes (older potatoes may take a little longer, so be sure to check). For the grilling, rub the potatoes with olive oil, sprinkle them with salt and pepper, and set them aside. Grill the steak over a medium-hot fire to the desired doneness, about 2 minutes per side for rare. Rotate the meat a quarter turn halfway through cooking on each side to get nice crosshatch grill marks. Let the meat rest while you grill the potatoes, also rotating them a quarter turn on each side to get nice grill marks. Remove the potatoes to a platter and keep them warm. Slice the steak on a slight angle into 12 pieces, saving any meat juices you can.

Combine the cabbage, cilantro, chile, and bell pepper, and dress lightly with some of the *salpicón* dressing. Lightly dress the potatoes, too, and arrange them on a serving platter. Top each slice of potato with 2 slices of steak, and drizzle with the reserved meat juices. Top with a little mound of *salpicón* and another drizzle of dressing. Add a slice of avocado and 2 to 3 pieces of Asiago to finish.

Grilled Beef on Potato Rafts
with Salpicón (page 190)

Coquilles St. Jacques

Serves 6

3 tablespoons butter

2 tablespoons olive oil

1 tablespoon chopped garlic

3 beefsteak tomatoes, peeled, seeded, and sliced into wedges

½ cup white wine

Grated zest of ½ lemon

Juice of 1 lemon

Salt and freshly ground black pepper

1½ pounds sea scallops

3 or 4 leaves fresh basil cut into a chiffonade, plus some small leaves for garnish

¼ cup (loosely packed) chopped fresh Italian parsley, leaves and tender stems only

1 cup tiny croutons (¼-inch dice)

Whether you call them coquilles or scallops, these rich, sweet seafood delicacies should never be overcooked or they'll become tough and chewy. There are a number of steps you can take to avoid this disaster when you fix this dish. First of all, assemble all the ingredients and paraphernalia that you'll need ahead of time, including tongs to turn the scallops and a warmed plate to hold them after you've pan-seared them. Actually, you need two plates. My trick for holding the scallops is to invert the warmed plate and set it on a larger plate. After the scallops have been seared, they go on the inverted plate and onto a warming shelf or into a very low oven. Any excess juices will drain down, and the scallops won't lose their crispy caramelized edges.

Once you're ready to go, start making the sauce, set it aside for a moment while you sear the scallops and transfer them to the plate, and then finish the sauce. You'll probably be done in less than seven minutes. If you overcrowd the pan, they'll steam and overcook, so cook them in two batches or two pans.

For the sauce, put half the butter in a saucepan with enough olive oil to coat the pan nicely, and heat over medium heat. Add the garlic; sauté 1 minute, but do not let the garlic brown. Add the tomatoes and cook 2 minutes, or until the tomatoes exude some of their juices. Continue cooking until most of the liquid has evaporated. Throw in the wine, lemon zest, and lemon juice, season with salt and pepper, and let reduce a bit, about 3 minutes, until it is fairly thick.

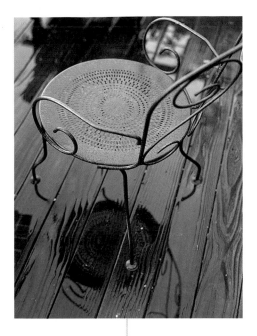

While the sauce is reducing, coat 1 large or 2 medium sauté pans liberally with the remaining olive oil and set them over high heat. Sprinkle a little salt and pepper on the scallops. When the pans are very hot, add a small amount of the remaining butter and put the scallops flat in the pan. Cook 1 minute, until golden brown on the bottom; turn them, using tongs, and cook another minute, until golden brown on the other side. (Keep an eye on the sauce while you're doing this, and take it off heat if it's done before the scallops.) Transfer the scallops to the warmed plate.

To finish the sauce, return it to the heat. Add any liquid that has drained from the scallops, and stir in the basil chiffonade and half the parsley.

To serve, put a spoonful or so of sauce on each plate, and place a few scallops on top. Sprinkle with croutons, small basil leaves, and the remaining parsley.

Rabbit Tostadas with Cumin-Scented Black Beans and Lime Crème Fraîche

Serves 6

A lot of our regular customers at Cindy's Backstreet Kitchen order this every time they come in and never try anything else. Though this recipe is fairly complicated, you can do almost everything ahead of time and have very little to do once the guests arrive. In fact, you could even have them assemble their own tostadas.

Check the recipe out carefully and figure out your own time line. Just consider that the beans need to soak overnight and will take about an hour to cook after that. The chiles for the chile paste need to soak for an hour, and you need to make the chile paste before you cook the rabbit. You can work the other parts of the recipe in around the beans and the rabbit. If rabbit is not to your liking, this dish could also be made with chicken thighs or turkey legs. And if cooking the beans seems like too much trouble, you can use canned black beans instead (see the note following the Cumin-Scented Black Beans recipe on page 201).

One of the key flavor components in this recipe is the guajillo chiles. They are rust-colored, about four inches long and an inch and a half wide, a little fruity, and only mildly hot. Guajillos are so common in California, all Latin American markets carry them, and you might even find them in some regular markets, too. You need five of them altogether, four for the rabbit and another for the black beans. There's a hefty

(continued)

chile paste

4 dried *guajillo* chiles, stemmed and seeded

2 cloves garlic

1 tablespoon fresh oregano leaves

½ tablespoon ground toasted cumin seeds

½ teaspoon salt

¼ teaspoon freshly ground black pepper

2 to 4 tablespoons olive oil

2 rabbits, cut into 6 to 8 pieces each

½ teaspoon salt

¼ teaspoon freshly ground black pepper

½ cup chopped celery

½ cup chopped peeled carrot

½ cup chopped onion

Rabbit or chicken stock (you'll need about 3 to 4 cups; use some water if you don't have enough stock)

amount of ground cumin called for—5½ teaspoons in all—so you might find it easiest to toast and grind enough seeds for the whole recipe all at once. Cumin has strong flavors, so start with a bit less than called for, and add to your taste.

For the chile paste, toast the chiles until aromatic, then put them in a small pot with just enough hot water to cover. Soak the chiles 1 hour until soft, then drain them, reserving some of the soaking liquid. Puree the chiles in a blender along with the garlic, oregano, cumin, salt, and pepper, adding a little of the soaking liquid as needed. You want the chile paste to be slightly thinner than warm peanut butter. Strain and reserve.

To cook the rabbit, heat the oil in a heavy-bottomed pan over medium-high heat. Toss in the rabbit, season with the salt and pepper, and cook until golden brown on all sides. Transfer the rabbit to a platter. Add the celery, carrot, and onion to the same pan and cook until browned. Stir in the chile paste, and cook 1 to 2 minutes to bring out the flavor. Add the rabbit back to the pan and stir everything to coat the meat nicely. Pour in just

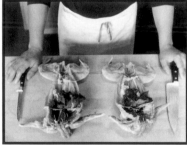

enough stock to cover and bring to a boil. Reduce to a simmer and cook until the meat is very tender, 30 to 40 minutes.

Pull the meat out of the broth and let it cool on a rack set over a baking sheet. Strain the broth into another pot. Simmer the broth to reduce by half, until it is thick enough to coat a spoon. Chill this sauce until you're ready to serve. When the rabbit is just cool enough to handle, carefully pull the meat from the bones, leaving it in big pieces as best you can. It will break up some when you reheat it. Watch out for small bones as you do this. The meat can also be chilled until you're ready to finish the dish.

To finish the rabbit, add the meat to the sauce. Stir everything to combine, and cook just long enough to heat it through.

For the crème fraîche, combine all the ingredients in a small bowl and mix well. Cover and chill until needed.

To crisp the tortillas, pour the oil to a depth of 1 inch into a cast-iron or other heavy skillet and heat to 375°F. Prick the tortillas several times with a fork to keep them from curling up, and cook them one by one until golden brown. This shouldn't take more than a minute or so on each side. Transfer the crisped tortillas to paper towels to drain. You can stack them after they are drained and cool. You can also cook the tortillas in the oven: put them in at 350°F for 18 to 20 minutes, until firm and crisp. (Stale tortillas crisp more quickly.)

To make the vinaigrette, whisk together the garlic, salt, lemon juice, red wine vinegar, sugar, and optional cumin and chile flakes. Continue whisking as you add the oil in a slow, steady stream and whisk until well emulsified.

Just before serving, reheat the beans and the rabbit. Combine the cabbage, radishes, arugula, and cilantro in a bowl, and dress with just enough of the vinaigrette to moisten. To serve, smear each of the tortillas with about ¹/₃ cup of black beans, then top with some braised rabbit meat and sauce, greens, and crumbled cheese. Drizzle with crème fraîche and garnish with lime wedges. After all this, you deserve a treat: go eat!

lime crème fraîche

1 cup crème fraîche

Finely grated zest of 1 lime

1½ to 2 tablespoons freshly squeezed lime juice

Tiny pinch of salt

A few grindings of black pepper

Peanut or vegetable oil, for frying

6 (6-inch) corn tortillas, or 12 to 18 (3- to 4-inch) tostaditas

vinaigrette

1 clove garlic, chopped

¼ teaspoon salt

¼ cup freshly squeezed lemon juice

2 tablespoons red wine vinegar

2 teaspoons brown sugar

2 teaspoons ground toasted cumin seeds (optional)

Pinch of chile flakes (optional)

¾ cup olive oil

Cumin-Scented Black Beans (page 201)

1½ cups finely shredded cabbage

4 to 6 radishes, sliced

1 cup arugula

⅓ bunch cilantro, leaves only

¾ cup crumbled feta cheese or soft fresh goat cheese

1 or 2 limes, cut into wedges

cumin-scented black beans

These beans were designed especially for the Rabbit Tostadas, but we also use them with the Salt-Roasted Salmon Tostadas (page 204), the Tuna Tostadas (page 208), and in the Stuffed Pasilla Chiles (page 295) make a great change of pace when served on the side with a grilled steak. This recipe will yield about three cups of cooked beans. The flavor improves with a day of refrigeration, and they will keep three or four days.

Ideally, you should soak the beans overnight, but if you didn't plan ahead, don't fret. Just rinse the beans well, picking through them to remove any small stones, put them in a big pot, and cover liberally with water. Bring the water to a boil, then turn off the heat and let the pot sit for five minutes. Drain, rinse again, and start the recipe. Or you can use canned black beans (see the note on the next page).

8 ounces black beans

1 small dried *guajillo* chile or
   2 dried *chiles de árbol*,
   stemmed and seeded

1 bay leaf

4 to 5 cups water, vegetable
   stock, or chicken stock

1 tablespoon olive oil

⅓ onion, diced

1 large clove garlic, minced

2 teaspoons ground toasted
   cumin seeds

1½ teaspoons salt

½ teaspoon freshly ground black
   pepper

⅓ bunch cilantro, leaves and
   tender stems, minced

Rinse the beans well, picking through to remove any small stones. Put the beans in a large pot with enough water to cover by 2 or 3 inches and soak overnight. The next day, pour off the soaking water and add fresh water or stock to cover. Toast the chile and add it to the beans, along with the bay leaf, and bring to a boil. Reduce the heat to a simmer and cook about 1 hour, until the beans are tender, but not so long that they are breaking apart. Skim off any foam that rises to the surface as the beans are cooking. If the beans dry out before they are cooked, add a little water and reduce the temperature further. When the beans are done, drain them, reserving the liquid for finishing the dish; return the beans to the pot and set aside.

Heat the oil in a small sauté pan over medium-high heat. Add the onion and garlic and cook until translucent. Add the cumin, cook a minute longer, then scrape this mixture into the pot with the beans. Add just enough of the reserved liquid to make the beans saucy but not watery. Stir everything around well and

(continued)

cook over low heat for 15 to 20 minutes more, to infuse the flavors. Add more of the liquid if the beans become too dry.

To finish the beans, blend about one-third of them with just enough of the remaining liquid to make a thick paste. Stir this paste back into the whole beans and add a little more liquid, just enough to get a nice consistency that will stay on the tostada. Season with the salt and pepper. Just before serving, stir in the cilantro.

Note: If you want to use canned beans, two 14¹/₂-ounce cans should do it. Rinse the beans well and put them in a saucepan. Add the toasted chile, bay leaf, sautéed onions and garlic, and ground cumin. Add enough stock to moisten, and simmer 15 or 20 minutes. Finish as described in the preceding paragraph, but be careful with the seasoning, as some brands of canned beans are already pretty salty.

jicama slaw

8 ounces jicama, peeled and cut into matchstick-size strips

1 red Fresno or jalapeño chile, stemmed, seeded, and julienned

1 Anaheim or *pasilla* chile, stemmed, seeded, and julienned

1 scallion, white and light green parts only, sliced

½ cup cilantro leaves and tender stems

Juice of 1 lime

2 tablespoons extra virgin olive oil

¼ teaspoon salt

1 or 2 pinches cayenne pepper

12 to 14 ounces halibut

Olive oil, for brushing

Salt and freshly ground black pepper

¼ teaspoon ground toasted cumin seeds

1½ cups canned black beans, or ½ recipe Cumin-Scented Black Beans (page 201)

6 (3-inch-diameter) corn tortillas, fried or baked until crisp (see page 205)

½ recipe Lime Crème Fraîche (page 199), or ½ cup sour cream thinned with cold water

6 lime wedges, for garnish

Halibut Tostadas with Jicama Slaw

Serves 6

How about a tostada party? You can set everything out on a table and let your guests build their own tostadas. Or you can serve them all assembled, if you prefer. Cooked shrimp, crab, or lobster could easily replace the fish to make this dish more elegant. The tortillas can be either fried or baked (see page 205).

The jicama slaw is very versatile. It's good with just about any fish tostada or taco, and I often tuck some of it into fried-fish sandwiches. Or try mixing it with greens for a refreshing salad. It is excellent chopped finely and used to stuff an avocado.

Combine all the slaw ingredients in a bowl and mix well. Cover and set aside till needed.

The halibut can be either roasted or grilled. To roast it, preheat the oven to 375°F. Brush the fish with a little olive oil; season with salt, pepper, and cumin and roast 8 to 10 minutes per inch of thickness. To grill the fish, cut it into 6 pieces, rub with olive oil, season, and grill to the desired doneness, 2 to 3 minutes per side.

To assemble the tostadas, reheat the beans, and smear the crisped tortillas with warmed beans. If you roasted the halibut, flake some of it onto each tortilla. If it's grilled, just place a piece of fish on each. Garnish with some of the jicama slaw and a drizzle of Lime Crème Fraîche. Serve with the lime wedges on the side.

Salt-Roasted Salmon Tostadas with Cindy's Backstreet Tomatillo-Avocado Salsa

3 cups (loosely packed) arugula

1 cup very thinly sliced red radishes (use a mandoline)

1 cup (loosely packed) watercress, coarse stems removed

1 pound salmon fillet

2 large egg whites

4 cups kosher salt or sea salt

1 tablespoon rice vinegar

3 tablespoons olive oil

1 recipe Cumin-Scented Black Beans (page 201)

6 (3- to 4-inch) corn tortillas, fried until crisp (see page 205)

Cindy's Backstreet Tomatillo-Avocado Salsa (page 207)

4 ounces soft fresh goat cheese or *queso fresco*, crumbled

6 lime wedges, for garnish

Serves 6

Salt-roasting calls for encasing a piece of fish in a crust made of egg whites beaten together with salt until stiff, and then roasting the fish at high temperature. The crust seals in the juices, and the fish almost steams as it roasts, coming out very moist, tender, and sweet. This process works especially well with salmon and bass. For a big party, try roasting a whole salmon (ten to twelve pounds). Triple the crust and cook the salmon with the skin on at 500°F. Cook for ten minutes per inch of thickness. You can break the crust and let your guests build their own tostadas tableside. Increase the number of tostadas, salsa, and greens according to the number of guests.

This is a pretty substantial small plate, so you'd probably need to serve it with only one other dish and a light dessert. If you are serving fancy, with a knife and fork, putting just a dab of beans on the plate first will hold the tostada in place. Otherwise, put out plenty of paper towels and napkins, as eating this could get messy!

Combine the arugula, radishes, and watercress in a large bowl. Cover and refrigerate until you're ready to put the tostadas together.

To prepare the fish, preheat the oven to 500°F. Remove the skin if any, from the fillet, and the blood fat line (the dark brown

streak that runs down the length of the fillet). Whip the egg whites till frothy and fold them into the salt. Sprinkle with a touch of water if the mixture seems too dry. You want something like the consistency of moist sand. You need a baking dish that will hold the fillet lying flat. Cover the bottom of the dish with half the salt, lay the salmon on top of it, and then cover the fish with the remaining salt. Bake 7 to 10 minutes for medium-rare. When the salmon is ready, remove it from the oven and allow it to cool a bit. Crack and discard the salt crust, then gently break the meat into bite-size pieces with your fingers. (Unless it has been overcooked, the meat will be very moist and tender.)

Shortly before serving, whisk together the vinegar and oil, and dress the greens with just enough of this to coat. Reheat the black beans in a small pot.

To serve, place a crisp tortilla on each plate and top each with a portion of the black beans. Next, layer on some of the salmon, then a small mound of greens. Top with a couple tablespoons of the tomatillo-avocado salsa and a sprinkling of cheese. Finish each plate with a wedge of lime.

TOSTADAS

A tostada is a corn tortilla that has been fried or baked to make it nice and crispy. Like a piece of toast or a waffle, the tostada can be eaten plain, but why do that when you can load it up with all kinds of tasty foods? For example, elsewhere in this chapter you'll find recipes for rabbit tostadas, halibut tostadas, and tuna tostadas, each with their own salsas and garnishes.

To make tostadas by frying the tortillas, heat a small amount of oil to 375°F in a small frying pan, prick the tortillas several times with a fork to keep them from bubbling up and curling, and fry them one by one until crisp. Alternatively, you can bake

(continued)

them at 350°F for 18 to 20 minutes. Normally, corn tortillas measure 5 or 6 inches in diameter, but for special occasions, you might want to serve tiny tostadas, or tostaditas. You can cut them out of regular-size tortillas with a cookie cutter. For hors d'oeuvres you could do 1-inch tostadas; for a small-plates meal, 3- or 4-inch tostadas work well. You have to cut the tortillas before baking or frying them, or else you'll just have crumbs. Scrap pieces of tortillas can be crisped and crumbled up to use as a garnish for soups, or as a last-minute addition to scrambled eggs or omelettes.

cindy's backstreet tomatillo-avocado salsa

8 ounces tomatillos, papery husks removed, cut into ¼-inch dice

1½ avocados, pitted, peeled, and cut into ¼-inch dice

3 scallions, white and light green parts only, minced

1 jalapeño chile, stemmed, seeded if you wish, and minced

3 tablespoons minced cilantro leaves

½ teaspoon sea salt

¼ teaspoon freshly ground black pepper

½ teaspoon ground toasted cumin seeds (optional)

1 tablespoons rice vinegar

3 tablespoons olive oil

A few thoughts before you get started on the salsa: Look for avocados that are ripe but still firm—the ones on which the stem at the end still wiggles. Depending on the juiciness of your tomatillos, you may need a teaspoon or so more rice vinegar and a tablespoon of additional olive oil. A little ground cumin would be a nice addition, if you like. And finally, if you don't want too much heat, remove the seeds from the jalapeño.

This salsa can be made up to a day ahead, though the fresher it is, the brighter it will be.

To make the salsa, combine all the ingredients except the vinegar and oil in a bowl. Mix well but gently, taking care not to mash the avocado. Whisk together the vinegar and oil until emulsified, and add just enough of this to the salsa to moisten it. Reserve any leftover vinaigrette to use in other salad dressings.

watermelon salsa

2 cups diced watermelon

2 cups watercress leaves

1 or 2 jalapeño, Fresno, or serrano chiles, stemmed and cut on the diagonal (seeds removed if you prefer less heat)

3 scallions, white and light green parts only, minced

Juice of 1 lime

2 to 3 tablespoons extra virgin olive oil

½ teaspoon salt

¼ teaspoon freshly ground black pepper

tomatillo salsa

20 ounces tomatillos, papery husks removed

3 serrano chiles, stemmed and seeded

2 to 3 tablespoons peanut or olive oil

¼ onion, chopped

1½ teaspoons minced garlic

¼ bunch cilantro, leaves only

½ teaspoon salt

¼ teaspoon freshly ground black pepper

Tuna Tostadas with Watermelon and Tomatillo Salsas

Serves 6

These are so much fun. You can make them on mini tostadas (one to three inches in diameter) as well as on the regular four-inch rounds. If you want to do the cocktail-size ones, cook the tuna in one piece to medium-rare and slice it into bite-size pieces to fit the bite-size tostadas. Use number 1 grade yellowfin or ahi tuna, if possible.

As for the salsas, if you want them really spicy, don't remove the seeds and membranes of the chiles. And if you have leftovers, either salsa would be great as a topping for scrambled eggs or a cheese omelette.

This recipe calls for a batch of Cumin-Scented Black Beans; you'll want to get a head start on making those.

For the watermelon salsa, combine the watermelon, watercress, chiles, and scallions in a small bowl. In a second bowl, mix together the lime juice, olive oil, salt, and pepper. Reserve separately until needed. If you're making this a long time ahead, refrigerate the watermelon, but give it time to come back to room temperature before you finish and serve it.

For the tomatillo salsa, put the tomatillos and serrano chiles in a pot with just enough water to cover. Bring to a boil and reduce to a simmer. Cook till just tender, 3 to 5 minutes, depending on how ripe your tomatillos are. In the meantime, heat the oil in a sauté pan and sauté the onion and garlic until translucent. Once

12 to 14 ounces tuna

Salt and freshly ground black
  pepper

Extra virgin olive oil, for brushing

1 recipe Cumin-Scented Black
  Beans (page 201)

6 small (4-inch) corn tortillas,
  fried until crisp

6 ounces feta cheese, crumbled

3 tablespoons toasted pumpkin
  seeds

1 lime, cut into wedges

the tomatillos and chiles have softened, drain them and put
them in a blender with the sautéed garlic, onion, cilantro, salt,
and pepper. Blend until smooth. Strain if desired (we don't),
and set aside until needed.

When you are ready to put the dish together, season the tuna to
taste with salt and pepper and brush it lightly with olive oil. Sear
it in a hot pan or grill over a hot fire until medium-rare. This
should take 2 to 4 minutes, depending on the thickness of your
fish and how hot your pan or grill is. In the meantime, reheat
the beans. To finish the watermelon salsa, pour the lime and
olive oil dressing over the watermelon and mix gently.

To serve, smear the tostadas with black beans, then
top them with some of the tuna and the watermelon salsa. Over that, spoon some tomatillo salsa,
then sprinkle on the cheese and pumpkin seeds.
Serve lime wedges on the side for squeezing.

lime-cumin-dijon vinaigrette

2 tablespoons freshly squeezed lime juice

2 teaspoons Dijon mustard

¾ teaspoon ground cumin

¼ teaspoon salt

⅛ teaspoon freshly ground black pepper

6 tablespoons extra virgin olive oil

2 to 2½ cups roughly flaked cooked halibut (about 12 ounces)

3 tablespoons good-quality mayonnaise

1 scallion, white and light green parts only, minced

½ cup minced celery leaves and stalks

¼ cup chopped green olives (optional), or serve olives as a garnish

1 cup small arugula or other peppery green

1 cup cilantro leaves

6 small (4-inch-diameter) stone-ground corn tortillas

½ to 1 cup Tomatillo Salsa (page 208)

¼ cup plain yogurt

½ cup mild soft fresh goat cheese

1 avocado, thinly sliced

1 lime, cut into wedges

Pacific Halibut Soft Tacos

Serves 6

I invented these fish tacos after a Valentine's Day ferry ride to the San Francisco Ferry Plaza Farmers' Market. I always try to limit myself to shopping just for our dinner, but no matter how many restraints I put on myself—you know, only one bag, just what I can carry in one hand (it's amazing how much you can carry in one hand!)—I end up with enough food for several meals. On this occasion, one of the extras I just couldn't pass up was some wonderful stone-ground tortillas from a great Sonoma vendor. They are thick and a bit chewy in just the right way. So the next day, I had the perfect use for the leftover roasted halibut from our Valentine's Day dinner.

I like to serve this as soft tacos, on tortillas that are warmed in a hot skillet with no oil added. Of course, you could easily turn this dish into a tostada by frying the tortillas in a little oil until crisp.

To make the vinaigrette, combine the lime juice, mustard, cumin, salt, and pepper in a small bowl. Whisk in the olive oil in a slow steady stream, and continue whisking until well emulsified.

To make the taco filling, combine the fish, 2 tablespoons of the vinaigrette, the mayonnaise, scallion, and celery in a bowl and mix gently. Do not break up the fish too much. If you're using the chopped olives, add them now. In a separate bowl, mix together the arugula and cilantro, and toss them with just enough of the vinaigrette to coat.

When you are ready to serve, heat the tortillas over a gas flame or in a dry skillet until just warm and softened, keeping them warm under a kitchen towel as you go. Place the tortillas on

If you don't have any leftover fish, it's easy enough to roast a fillet of fish. Preheat the oven to 375°F. Remove any stray bones from the fillets, then sprinkle with sea salt and freshly ground black pepper, and drizzle liberally with olive oil. Roast for ten minutes per inch (so if your fillet is half an inch thick, roast for five minutes). Let it cool, then roughly flake the fish.

plates, spoon on a layer of the fish, and sprinkle with some of the salsa. Top this with a little mound of greens and a drizzle of yogurt. Finish by crumbling some cheese over all, and top with a slice or two of avocado. Serve with lime wedges. The way to eat these is to fold the taco in half and eat by hand; it can be messy, so have plenty of napkins on hand!

BURGERS

When I think *burgers*, I think of Sundays with my father. If we were good in church, my father would take us to the White Castle on Lake Street and order "sliders" for us. I can still picture it: we'd be munching on them, all dressed up in our Sunday best, with all that fried onion grease running down our arms.

We do a lot of mini burgers at the restaurant. They fit right in at Cindy's Backstreet Kitchen with all the parties we do in our upstairs dining room. There are so many possibilities— different burgers, different buns, different dressings. And people love them. One Fourth of July, I did a "sliders" party: we made up trays of burgers, set out a huge spread of condiments and cheeses, and let everyone assemble their own mini burgers. It's still being talked about, fifteen years later. Well, actually, the fact that I made the buns and biscuits from scratch is what's still being talked about.

There are four burger recipes in this chapter. If you want tradition, try the Sunday Supper Burgers (page 216). If you want a little heat, try the burgers with the Roasted Chile Relish (page 222). And if you're feeling adventurous, make the Mini Duck Burgers with the Shiitake Mushroom Ketchup (page 226) or the Spicy Lamb Burgers (page 232).

Sunday Supper Burgers with Thousand Island Dressing

Serves 6

thousand island dressing

½ cup mayonnaise

¼ cup sweet pickle relish

2 to 3 tablespoons ketchup

3 or 4 drops Tabasco sauce

1 drop Worcestershire sauce

1 tablespoon chopped fresh
parsley leaves

1 tablespoon cognac or brandy

2 strips applewood-smoked
bacon

2 large onions

12 to 14 ounces ground beef

Salt

Freshly cracked black pepper

½ cup grated sharp Cheddar
cheese

6 poppy seed brioche buns

1 cup whole arugula leaves

2 tablespoons minced pickles or
6 slices bread-and-butter
pickle

1 tablespoon minced scallions

Whenever we have an open house or any other celebration, we serve these burgers, and they fly off the platters. I've heard talk that a person could eat about a hundred of them. The main reason for their popularity, I think, is that they are no-frills basic, and quite often, that's what people really crave.

For the ground beef, get a high-quality organic meat, if possible, with about 18 percent fat content. The patties can be cooked in a dry skillet on the stove top or over a grill, grilling being my favorite method. As for the rolls, most bakeries have small rolls of some kind available: try different ones, or cut up some bagels. French bread cut into small squares makes great bite-size patty melts. Or go wild! Make your own tiny biscuits. (There's an excellent recipe for Black Pepper Mini Biscuits on page 219.) Any extra Thousand Island Dressing can be used on a wedge of iceberg lettuce or a salad of romaine lettuce.

To make the dressing, combine all the ingredients and mix well. Cover and refrigerate until needed.

Cut the bacon crosswise into 1-inch strips. Cook the bacon until crisp, transfer to a layer of paper towels, and set aside. Slice the onions into ¼-inch-thick rings, and pick out the small rings in the center that will fit snugly on top of the little burgers. You'll need a couple of rings per burger. Set these aside, too.

(continued)

Form 6 small burger patties (they should take about ¼ cup of ground meat each) and season them with salt and pepper. Final preparation goes quickly, so line up everything you'll need before you get started cooking—dressing, bacon, onion rings, cheese, buns, and so on. Cook the burgers over high heat, 1 minute on each side for rare, or longer if desired. Remove from the heat, and immediately pile a tablespoon of cheese on each burger. After the cheese melts, top each with a couple of onion rings.

While the cheese is melting on the burgers, cut the buns in half, toast them, and generously spread some dressing on the bottoms. Top with some arugula, then the burgers, and then some pickles. Finally, sprinkle on a spoonful of bacon and a few scallion bits, and close off with the bun tops.

Black Pepper Mini Biscuits

Makes 12

These two-inch-diameter biscuits are great for making mini burgers, tiny Sloppy Joes, or miniature chicken-on-a-biscuit rounds—all the familiar American dishes done small. They are best used fresh, but they can be reheated by placing them in a 300°F oven for a few minutes.

2 cups flour

1 tablespoon baking powder

1 teaspoon salt

½ teaspoon freshly ground black pepper

6½ tablespoons unsalted butter, chilled and cut into small cubes

¾ cup plus 1 tablespoon buttermilk

1 large egg

Preheat the oven to 400°F. Grease a baking sheet and set it aside.

Combine the flour, baking powder, ½ teaspoon of the salt, and the pepper in a food processor or a large mixing bowl. Work in the butter until the mixture resembles coarse meal, using short bursts of the food processor, the paddle attachment on a mixer, or a pastry blender if mixing by hand. Add the buttermilk and mix quickly, just until everything clumps together. Turn the dough out onto a smooth, lightly floured surface and finish it with a few pats of the hand. Roll the dough out to a ³/₄-inch thickness. Cut into 1¹/₂- or 2-inch rounds with a pastry cutter, and place the biscuits on the baking sheet. Gently press the scraps together, being careful not to overwork the dough, and cut out more biscuits.

Make a glaze by whisking the egg and the remaining ¹/₂ teaspoon of salt till frothy, and brush this over the biscuits. Bake until golden, about 12 to 14 minutes. Cool on a wire rack.

I love the light lime-green of Anaheim chiles, so that's what we use for the relish.

Mini Beef Burgers with
Roasted Chile Relish and
Pablo's Pickled Onions
(page 222)

pictured on page 221

pablo's pickled onions

1 medium-size red onion, julienned

Juice of 1 lime

Tiny pinch of salt

roasted chile relish

2 Anaheim chiles, roasted and peeled

2 *pasilla* chiles, roasted and peeled

1 tablespoon extra virgin olive oil

1 scallion, white and light green parts only, minced

1 teaspoon minced fresh oregano leaves

6 sprigs cilantro, minced

Salt and freshly ground black pepper

1 pound ground beef

3 to 4 ounces soft Monterey Jack cheese

Salt and freshly ground black pepper

6 small buns or 12 Black Pepper Mini Biscuits (page 219)

½ cup shredded iceberg lettuce

6 to 8 tablespoons butter, softened

6 sprigs cilantro

Mini Beef Burgers with Roasted Chile Relish and Pablo's Pickled Onions

Serves 6

For better flavor, I recommend using ground beef that is not too lean: we use a local beef that is free of additives and has a ratio of 82 percent lean to 18 percent fat. If you use anything leaner, the burgers will be pretty dry and tasteless. I love the light lime-green of Anaheim chiles, so that's what we use for the relish. They are not screaming hot, either. You can substitute a hotter chile if heat is what you want, or sweet bell peppers, if not. Just don't skip the roasting and peeling step. It really makes a difference. You can make the relish a day ahead. And if you have any left over, it is great in egg dishes or mac and cheese or on bruschetta.

There's nothing much to the pickled onions—just lime juice and the onions—but I love them for their bright pink color. The lime juice bleeds the red out of the outer layer of the onion and turns everything pink. These onions are often used in Mexican cooking to top off tostadas or quesadillas. The pickled onions can also be made a day ahead.

Vella Cheese produces many Monterey Jack cheeses, but my favorite for these burgers is the one called Original High Moisture Monterey Jack. It melts well and helps hold everything together. Other options would be a fontina, mild Cheddar, or buffalo mozzarella.

To pickle the onions, combine the onions, lime juice, and salt in a ceramic or other nonreactive bowl and mix well. Cover and let

sit a couple of hours at room temperature. The onions should become soft and turn a bright pink.

To make the relish, tear the chiles into ¹/₄-inch-wide strips and put them in a small bowl. In a separate bowl, combine the olive oil, scallion, oregano, minced cilantro, salt, and pepper, and mix thoroughly. Pour this mixture over the peppers and stir, making sure that all surfaces get nicely coated. Cover and put in the fridge at least 30 minutes.

Divide the ground beef into 6 or 12 portions, depending on what size buns you're using, and form them into patties that will just about fit the buns. Cut the cheese into 6 or 12 squares. When you're about ready to serve, season the burgers with salt and pepper, and cook in a large dry cast-iron pan over high heat, or on the grill. Cook to the desired doneness, about 1¹/₂ to 2 minutes each side for medium-rare. Put a square of cheese on top of each burger right after flipping them over.

Toast and butter the buns. Place some of the shredded iceberg lettuce on each of the bun bottoms and top with the burgers, cheese side up. Add some of the chile relish, then 1 or 2 slices of pickled onion. Finish with a sprig of cilantro and close off with the bun tops. You may want to use a sandwich pick to keep everything together.

CALIFORNIA GROWN
ORGANIC MUSHROOMS

CERTIFIED ORGANIC
SHIITAKE
8 00
lb.

Mini Duck Burgers with Shiitake Mushroom Ketchup and Chinese-Style Mustard Sauce

Serves 6 to 8 (makes 16)

duck burgers

1 pound ground duck

1 scallion, white and a bit of the tender green, minced

1 teaspoon grated peeled fresh ginger

1½ teaspoons minced garlic

1 tablespoon Mongolian Marinade (page 76)

1 teaspoon salt

¼ teaspoon freshly ground black pepper

shiitake mushroom ketchup

2 to 3 tablespoons olive oil

1 pound shiitake mushrooms, stemmed and quartered

1 onion, finely diced

½ teaspoon salt

½ teaspoon freshly ground black pepper

¼ cup balsamic vinegar

2 teaspoons minced garlic

2 tablespoons molasses

¼ bunch basil leaves, chopped

¼ cup Mongolian Marinade (page 76)

(continued)

Here's a great departure from the standard American hamburger—a duck burger on a sesame bun. You can buy ground duck meat or, if you have a meat grinder, you can grind it at home on a medium-size disk blade (you'll need two ducks, about four pounds each). I use about 85 percent meat to 15 percent fat and skin. You should have pretty good luck finding sesame brioche buns at a local bakery, but if you have trouble and don't feel like baking your own, any sesame seed bun you like would work as well. If the duck sounds good, but not as a sandwich, try serving it on a bed of arugula, lightly dressed with sesame vinaigrette and toasted sesame seeds.

As for the Shiitake Mushroom Ketchup, it was inspired by a dish my friend Annie Gingrass made for me one Christmas. It's more like a vegetable condiment than a tomato ketchup, as it is much thicker. Any extra would be really good on beef burgers or scrambled eggs, or in fried rice or an Asian duck-and-noodle dish.

You'll need one recipe of Mongolian Marinade, which you should prepare first. It goes into the duck burger mixture and the Shiitake Mushroom Ketchup, and is used to baste the burgers as they grill.

(continued)

Combine all the duck burger ingredients in a large bowl and mix well. Cover and chill for at least 1 hour and up to overnight. Meanwhile, prepare the ketchup and the mustard sauce.

To make the ketchup, heat the olive oil in a large sauté pan over medium-high heat. Add the mushrooms and cook until tender. Add the onions and cook until they are translucent. Then add the remaining ingredients. Give the pan a good stir to make sure everything is evenly coated, reduce the heat, and simmer until the liquid is thick enough to coat the mushrooms, 3 to 5 minutes. Refrigerate, if you make this ahead, and warm it up before serving.

For the mustard, combine the sugar and mustard powder in the top of a double boiler and mix with a whisk. Be sure to do this thoroughly, otherwise you will end up with lumpy mustard. When well combined, whisk in the egg yolk and vinegar. Cook over simmering water, stirring occasionally, 10 to 15 minutes, until the mixture is thick enough to form ribbons when drizzled from the spoon. Remove from the heat and allow to cool. When cool, fold in the crème fraîche. Keep refrigerated until needed.

When you're about ready to serve, portion the chilled duck mixture out into 2-ounce (¼-cup) mini patties. Grill or griddle the patties over medium-high heat 2 to 3 minutes per side, basting with some of the marinade as you go. Toast and lightly butter the buns. Place the burgers on the bun bottoms, and top each with some shiitake ketchup, arugula, and a drizzle of the mustard sauce. Close off the sandwiches and serve with any extra mustard and ketchup on the side.

chinese-style mustard sauce

¼ cup sugar

2 tablespoons Colman's mustard powder

1 large egg yolk

¼ cup red wine vinegar

6 tablespoons crème fraîche or sour cream

Additional Mongolian Marinade, for basting

16 small sesame brioche buns, split

1 to 2 tablespoons butter

2 cups arugula

If you find lamb too rich and maybe too strong for your taste, give these burgers a try.

Spicy Lamb Burgers with
Vietnamese Herb Salad
and Tamarind Vinaigrette
(page 232)

pictured on page 231

Spicy Lamb Burgers with Vietnamese Herb Salad and Tamarind Vinaigrette

Serves 6

If you find lamb too rich and maybe too strong for your taste, give these burgers a try. The lamb burgers here are lightened and brightened by the addition of cilantro and mint to the patty mix, and if you want to lighten it even further, you can add some lime juice to it. To get it all just right, serve them with the cooling herb salad and tart-sweet tamarind vinaigrette.

Tamarind paste is the brownish-reddish pulp in the pod-shaped fruit of the tamarind tree: you can buy tamarind pods at Asian and Latin American markets and scrape out your own paste, but you can find jars or cans of prepared tamarind paste there, too. Tamarind has a pleasant sweet-sour taste and is very commonly used in cooking throughout Southeast Asia, India, Africa, South America, and the Caribbean. Even if you've never used tamarind yourself, you've probably had a taste of it somewhere along the line, as it is used commercially to flavor candies, jams, chutneys, and soft drinks.

Oyster sauce is a Chinese condiment, used as a dip and in stir-fries and marinades. The best brands come from Hong Kong, but you may find domestic brands right in your local supermarket. Once opened, the container should be refriger-

tamarind vinaigrette

4 tablespoons brown sugar

3 tablespoons water

2 tablespoons tamarind paste

1 tablespoon soy sauce

6 tablespoons olive oil

lamb burgers

5 cloves garlic, minced

1½ tablespoons oyster sauce

½ serrano or jalapeño chile, seeded and minced

2 tablespoons chopped fresh mint leaves

1½ tablespoons minced cilantro leaves

½ sweet onion, minced

Juice of ½ to 1 lime (optional)

1 pound ground lamb

vietnamese herb salad

2 scallions, white and light green parts only, cut into 1½-inch julienne

2 Thai or serrano chiles, seeded and julienned

½ bunch basil, any kind, small leaves only

¼ bunch cilantro, leaves only

¼ bunch mint, small leaves only

½ bunch chives, cut into ½-inch pieces

1 bunch ancho cress or watercress, leaves only

ated. If you can't find oyster sauce but have some hoisin sauce, use that instead. It's different but nice.

These brightly flavored burgers are best cooked over a charcoal or wood fire, but they can be seared instead in a cast-iron pan, or cooked under an oven broiler. Maxine, one of my testers, set off her smoke alarm broiling her burgers in the oven, though, so you might want to start up the grill.

To make the vinaigrette, combine the sugar and water in a small sauté pan. Cook over medium heat, stirring, until the sugar has dissolved. Add the tamarind and soy sauce, and stir until smooth. Remove from the heat and whisk in the olive oil. Reserve until needed.

To make the lamb burgers, first combine the garlic, oyster sauce, chile, mint, cilantro, onion, and lime juice, if desired, in a large bowl and mix well. Then mix in the ground lamb meat, making sure everything is well combined. Divide the mixture into 6 equal parts, or 12 if you want to make mini patties. Moisten your hands with water before forming the patties, as this makes it easier. Shape the patties with the palm of your hand more than your fingers, and make them flat but not too thin: ½ to ¾ inch thick is ideal, otherwise the burgers will over cook before they caramelize nicely. Regular patties should be 2 to 3 inches in diameter, minis about 1½ inches.

When you're ready to serve, cook the burgers to the desired doneness, about 1½ minutes per side for rare, 2 minutes for medium. Combine all the ingredients for the salad and toss it with just enough of the vinaigrette to coat. Serve the dish with the salad piled alongside or on top of the lamb patties and an extra drizzle of the vinaigrette over all.

Fried Green Tomatoes with Spicy Rémoulade

Serves 6

Make sure the tomatoes you use for this dish are nice and hard, with no hint of ripening. You want that firm crispness and tart taste to contrast with the rich creaminess of the rémoulade. Don't use the special green variety of heirloom tomatoes, as it remains green even when it's fully ripe, which could lead to some confusion.

Think of a rémoulade as a dressed-up mayonnaise, and feel free to play around with the recipe given here. A classic French rémoulade is made with tarragon and cornichons and a French coarse-grained mustard. Long ago, the Creole cooks in New Orleans modified the French-style rémoulade by using finely chopped sweet or dill pickles instead of the cornichons, and minced green onions instead of tarragon. But the biggest change was to use Creole mustard, which is much spicier than the French mustard. If you want to experiment with that, try Zatarain's Creole mustard. It's my favorite. The rémoulade below has capers instead of pickles.

Plan on one or two half-inch slices of tomato per person, depending on how many other dishes you are making. For something a little more substantial, make a sandwich with a couple of slices of fried green tomatoes, a big dollop of rémoulade, and some shaved lettuce. To make it even more filling, tuck a slice of buffalo or other fresh mozzarella between the slices of fried tomatoes. If you have extra rémoulade, it would be great in a potato salad.

spicy rémoulade

1 cup mayonnaise

1 tablespoon Dijon or Creole mustard

1 scallion, white and light green parts only, minced

1 tablespoon capers, rinsed and minced

2 tablespoons minced fresh tarragon or chervil

2 tablespoons minced fresh parsley leaves, rinsed and squeezed dry

½ teaspoon freshly ground black pepper

1 cup watercress, trimmed of coarse stems

2 cups small-leaved arugula, preferably Italian wild *rucola*

2 tablespoons balsamic vinegar or aged sherry

½ clove garlic, smashed and minced

¼ teaspoon dried crushed red pepper

Salt and freshly ground black pepper

6 tablespoons extra virgin olive oil

3 or 4 large hard green tomatoes

1 cup flour

1 cup *panko*

2 large eggs

Olive oil or vegetable oil, for frying

To make the rémoulade, combine all the ingredients and mix well. Cover and refrigerate until needed.

Combine the watercress and arugula in a mixing bowl, and set it aside. To make the dressing, combine the vinegar, garlic, crushed red pepper, salt, and pepper. Stir until the salt has dissolved, then gradually whisk in the oil. Whisk until well emulsified. Set aside until needed.

To prepare the tomatoes, core them and cut them crosswise into ½-inch-thick slices. Place the slices on a tray or in a casserole dish, and sprinkle them on 1 side with 1 teaspoon of salt to draw out excess moisture. Let them rest undisturbed for 30 minutes, then blot them with clean kitchen or paper towels.

Put the flour in a shallow bowl, and combine it with 1 teaspoon of salt and ½ teaspoon of pepper. Put the *panko* on a small plate. Beat the eggs in another shallow bowl, and set that between the flour mixture and the *panko*. Dredge the tomatoes in the flour mixture and shake off the excess. Dip immediately in the eggs, drain, and dip in the *panko*, pressing firmly to coat. Let the tomatoes rest, not touching them, for 20 minutes or so.

When you are ready to fry the tomatoes, preheat the oven to 200°F and heat ¼ inch of oil in a skillet over medium-high heat. When the oil is hot but not yet smoking, add some of the tomatoes, being careful not to overcrowd the pan. Fry until golden brown and crisp on the bottom, then turn them over and repeat. About 2 minutes on each side should do. Drain the tomatoes on a baking sheet lined with paper towels. Keep in the warm oven while you fry the remaining slices.

If you're arranging the tomatoes on a large platter, they'll look best on an oval one. Toss the greens with just enough of the dressing to coat them lightly, and put the greens on the platter first. Tuck tomato slices into the greens, and put a dollop of rémoulade on each slice. Pass additional rémoulade for your guests to help themselves. For individual servings, put 1 or 2 tomato slices in the center of each small plate, and top with ½ tablespoon or so of rémoulade. Toss the greens with the dressing, and sprinkle them around the tomatoes.

Cindy's Supper Club Escargots

6 half-inch-thick slices baguette or *bâtard*, sliced on the diagonal

2 tablespoons olive oil, plus additional for brushing

6 to 8 paper-thin slices Serrano ham or prosciutto, julienned

¼ cup red wine

2 shallots, thinly sliced

6 cloves garlic, thinly sliced

1 large tomato, peeled and diced, or ¾ cup canned diced tomatoes

1 to 1½ cups chicken stock

2 to 3 tablespoons butter

1 to 1½ ounces dry sherry, Pernod, or Ricard

18 large canned snails, halved

1 tablespoon finely chopped fresh thyme leaves

2 tablespoons chopped fresh parsley leaves

Salt and freshly ground black pepper

At Cindy's Backstreet Kitchen, we do a monthly event called Cindy's Supper Club. It's held in one of our upstairs dining rooms, and we do a set menu with selected wines. We always try to have a course or two that people don't usually order, like this one, which has converted many non-snail-eaters. The idea for this dish came from a wonderful braised pork and snail stew that Paula Wolfert makes. We serve our version over half-inch-thick slices of baguette that have been grilled. A few other excellent ways to serve this would be over smaller croutons or—seasoned with a touch of grated Parmesan cheese—over soft polenta or grits. It would even be good over pasta.

To make the toast, lightly brush the bread slices on each side with olive oil and toast over a grill or on a baking sheet in a 375°F oven until crispy and golden on the outside, but still a little soft in the center.

For the sauce, heat the 2 tablespoons of oil in a large sauté pan over medium-high heat. Add the ham and sauté till it is well heated through and just a touch caramelized. Add the wine and deglaze the pan. Add the shallots and half the garlic; cook 1 to 2 minutes, until translucent. Add the tomato and continue cooking, stirring, till the liquid in the pan has almost completely evaporated. Add the stock and cook till reduced by half. The dish can be made a bit ahead to this point, and set aside.

Just before serving, heat the sauce over medium-high heat, bringing it to a simmer, and add the remaining garlic along with the butter, sherry, and snails. Reduce the heat to medium, add the herbs, season with salt and pepper, and cook till emulsified, 1 to 2 minutes. Take care not to boil the snails, as they will become tough if you do. To serve, lay out the toasted bread in the center of 6 small soup plates, and spoon the snails and sauce over all.

2 jumbo eggs

1 teaspoon salt, plus a pinch more for the egg salad

1 small center rib of celery with leaves, finely minced

1 scallion, white part only, finely minced

½ red Fresno chile, seeded and finely minced

1½ teaspoons Indian (not Thai) curry paste

1½ teaspoons finely minced fresh dill weed

2 or 3 drops freshly squeezed lemon juice

1 or 2 drops Tabasco sauce

1 to 1½ tablespoons mayonnaise, preferably homemade

12 thin 2-bite-size slices of European-style rye bread

Olive oil, for coating

12 paper-thin slices of smoked salmon

1 Japanese cucumber, finely minced

Coarsely ground black pepper

Smoked Salmon with Curried Egg Salad and Rye Toasts

Serves 6

My niece Aimee, who is also one of our recipe testers, says these make the best Sunday football snack. One of the tricks to them is not to overcook the eggs: the yolks should be just set. If you absolutely must have harder-cooked eggs, add a minute or two to the cooking time.

Try to get salmon that has been smoked over alder wood, as it is the most flavorful. If you can't find nice sliceable smoked salmon of any kind, smoked trout will work, too. Just don't use lox.

To cook the eggs, put them in a small pot with enough water to cover, and add 1 teaspoon of salt. Bring the water to a boil, reduce the heat to a strong simmer, and cook the eggs for 7 minutes. Run them under cold water till cool, or put them in an ice bath.

For the salad, peel and finely chop the eggs (I often grate eggs using a box grater held over a bowl). Put the eggs in a small mixing bowl along with the celery, scallion, chile, curry paste, dill, lemon juice, Tabasco, 1 tablespoon of mayonnaise, and a pinch of salt. Mix gently but thoroughly, using a fork. If the mixture seems too dry, add a little more mayonnaise. You can make the egg salad ahead, and chill it until needed.

To make the toasts, preheat the oven to 375°F. Brush both sides of the bread with olive oil and toast until crisp.

To serve, spread 1 to 2 tablespoons of egg salad on each toast and top with a piece of salmon. Finish with a sprinkle of cucumber and coarsely ground black pepper.

Roasted End o' Summer Tomatoes with Red Wine–Honey Vinaigrette

Serves 6

You can make this with any variety of tomato, but be sure they are really tasty. Roasting will intensify and sweeten the flavors, but you can't expect much if you start with bland tomatoes. If you want to have a little fun with this, buy two different colors of tomatoes, and roast them separately. It will make very colorful bruschetta.

For the cheese, you want something with sharp, bright flavor to contrast with the richness of the roasted tomatoes. Some of my favorites are Cabrales, Valdeón, or Picón, which are all blue cheeses from Spain; or Laura Chenel's aged Crottin, Ig Vella's dry-aged Monterey Jack, or Bellwether Farms' pecorino. I've even done it with crumbled feta cheese. This recipe will give you a chance to experiment (or to use up leftover cheese).

The vinaigrette is more like a sauce than a salad dressing. It is cooked, which smooths it out, sweetens it, and keeps it from "fighting" with any table wine you might be serving with the meal. I've been using a French red-wine vinegar called vinaigre de Banyuls. It is made from Grenache grapes, so it has some fruit and lightness, and isn't thick or super-rich. Like balsamic vinegar, vinaigre de Banyuls undergoes a long aging process. You can find it at specialty gourmet shops.

red wine–honey vinaigrette

2 tablespoons red wine

2 tablespoons red wine vinegar

½ tablespoon honey

⅛ teaspoon salt

Pinch of freshly ground black pepper

1 tablespoon Dijon mustard

¾ cup extra virgin olive oil

2 pounds vine-ripened tomatoes

1 Maui or other sweet onion, cut into wedges

1 tablespoon chopped fresh oregano

2 tablespoons extra virgin olive oil

½ tablespoon sea salt

¼ to ⅓ teaspoon freshly ground black pepper

6 half-inch-thick slices rustic country, sourdough, or semolina bread

1 cup arugula leaves

1 tablespoon minced chives

½ cup crumbled blue cheese or goat cheese

Minced fresh oregano, for garnish

For the vinaigrette, combine the red wine, red wine vinegar, and honey in a small pot. Bring to a boil, lower the heat to a strong simmer, and reduce by half. Allow to cool to room temperature, then add the salt, pepper, and mustard; whisk till the salt dissolves. Add the olive oil in a slow steady stream, whisking all the while. Whisk till well emulsified and set aside. This can be done up to 4 hours before serving.

Preheat the oven to 425°F. Peel and core the tomatoes, then quarter them and remove the seeds. Gently mix together the tomato, onion, chopped oregano, oil, sea salt, and pepper. Spread this mixture out in an even layer in a large ceramic baking dish. A Spanish earthenware dish called a *cazuela* would work well. Roast, stirring occasionally, until the juices from the tomatoes have evaporated and the edges of the vegetables have caramelized well, 15 to 20 minutes. The tomatoes should reduce to a very concentrated, chunky puree.

To serve, toast or grill the bread, and toss the arugula and the chives with the vinaigrette. Smear the tomatoes liberally on the toasts. Sprinkle the greens over the tomatoes, crumble on some cheese, and finish with a sprinkle of minced oregano.

Roasted Peppers with Anchovies and Capers

Serves 6 to 8

3 red bell peppers

3 yellow bell peppers

2 ounces anchovies, plus additional for garnish (optional)

1 handful fresh basil leaves

Pinch of fresh oregano leaves, finely chopped

3 cloves garlic, minced

2 tablespoons capers, rinsed

Sea salt (Maldon flake, if possible)

Freshly ground black pepper

1 tablespoon extra virgin olive oil, plus additional for brushing

12 to 16 slices bread (3-inch-long ovals or rectangles)

I am a roasted pepper junkie. I love them in all their colors, even the green ones, and use them with abandon on just about whatever will hold still long enough for me to plop them on. The best way to roast peppers is over a wood fire. It gives them far superior flavor. I can't count how many times over the past twenty-two years people have told me how good the food tastes at Mustards because it's cooked over a wood fire. I will never understand the idea of outdoor gas grills. You might as well just cook in the kitchen! So I always roast peppers over a wood fire unless there's an absolute downpour, and then I'd do it over the gas stove burner or under a broiler.

The very best anchovies of all are the salt-packed anchovies from Italy and Spain. They are shipped in large cans, but if you live in a large city, there's probably a specialty store there where you can buy just what you need. Soak and rinse well before using. If you can't get the salt-packed ones, buy the oil-packed anchovies that come in glass jars. That way you can be sure of what you are getting. I have never found a good anchovy paste, and I don't recommend that as a substitute.

This dish is great with the Roasted End o' Summer Tomatoes (page 240). Serve them on bite-size croutons as stand-up cocktail party hors d'oeuvres.

Roast the peppers till nicely blackened all over, then pop them into a plastic bag or put them in a bowl and cover it tightly. When the peppers are cool enough to handle, peel off the blackened skin and remove the stem, seeds, and membranes. Tear the peppers into strips over a mixing bowl so as not to lose any of their juices, and drop them into the bowl.

(continued)

Chop the anchovies really finely, then smash them into a paste with the side of the knife blade. Add this to the bowl of bell peppers. Shred the basil by hand (don't use a knife, as the basil will turn black). Add this to the bowl, too, along with the oregano, garlic, capers, salt, pepper, and the 1 tablespoon olive oil. Set aside until needed (this will hold up to 2 hours).

When you are ready to serve, preheat the oven to 375°F. Brush the bread on each side with olive oil, place on a baking sheet, and toast in the oven till crispy and golden. (If you have the grill fired up, you can toast the bread on the grill instead.) Pile a nice amount of the bell pepper mix on each crouton, and sprinkle gingerly with additional sea salt and freshly ground black pepper. If you like, top each off with a half fillet of anchovy as a garnish.

Wilted Winter Greens on Bruschetta

Serves 6 to 8

You may be surprised to know that chard comes in a variety of colors, including red, pink, orange, and yellow (the color is in the stalks, not in the leaves). There is even a rainbow chard, which has stalks of five different colors on each plant. The taste differs little from variety to variety, so if you can't find red or rainbow chard, you can use regular green Swiss chard, and substitute white wine or vermouth for the red wine in the recipe. In preparing this dish, be sure to wash all the greens very well: nibble on a leaf or two to make sure they're clean, as even the tiniest bit of dirt or sand will ruin it.

If you want to be fancy, you can fry the capers in one or two tablespoons of olive oil until crisp and drain them, then sprinkle them on top at the end as a garnish. If you don't care for capers, you can sprinkle on Parmesan or an aged goat or Monterey Jack cheese as the topping instead.

Another great way to serve the greens would be to toss them with pasta or spoon them over polenta or risotto. Mascarpone would be a wonderful addition to the polenta alternative.

To make the bruschetta, preheat the oven to 375°F. Cut the bread slices in half. Coat both sides with butter or olive oil, place on a baking sheet, and toast in the oven until just starting to turn golden. You want the bread to be crispy on the outside but still tender and chewy in the middle. Grilling the toasts would be extra-good if you happen to have one going.

Wash all the greens thoroughly. Working with the chard first, pull the leaves from the stems, tear them into large pieces, and set them aside. Finely julienne the stems crosswise, and keep them separate from the leaves. Tear up the other tender greens into large pieces, and add them to the chard leaves. Heat the olive oil in a large saucepan over medium heat and add the onion and leek. Cover and let cook for 3 to 5 minutes, stirring a couple of times. Add the chard stems and garlic, stir again, then cover and cook several minutes longer, until tender. Remove the lid and reduce the liquids. When the ingredients begin to caramelize, add the wine and cook till dry. Add the chard leaves, the other greens, and the stock; cook, covered, another minute. Remove the lid and continue to cook, stirring, till all the greens are wilted and tender and almost all the liquid has evaporated. Season to taste with salt and pepper. Stir in the crushed red pepper, chopped mint or thyme, and capers. Serve mounded on the bruschetta.

3 or 4 half-inch-thick slices rustic country bread or *bâtard*

Butter or olive oil, for coating

1 bunch red or rainbow chard

8 ounces other tender greens, such as Japanese red mustard, turnip, or beet greens

3 or 4 tablespoons olive oil

½ medium onion, finely diced

1 small leek, white and light green parts only, sliced into thin circles and rinsed

2 cloves garlic, finely minced

¼ cup red wine

¼ cup chicken or vegetable stock or water

Salt and freshly ground black pepper

1 teaspoon crushed dried red pepper

1 tablespoon chopped fresh mint or thyme (not both)

1 tablespoon capers

knife and fork

...but there are times when even I have to give in and use a knife and fork.

chapter 5: Knife and Fork

Like most chefs, I prefer to eat everything with my fingers, but there are times when even I have to give in and use a knife and fork. That's what this chapter is all about—dishes you really can't (or shouldn't) eat with your hands because the food needs to be cut up, or because the food will fall in your lap if you don't use a utensil or two. Most of these dishes are fairly substantial—main courses, in other words, even though the portions are small.

Quite a number of the recipes in this chapter feature stuffed peppers or chiles. These are especially good for entertaining because they make neat individual servings that look spectacular when "plated up," as we say in the restaurant business. There are more steps involved in making these dishes, but much of the work can be done ahead. The Crisp-Fried Squash Blossoms and the Wild Mushroom Tamales fit into this category, too. If you want something simpler, try Oysters Pablo (a restaurant favorite) or Bubbly Baked Brie. If you're looking for something unique, try the Rabbit Sausages or Japanese Crab and Shrimp "Pizzas."

There are plenty of vegetarian dishes in this chapter, in case that is a concern. In addition to the fried squash blossoms, mushroom tamales, and baked Brie dishes mentioned above, the Morel Mushroom– and Goat Cheese–Stuffed Crêpes and the Poached Eggs with Sherried Mushrooms are meatless, as is the Sweet Corn Custard (just be sure to make it with a vegetable stock).

One of the easiest ways to organize a small-plates meal is to select one recipe from this chapter, and then build the rest of your menu around it. Any way you look at it, this chapter has a lot to offer, and you should feel confident enough to mix things up and have some fun.

tomatillo–ancho chile salsa

16 large tomatillos, husked and rinsed

2 whole cloves garlic

2 dried ancho chiles, seeded

2½ cups water

¼ cup good-quality tequila

1 tablespoon salt

1 teaspoon freshly ground black pepper

18 squash blossoms

stuffing

2 ears fresh corn

1 teaspoon olive oil

1 cup ¼-inch dice summer squash

½ cup grated Monterey Jack cheese

½ cup soft fresh goat cheese, at room temperature

2 tablespoons minced cilantro leaves

2 tablespoons minced fresh oregano

2 tablespoons minced fresh epazote (optional)

Crisp-Fried Squash Blossoms with Tomatillo–Ancho Chile Salsa

Serves 6

If you're lucky enough to have squash growing in your own backyard, then you'll have a ready source for squash blossoms. In fact, picking the blossoms is the best way to control overpopulation in the summer squash garden. When picking the blossoms, look for the ones that are starting to open or are already open, as they are easier to work with. And try to get the male flowers—the ones that grow out of the vines rather than out of the baby squash. Watch out for ants and honeybees: they love squash blossoms, too! Early morning is the best time to harvest the blossoms, and you should plan on using them the same day they're picked. We get a good supply of blossoms from the Mustards garden, but we still have to supplement with some from the produce market. For more on squash blossoms, see page 260.

In the restaurant kitchen, we call the Tomatillo–Ancho Chile Salsa "Sauce Forty-One," which stands for forty chiles and one tomatillo. It's just one of Pablo's jokes. Obviously, we've toned it down a little here.

Have some fun serving these by bringing them out in large assorted serving spoons or on tiny plates. I have a collection of mismatched silver soupspoons and serving spoons I often use.

To make the salsa, spread the tomatillos and garlic out on a baking sheet and pop them under the broiler for 1 to 2 minutes, until aromatic and slightly dry. Combine the tomatillos, garlic, ancho chiles, and the 2¹/₂ cups water in a big pot and bring to a boil. Cook until tomatillos are tender, about 5 minutes. Cool slightly, then pour into a blender and blend until smooth. Do this in batches, if necessary. Pour into a bowl and whisk in the tequila, salt, and pepper. Reserve until needed.

Gently clean the blossoms of any dirt and/or ants. Remove the stamens and pistils from the inside and the prickles at the base of the blossom on the outside.

To make the stuffing, cut or grate the kernels off the corn cobs into a bowl. Heat the olive oil in a sauté pan over medium-high heat, and sauté the corn and squash 2 to 3 minutes. Allow the mixture to cool and combine it with the Monterey Jack cheese, goat cheese, cilantro, and 1 tablespoon of the epazote, if desired. (Save the remaining tablespoon of epazote for a garnish.)

Fill the blossoms with some of the mixture, being careful not to break any of them, and leaving enough room at the top so that you can fold the petals back over to get a nice seal. Place the blossoms on waxed paper and put them in the refrigerator to chill a bit before frying them.

For the coating, mix the cornstarch, cornmeal, flour, salt, black pepper, and cayenne pepper together in a shallow bowl. Pour the buttermilk into another bowl. Dip the blossoms into the buttermilk, shaking off the excess, then into the cornstarch-flour mixture, again shaking off the excess. Allow the blossoms to rest for a couple of minutes in the fridge.

To cook the blossoms, heat 2 inches of oil to 375°F in a heavy-bottomed frying pan. Working away from yourself so the hot oil doesn't splash on you, carefully place only as many blossoms in the oil as will comfortably fit in the pan without crowding. You want some space around each blossom to allow good movement without touching. When the undersides are golden-brown and crispy, turn the blossoms and continue cooking until the other side is the same. Gently transfer the crispy blossoms with a spider or slotted spoon to paper towels to drain. Skim out any bits

coating

½ cup cornstarch

½ cup cornmeal

½ cup flour

1 teaspoon salt

½ teaspoon freshly ground black pepper

¼ teaspoon cayenne pepper

1 cup buttermilk

2 cups vegetable or canola oil, for frying

¼ bunch cilantro, leaves only

¼ cup pumpkin seeds, toasted

⅓ cup Lime Crème Fraîche (page 199) or sour cream thinned with water

(continued)

left in the pan and allow the oil to return to 375°F before starting on the next batch.

Serve the blossoms over spoonfuls of the salsa. Garnish with cilantro, pumpkin seeds, crème fraîche, and the reserved epazote, if desired.

Bubbly Baked Brie and Asparagus with Toasted Hazelnuts

Serves 6

To make a very elegant starter, use big fat spears of asparagus for this dish. If you can find it, use white asparagus, or a combination of the two (one spear of white and two of the green makes a really lovely plate). The Brie and cream sauce makes this dish quite rich, so the rest of the plates on your menu need to be on the light side. Cut this recipe down to an appropriate size, and surprise someone with breakfast in bed. Serve it up with the Sunday paper and a bottle of bubbly.

6 to 8 tablespoons hazelnuts (about 4 ounces)

18 spears of asparagus

½ cup heavy cream

8 to 10 ounces Brie cheese, trimmed of the rind

6 tablespoons lightly toasted bread crumbs

Lightly toast the hazelnuts. Briskly rub them together in a kitchen towel to remove the skin. You don't need to get all the skin off, but do the best you can. Roughly chop the hazelnuts and set them aside.

Snap off the tough ends of the asparagus where they break naturally. Blanch the asparagus until they are just barely done, about 2 minutes for fat spears. Test them for doneness with a fork. You want green asparagus just tender; white asparagus a little softer. Drain the asparagus and place in 6 individual dishes or in 1 large oval baking dish. (If you're going to hold the asparagus for later serving, chill them quickly in an ice bath.)

Shortly before serving, preheat the oven to 400°F. Heat a saucepan over medium heat and pour in the cream. Bring the cream to a boil and let it reduce a bit, about 1 minute. Add the Brie and cook, stirring, until the cheese has melted and the sauce is thick enough to coat a spoon. Pour the sauce over the asparagus and sprinkle with bread crumbs. Place under the broiler and cook until golden and bubbly, 1 to 3 minutes, depending on your broiler. Place on plates lined with napkins to keep the baking dishes from sliding around, and sprinkle 1 to 1¹/₂ tablespoons of hazelnuts over each. Warn your guests about the hot dishes.

Chiles en Nogada

Serves 8

According to food historians, the origins of this dish go back to 1821 and a victory banquet in Pueblo, Mexico, commemorating the defeat of the Spanish. All the dishes at that meal had the colors of the Mexican flag: chiles en nogada (chiles in walnut sauce) had the white of the walnut sauce, the red of the pomegranate seeds, and the green of the chiles to represent the flag. It's a celebratory dish, especially good for Christmas and weddings.

It's a bit of work, but to make the sauce in the traditional way, you must soak the walnuts in milk overnight, then peel them as best you can before pureeing them. You can skip this step, but the sauce won't be as pretty and white.

When you buy pomegranates, look for firm, smooth, round fruits. Be careful when you cut them open to get at the seeds, as they have tons of juice and squirt all over. I usually work over a sink, and I never wear white. The seeds are attached to inner membranes that peel off easily. Break off a lobe, remove the membrane, and separate the bright red seeds. If you want pomegranate juice, just cut the fruit in half, as you would an orange, and juice it on a citrus juicer. If pomegranates are not in season, you could substitute minced red peppers, chiles, or pimientos to get a touch of red in the dish.

The chiles in this dish are stuffed with a pork and beef filling, then dipped in a light batter and fried. If the batter-and-fry steps seem too much, turn it into a baked dish instead (see directions on the following pages).

(continued)

walnut sauce

2 cups shelled walnuts

1½ cups milk, plus additional to thin the sauce, if needed

1½ cups sour cream

Salt

8 poblano chiles

filling

3 tablespoons vegetable oil

1 small onion, finely chopped

2 cloves garlic, minced

3 tablespoons chopped golden raisins

1 apple, peeled, cored, and diced

12 ounces ground pork

12 ounces ground beef

1 teaspoon salt

¼ teaspoon freshly ground black pepper

½ teaspoon ground cinnamon

1 tablespoon white wine vinegar

4 large eggs

Pinch of salt

Canola, vegetable, or peanut oil, for frying

Flour, for dusting

Seeds of 1 pomegranate

2 tablespoons coarsely chopped cilantro leaves

For the sauce, soak the walnuts in 1½ cups of milk overnight in the refrigerator. The next day, pour off and discard the milk. Rub the walnuts between your fingers to break up the skin, and pick it off with the tip of a sharp paring knife. It's a pill of a job, but it makes a big difference in taste and appearance. Puree the walnuts and sour cream in a food processor or blender, taste, and add salt if needed. If the sauce seems too thick, thin it with a little milk or half-and-half. Keep chilled till needed, but bring back to room temperature before using.

Roast the chiles and peel them, being careful not to tear them in the process. Don't remove the stems, as they will serve as a handle as you work with the chiles. Cut a neat slit down the length of each chile, stopping about ½ inch from the bottom. Carefully scrape out the ribs and seeds, and set the chiles aside.

To make the filling, heat the oil in a large skillet over medium-low heat. Add the onion, garlic, raisins, and apple; cook until soft, about 20 minutes. Increase the heat to medium-high; add the pork and beef and cook 6 to 8 more minutes to brown the meat, breaking it up as it's cooking. Stir in the salt, pepper, cinnamon, and vinegar, and cook another 2 to 3 minutes. The filling should be moist but not saucy. It can be made a day ahead, and kept refrigerated.

About an hour before serving, remove the walnut sauce from the refrigerator. Dry the chiles with paper towels and carefully fill them with the meat mixture, a couple of tablespoons per chile. Don't rush this step, as you don't want to tear the chiles.

If you are going to bake the chiles, skip down to the last paragraph of this recipe. If you are going to fry them, continue on. Separate the eggs, with the whites going into the bowl of a mixer or another medium-size bowl, and 2 of the yolks into a smaller bowl (discard the 2 remaining yolks or keep them for another use). Using the mixer or by hand, beat the egg whites until foamy. Add a pinch of salt and continue to beat until soft peaks form. Lightly beat the yolks, then fold these into the whites. In a large skillet, heat 1 inch of oil to 375°F. Coat the chiles lightly with flour, shake off the excess, then dip them in the egg. Fry the chiles in small batches to avoid overcrowding (the chiles should not touch). Cook them until they are golden brown on 1 side, then turn and cook until golden brown on the other. Adjust the temperature as needed. If the chiles brown too fast, the insides will not be hot, and if the temperature is too low, the chiles will absorb oil instead of getting crisp and brown. As the chiles finish, remove them to drain on a metal rack or on paper towels. Skim out any bits that have fallen into the oil, and let the oil come back to 375°F between batches.

This is one of those dishes that should be served immediately. To serve, pool the walnut sauce in the center of a large platter. Place the chiles in the center of that, and sprinkle with the pomegranate seeds and cilantro. Alternatively, you could pour the sauce out onto individual plates (dark plates look good), top with a chile, then sprinkle on the garnishes. Serve right away.

To bake the chiles, preheat the oven to 375°F. Tuck the chiles into a casserole dish, drizzle with a bit of chicken or veal stock, and bake uncovered 15 to 20 minutes, until they are steamy and hot through. Place the chiles on a bed of walnut sauce, and sprinkle pomegranate seeds and cilantro about.

Sweet-Corn Custard with Shiitake Mushroom Sauce

Serves 5 to 10

custard

3 ears fresh corn

2 cups heavy cream

4 large eggs

1 cup (loosely packed) grated
  Monterey Jack cheese

1 tablespoon Dijon mustard

½ teaspoon salt

¼ teaspoon freshly ground white
  pepper

mushroom sauce

2 cups rich veal or chicken stock

2 tablespoons olive oil

6 shiitake mushrooms, stemmed
  and quartered

2 tablespoons butter

2 scallions, minced

Salt and freshly ground black
  pepper

Minced fresh chives, for garnish

This rich, savory custard was a brunch favorite at one of my past restaurants. At the restaurant, the mushroom sauce is made with reduced veal stock. I don't think very many home cooks have reduced veal stock on hand, but chicken or mushroom stock will do just fine. The dish will be yummy without that gilding of the lily. If you make them in tiny ramekins (an inch and a half in diameter), the recipe will yield ten servings; larger ramekins (three inches in diameter) will yield five. The custards can be kept warm while you make the sauce, but if you want to hold them any longer than twenty minutes, they should be refrigerated and reheated before serving.

Using a coarse grater or corn cutter, cut the kernels off the ears of corn into a bowl. Transfer the corn to a medium-size saucepan, add the cream, and heat to a simmer. Cook 5 to 10 minutes, till the corn is tender. Allow the mixture to cool, then puree it in a blender. Strain the puree through a fine sieve into a bowl, pressing well to extract all the liquids and flavors. Put the eggs, cheese, mustard, salt, and pepper in a large bowl. Mix well, but don't beat in any air, as this will cause a foamy ridge to form around the edges of the custard. Stir in the corn mixture.

Preheat the oven to 325°F and butter ten 2-ounce ramekins or five 4-ounce ones. Pour some custard into each of the ramekins. You will want to stop at least ¹/₄ inch from the rims to allow for rising. Place the ramekins in a large, shallow pan and carefully fill the pan with enough hot water to go two-thirds of the way up the ramekins. Cover the pan with aluminum foil and prick a few small holes in the foil. Bake in this water bath for 35 to 40 minutes, till the custards are set. Keep them warm while you prepare the mushroom sauce. (If you're not going to serve them right away, let them cool a bit, then cover and refrigerate them. When you're ready to serve, reheat the custards in a water bath, 5 to 6 minutes for the small ones, 8 to 10 minutes for the larger ones. Meanwhile, you can prepare the sauce.)

To make the sauce, put the stock in a sauté pan over high heat to reduce it by half; this should take about 15 to 20 minutes. Meanwhile, heat the oil in a sauté pan over medium-high heat. Add the mushrooms and cook, stirring, until the mushrooms have released their juices and are tender, and the pan has dried out a bit, 10 to 15 minutes. When the mushrooms are done, increase the heat to high and pour the stock over. Let it bubble up, and cook 1 to 2 minutes. Add the butter and scallions, swirling to melt the butter into the sauce. Season to taste with salt and pepper.

To serve, turn the custards out onto individual plates. Pour some sauce around each of the warm custards and garnish with minced chives.

Crêpes "Croque-Monsieur" with Horseradish-Mustard Cream

Serves 6

A real croque-monsieur is nothing more than a ham and Gruyère cheese sandwich that is sautéed in butter to crisp it up and to melt the cheese. France's answer to fast food! In this dish, crêpes take the place of the bread. They are filled with ham and cheese, but then they are bathed in a tangy cream sauce and heated in the oven. They are delicious! They are also very rich, so you'd want them as the main course of a small-plates dinner. Or they would be the perfect snack on a cold winter's evening: just add a fire in the fireplace and a nice glass of Chardonnay to complete the picture.

If you cook the crêpes ahead of time and freeze them, this dish comes together quickly. Of course, if you can swing it, fresh crêpes are always better. (Crêpe batter will keep, covered, in the refrigerator for a couple of days, so that's another plan-ahead option.) This recipe will make about a dozen crêpes, so you'll have plenty left over to freeze for another time, or to use for the Morel Mushroom–and Goat Cheese–Stuffed Crêpes (page 264).

A good-quality ham makes a big difference. Try Westphalian or another flavorful, well-made, old-fashioned ham, like a honey-baked ham or an applewood-smoked ham. We have a great local source (Hobb's, in El Cerrito), and you can probably find a good one in your area, too. For instance, in the mid-Atlantic area you can buy Edwards hickory-smoked

(continued)

hams from Virginia Traditions. Don't use prosciutto or Serrano ham, as they don't have the right texture.

It's best to bake the filled crêpes in dishes with sloped sides. Shirred egg dishes would be ideal, if you have them. But even individual flat plates would work. What you definitely do not want to do is to bake the crêpes in dishes with high straight sides. Doing so will result in steaming and boiling and a soggy situation, versus baking and caramelizing into a bubbly richness.

crêpe batter

⅓ cup corn flour

⅔ cup all-purpose flour

1 tablespoon sugar

¼ teaspoon salt

3 large eggs

1½ cups whole or 2 percent milk

1 tablespoon melted butter, plus extra butter or a pure pan spray for cooking the crepes

horseradish-mustard cream

1½ cups heavy cream

3 tablespoons Dijon mustard

1 to 2 tablespoons prepared horseradish

3 thin slices good-quality ham

½ to ⅔ cup finely grated Gruyère or Jarlsberg cheese

2 tablespoons minced fresh chives

Freshly ground black pepper

To make the crêpe batter, whisk together the 2 flours, sugar, and salt in a mixing bowl. In a separate bowl, beat the eggs with the milk until blended. Now quickly mix the wet ingredients into the dry ones, stirring just enough to combine. Whisk in the tablespoon of melted butter at the end. Cover and let the batter rest for at least 1 hour in the refrigerator. (The batter can be made ahead as much as 24 hours.)

To make the crêpes, heat an 8-inch sauté pan over medium-high heat and brush the pan with some butter. Be sure the pan is very hot before you start, otherwise your first crêpe will probably stick. Mix the batter well, and pour about ¼ cup into the pan, tilting the pan as you pour it in and swirling the batter around to cover the bottom of the pan and ¼ inch up the sides in a very thin layer. When the bottom is golden, the crêpe should release easily; turn it and cook the other side till just set. This will take about 1½ minutes on each side. Slide the crêpe out of the pan onto a plate. Recoat the pan with some butter, if needed; stir the batter again and carry on with the next crêpe. If you're going to use the crêpes right away, just stack them up. To freeze them, put a piece of parchment or waxed paper between the crêpes to keep them from sticking together, wrap the whole stack up in plastic wrap, and put it in a plastic freezer bag. When you need them, defrost them at room temperature and proceed with the recipe.

Shortly before serving, preheat the oven to 375°F.

To make the Horseradish-Mustard Cream, combine the cream, mustard, and horseradish in a small bowl and mix well. Set aside.

To assemble the crêpes, first trim the slices of ham to fit a folded crêpe. Place a slice of ham on the bottom half of each crêpe, sprinkle the ham slices with about half the cheese, and fold the crêpes back over the ham. Place each crêpe in its own baking dish or plate. Pour the horseradish cream over the crêpes, dividing it as equally as you can, and sprinkle with cheese. Bake 8 to 12 minutes, until bubbly and hot through and lightly golden brown.

While the crêpes are baking, get 6 plates ready to hold the baking dishes when they come out of the oven. Line each plate with a napkin (this will keep the baking dishes from sliding about when served). When the crepes are done, transfer the baking dishes to the napkin-lined plates and sprinkle each crêpe with chives and pepper. Be sure to warn your guests that the top plates are hot.

6 crêpes (page 262)

corn cream

2 ears fresh corn

2 cups heavy cream

¼ teaspoon salt

⅛ teaspoon freshly ground white
pepper

Pinch of cayenne pepper

pablo's oaxacan filling

1 to 1¼ pounds morel mushrooms

5 squash blossoms, petals only

1 tablespoon olive oil

1 tablespoon butter

¼ onion, minced

2 tablespoons thinly sliced fresh
epazote or chopped fresh
oregano

¼ teaspoon salt

Freshly ground white pepper

Pinch of cayenne pepper

4 to 6 gratings fresh nutmeg

4 ounces soft fresh goat cheese,
at room temperature

¼ cup finely shredded Parmesan
cheese

2 to 3 tablespoons finely minced
fresh chives

Morel Mushroom– and Goat Cheese–Stuffed Crêpes with Corn Cream

Serves 6

People do not usually associate crêpes with Mexican cuisine, but in fact there are various dishes made with thin pancakes that are identical to French crêpes. This one would make a nice first course or a great "main" part to a small-plates meal. The filling is a typical Oaxacan combination of corn, mushrooms, and cheese. Bake them in whatever dish you want to serve them from, as after they are baked you won't be able to move them around. Shirred egg dishes or some other cool baking dish with sloped sides would be ideal. I have also used small plates. Don't use dishes with high straight sides, as this will cause the crêpes to steam instead of bake.

If you can't find fresh morels, you can use dried morels (about four ounces), fresh chanterelles, or whatever fresh mushrooms you can get in your market; huitlacoche would be perfect. Any extra Corn Cream makes an excellent corn chowder base. As for the crêpes, if you have a batch in the freezer, take out six crêpes and let them defrost. Otherwise, start by making a new batch of crêpes.

To make the corn cream, cut the kernels off the ears of corn and set them aside for the filling. Chop the corn cobs into 3 or 4 chunks and place them in a pot with the cream and enough water to cover, about 1 cup. Bring to a boil; reduce to a simmer, and cook 30 minutes, or till a nice corn flavor has developed. You should have about 2 cups of corn cream. Season with the salt, white pepper, and cayenne. Remove the cobs and chill the cream until needed.

For the filling, clean the mushrooms with a soft dry pastry brush, stem them, then slice them into rings. Clean the squash blossoms of any dust or ants, and tear them into 4 pieces each. Heat the oil and butter in a medium saucepan over medium-low heat and sweat the onion 4 to 5 minutes, until tender. Increase

the heat and add the mushrooms. Cook until the mushrooms have released their juices and are tender and the pan has dried out a bit, 4 to 6 minutes. Add the reserved corn kernels and the epazote; cook 3 to 4 minutes more, until it looks like a succotash, moist but not too saucy. Stir in the salt, white pepper, cayenne, and nutmeg. Allow this mixture to cool, then stir in the cheese and the blossoms.

To finish the dish, preheat the oven to 500°F. Spread some of the filling on half of each crêpe, leaving a ¹/₂-inch border all around. Fold each crêpe in half, then cut each folded crêpe in half, making 2 pie-shaped wedges per crêpe. Place the wedges on plates or slope-sided baking dishes and top with the Corn Cream and the Parmesan, distributing both as equally as you can. Bake 2 to 3 minutes, until bubbly and golden brown. Serve sprinkled with chives.

Poached Eggs with Sherried Mushrooms and Piquillo Peppers

Serves 6

2 tablespoons butter or extra virgin olive oil (preferably Spanish)

1½ cups sliced mushrooms (button, crimini, chanterelle, or morel)

½ small onion, sliced

¼ cup medium-dry sherry (Oloroso Especial, if possible)

3 or 4 *piquillo* peppers, chopped, or ¾ cup chopped roasted bell pepper (peel and seed it first)

2 tablespoons cilantro or fresh parsley leaves, coarsely chopped

6 half-inch-thick slices rustic levain-style or herb bread

6 large eggs

6 cups water

1 tablespoon vinegar

2 teaspoons salt

Coarse sea salt

Freshly ground black pepper

This is a great small plate for breakfast, brunch, or a midnight snack. If you poach the eggs just right, when you dig in, the soft yolks will combine with the mushroom juices and create a luscious treat. My friend Gerry Dawes says egg yolks make the best sauce of all, and I do believe he's right. If you can't find the piquillos (see page 356), you could substitute roasted red or yellow bell peppers for them.

Heat the butter in a large flat sauté pan till very hot but not smoking. Add the mushrooms and cook 2 to 3 minutes. Add the onion and cook, stirring occasionally, until the onion is tender and the mushrooms are beginning to caramelize. Add the sherry and reduce until the pan is almost dry. Stir in the *piquillos* and cilantro and mix well. This mixture can be made earlier in the day, and reheated before the eggs are poached.

When you're ready to serve, toast the bread and reheat the mushrooms. To poach the eggs, combine the water, vinegar, and salt in a poacher or straight-sided sauté pan and bring to a boil. Reduce the heat just enough to maintain a strong simmer and poach the eggs 4 minutes (the whites should be set, but the yolks still runny). Scoop them out with a slotted spoon, and tap the spoon on a towel to shake off the water.

(continued)

To serve, place the toasts on plates and spoon some of the mushroom mix on the toasts, using up about half the mixture. Top each toast with a poached egg, then finish off with the remaining mushroom mix. Season with sea salt and pepper as you like.

Variation: If you want to make this for eating out of hand, use hard-boiled eggs instead of poached eggs. Cut the toasts to a two-bite size, and top each with mushrooms and half a hard-boiled egg.

Crispy Fried Rabbit with Dijon-Madeira Sauce

Serves 6 to 8

I just love rabbit, and I love creamy Dijon mustard sauces, too. I also have a thing for fried foods, so that's why this dish would have to go on the list of my top ten favorites. I know it's Charles Gatreaux's favorite dish. Charles owns one of the best table, china, and bed linens cool-stuff stores in Napa Valley. I should dedicate this recipe to him. Actually, I will.

The sauce could be prepared ahead up to the point of adding the butter. To finish it, gently reheat it so as not to reduce it any further, and add the butter and chervil. If you prefer, you can substitute tarragon for the chervil. I use a lot of chervil and tarragon in my cooking, depending on the season. All summer long, we grow tarragon in the Mustards garden, and in the cooler months, we grow chervil. Chervil is a more delicate herb, lightly anise-flavored, and lacy. It grows like a weed, and looks nice in the garden or in a window pot.

If you have extra crust mix, it also makes a great coating for fried calamari or fried green tomatoes. It keeps well, so you can double the recipe if you like. Just be sure to store it in a dry, airtight container.

1 rabbit (about 3½ pounds)

½ to ¾ cup buttermilk

1 teaspoon salt

1 teaspoon cayenne pepper

½ teaspoon freshly ground black pepper

rabbit stock

1 cup dry white or rosé wine

2 cloves

1 onion

2 carrots, peeled and chopped

1 stalk celery, chopped

3 sprigs thyme

3 sprigs parsley

6 cups chicken stock

crispy crust mix

¾ cup yellow or white cornmeal

½ cup all-purpose flour or corn flour

½ cup cornstarch

1 teaspoon salt

1 teaspoon cayenne pepper

½ teaspoon freshly ground black pepper

Peanut or vegetable oil, for frying

dijon-madeira sauce

3 tablespoons Madeira

2¼ cups rabbit stock

2 tablespoons heavy cream

3 tablespoons Dijon mustard

1 tablespoon butter

1 tablespoon minced fresh chervil, plus some whole sprigs for garnish

When you're cutting up the rabbit meat, try for pieces that are all about the same size (1½- to 2-inch chunks). Reserve all the bones for the stock. If you have to disjoint the rabbit yourself, separate the front legs and hind legs from the body first. Cut the front legs apart at the joint, and leave the bone in. Leave the bone in the smaller section of the hind legs, like a drumstick, but cut the thigh meat into bite-size pieces. Cut the loin away from the bone and cut the loin up, too. During the testing, I got 28 bite-size pieces, including the liver and kidneys.

Combine ½ cup of the buttermilk and the salt, cayenne pepper, and black pepper in a small bowl; mix well. Place the rabbit in a sealable plastic bag or a shallow dish and pour the marinade over, making sure that all surfaces are coated evenly. Add a bit more buttermilk if needed. Marinate in the refrigerator at least 1 hour (up to 6 hours is okay).

Meanwhile, make the stock. Put the rabbit bones in a baking pan and roast at 375°F 20 to 30 minutes, until golden brown. Remove the pan from the oven and put the bones in a stockpot. While the pan is still hot, deglaze it with the wine, scraping the pan to loosen all the browned bits at the bottom. Add this to the stockpot. Stick the cloves into the onion and add that to the pot, along with the carrots, celery, thyme, parsley, and chicken stock. Bring to a boil, skim, and reduce to a simmer. Cook 45 minutes to 1 hour, skimming as needed. Strain, and chill the stock until needed.

To prepare the rabbit, shake off the excess marinade and drain the rabbit well in a colander. While the rabbit is draining, combine all the ingredients for the crispy crust mix in a large bowl and mix thoroughly. To coat the rabbit, work with 3 or 4 pieces at time, tossing them around in the mix so they are well coated and shaking off the excess coating. You might find it easier to do this in a sieve. Place the pieces on a cooling rack over a baking sheet and continue with the remaining pieces. When all are done, refrigerate 20 to 30 minutes to set the coating.

(continued)

To fry the rabbit, pour oil to a depth of 1$^1/_2$ inches into a cast-iron or other heavy-bottomed skillet and heat it to 375°F. Starting with the bone-in pieces first, carefully add just enough rabbit to fill the pan but not overcrowd it. You want plenty of room around each piece so it all cooks quickly and evenly. Fry 3 to 5 minutes, turning occasionally to ensure the meat gets cooked through and you get a nice caramel-brown crispness on the outside. Transfer the fried rabbit to paper towels to drain, and keep in a warm oven until needed. Skim out any bits that have fallen into the oil, and let the oil return to 375°F before cooking the next batch. Continue until all the rabbit is fried.

To make the sauce, heat a saucepan over medium-high heat. Add the Madeira and allow it to reduce by half, then add the stock. Continue cooking until the liquid has reduced by about one-third, 15 to 20 minutes. Stir in the cream and mustard, and reduce a bit. The sauce can be held at this point, and finished just before serving. To finish, bring the sauce back to a simmer, add the butter, and cook until the sauce thickens enough to coat a spoon. Stir in the chervil and taste for seasoning.

To serve, pour equal amounts of the sauce onto individual plates, top with 3 to 4 pieces of the rabbit per serving, and garnish with sprigs of chervil.

Deep-Fried Soft-Shell Crabs with Ginger-Garlic Butter

Serves 8

Soft-shell crabs are in season from May through September. You can get frozen soft-shell crabs all year long, but I don't recommend them. If you are reading this at the wrong time of the year and have your heart set on this yummy combination, you're better off substituting jumbo shrimp for the soft-shells. For the sauce, young, thin-skinned ginger with pink-tipped roots is best.

8 soft-shell crabs

coating

⅔ cup all-purpose flour

⅔ cup cornmeal

1 teaspoon cayenne pepper

1 teaspoon freshly ground black
  pepper

¼ teaspoon salt

¾ to 1 cup buttermilk

Peanut or canola oil, for frying

ginger-garlic butter

3 to 4 tablespoons butter

3 tablespoons finely julienned
  peeled fresh ginger

3 tablespoons thinly sliced garlic

⅛ bunch Italian parsley, leaves
  only

¼ bunch chives, cut into ½-inch
  lengths

¼ bunch fresh basil, leaves only

1 lemon, cut into wedges

To prepare the crabs, snip off the eyes. Lift the back flaps and fold them back over the bodies, and remove the fibrous lung tissue. (If you're doing shrimp, peel them three-quarters of the way down, leaving the tails intact, and butterfly them.)

To prepare the coating, combine the flour, cornmeal, cayenne, black pepper, and salt in a bowl large enough to give you plenty of room for dusting the crabs. Pour the buttermilk into another bowl. To avoid a gummy mess when you bread the crabs, always use one hand for the buttermilk and the other for the dry ingredients. Dip the crabs 1 at a time in the buttermilk with the "wet" hand, drain, then drop them into the coating mix and use your "dry" hand to coat them evenly. Make sure you get the underside of the body and legs well coated. Shake off the excess.

To fry them up, pour the oil to a depth of 2 inches into a heavy-bottomed frying pan or pans and heat to 375°F. Working in batches, carefully slip the crabs into the hot oil, only as many as will fit in the pan without overcrowding. Cook 3 to 5 minutes, until golden brown and crispy. Transfer to absorbent paper or a metal rack to drain. Skim out any remaining bits and allow the oil to come back up to 375°F before starting the next batch.

To make the ginger-garlic butter, melt the butter in a saucepan. When it begins to foam, toss in the ginger, garlic, parsley, and chives. Cook just 1 minute. To serve, put the soft-shell crabs on individual plates, drizzle Ginger-Garlic Butter over them, and sprinkle on the basil. Put the lemon wedges on the side. If you prefer, you can put everything on a platter.

Glazed Scallops with Almond-Caper Butter Sauce

Serves 6

While working on recipes for this book, I came across this one, which I had completely forgotten about, and I thought, Madeira and soy sauce? How weird. What was I thinking? But when I retested it, it all came back to me. This is an absolutely delicious combination. I use the glaze on scallops here, but it is excellent with any firm white fish, too. Try it with medallions of monkfish, halibut, or sea bass.

Plan on two or three scallops per person, depending on what else you are serving. Final preparation for this dish takes less than ten minutes, so plan accordingly.

glaze

¼ cup Madeira

¼ cup soy sauce

½ cup mirin

¼ cup sugar

¼ cup minced peeled fresh ginger

almond-caper butter sauce

8 tablespoons (½ cup) butter, at room temperature

1 or 2 shallots, sliced into thin rings (ideally on a mandoline)

3 tablespoons capers, rinsed and coarsely chopped

3 to 4 tablespoons toasted sliced almonds

2 to 3 tablespoons fresh parsley leaves, minced

Freshly ground black pepper

Salt, if needed

12 large or 18 medium scallops

Salt and freshly ground black pepper

To make the glaze, combine the Madeira, soy sauce, mirin, sugar, and ginger in a medium-size saucepan. Heat to just below the boiling point, then reduce to a low simmer. Cook 5 minutes. Cover and set aside in a warm spot.

Just before you put the scallops on the grill, make the sauce. Heat a medium-size sauté pan over high heat till almost smoking. Spoon in ²/₃ of the butter: it will sizzle and melt and brown as soon as it hits the pan. Immediately toss in the shallots, capers, almonds, and half the parsley; cook, stirring, 1 minute. Add the remaining butter and a pinch of freshly ground black pepper. Swirl and stir to incorporate and melt the butter. Stir in the remaining parsley and taste for seasoning, adding salt only if needed. Remove from the heat.

(continued)

This recipe calls for grilling the scallops, but you could sear them in a cast-iron pan instead. Just be sure to coat them well with olive oil or vegetable oil, and a little oil in the pan wouldn't hurt. Go easy on the glaze. In other words, refrain from the dousing you can get away with over a grill, otherwise you'll end up with a gummy mess. Also, make sure you turn your hood vent on, as there will be some smoking.

Lightly sprinkle the scallops with salt and pepper. Brush them on both sides with some of the glaze and place them on a grill over a hot wood fire. Baste them liberally as they cook. Rotate them a quarter turn halfway through the cooking on each side to create nice crosshatch grill marks. Cook until they are nicely caramelized on the outside. This should not take more than a couple of minutes in all.

To serve, place the scallops on one large platter or on 6 small individual plates. Brush with the glaze again, then pour the sauce over.

Grilled Scallops Amandine

Serves 6

If you put almonds on or in anything, you get to call it "amandine"—coffee, ice cream, fish, or in this case scallops. There's more to this dish than the almondine sauce, though. The scallops are brushed with a delicate orange-mirin glaze as they are grilled.

The amount of time your scallops spend on the grill will, of course, depend on their size and how you like them cooked. I used two-ounce scallops to test this recipe and cooked them to medium-rare in three minutes. I prepare the shallots for the sauce by roasting them first. It takes an extra half hour, but it makes a big difference in the flavor. Roasted shallots are good with many other things—potatoes, steaks, and lamb chops, for instance—so you could roast extra while you're at it. If you're short on time, though, you could skip the roasting and simply sauté the shallots briefly. Instructions for both options are given below.

You can substitute any firm-fleshed fish, like swordfish or mahi mahi, for the scallops. Just cut the fish into two-ounce chunks and follow the recipe.

orange glaze

1 stalk lemongrass

1 fresh Thai or bird's-eye chile or
  1 dried *chile de árbol*

1¼ cups freshly squeezed orange
  juice

3 tablespoons mirin

4 thin slices peeled fresh ginger

amandine sauce

3 shallots

1 teaspoon olive oil

Salt and freshly ground black
  pepper

½ cup sliced almonds

1 tablespoon sesame oil

1 tablespoon peanut oil

2 scallions, white and light green
  parts only, thinly sliced

12 large or 18 medium scallops

Salt and freshly ground black
  pepper

3 tablespoons chopped cilantro
  leaves and tender stems

1 tablespoon toasted sesame
  seeds

Soak 6 bamboo skewers in enough water to cover at least 30 minutes.

For the glaze, peel off and discard the outer layers of the lemongrass, and cut off the bottom 2 inches of the bulb end. Chop this coarsely and put it in a small sauté pan. Score the chile to open it up and add it to the pan, along with the orange juice, mirin, and ginger. Bring to a boil and immediately reduce to a strong simmer. Continue cooking 3 to 5 minutes, until the liquid is reduced by half to a light syrup. Keep an eye on it as it's cooking. Strain, discarding the solids, and reserve in a warm spot until needed.

If you're going to roast the shallots for the sauce, preheat the oven to 375°F. Drizzle the shallots with the olive oil, season with salt and pepper, and roast 20 to 30 minutes, till tender and caramelized. (Toast the almonds 7 minutes, while you're at it.) Peel and slice the roasted shallots. If you elect to sauté the shallots, peel and slice them and set them aside. Toast the almonds at 375°F for 7 minutes. To make the amandine sauce, heat the sesame oil and peanut oil in a sauté pan over medium-high heat. Add the scallions and shallots, if you didn't roast them first, and sauté until the scallions are just tender. Toss in the almonds (and roasted shallots if you have them) and cook 1 minute more. Pour in 2 to 3 tablespoons of the glaze and continue cooking until hot and bubbly. Keep warm.

Thread the scallops onto the skewers and season them lightly with salt and pepper. Brush them with some of the glaze and grill over a hot fire 1 to 2 minutes. Turn the scallops and brush with more of the glaze. Continue grilling until nicely caramelized on the outside and cooked on the inside to your liking, 3 to 4 minutes in all.

To serve, spoon the amandine sauce over the scallops immediately. Finish with a sprinkling of cilantro and toasted sesame seeds.

People have told me
they're addictive.

Oysters Pablo
(page 278)

pictured on page 277

Oysters Pablo

Serves 6

These oysters have a rich, garlicky chile kick, and I'll bet you can't eat just one. They were on the opening menu of Mira-monte, and they continue to be a hit at Cindy's Backstreet Kitchen. People have told me they're addictive. I think it's the oyster-garlic combo. Chipotle chiles are smoked dried jalapeños: for this recipe, buy the chipotles canned in adobo sauce. Adobo is a somewhat spicy sauce made with tomatoes, onions, and vinegar. Both the chipotles and the sauce have multiple uses, so don't throw out the leftovers. I figure on three to four oysters per person, depending on the group and the rest of the menu.

Most of this dish can be prepared way in advance. You can make the sauce and the spinach a day ahead. Shuck the oysters a couple of hours ahead, and loosen them from the shell. Final preparation will just take three to four minutes.

sauce

2 cups mayonnaise

2 tablespoons minced shallots

1½ tablespoons minced garlic

1 tablespoon freshly squeezed
lemon juice

1 tablespoon good-quality
tequila

½ cup plus 2 tablespoons
(loosely packed) grated Asiago
cheese

⅛ teaspoon freshly ground black
pepper

spinach

1 pound fresh spinach leaves

1 to 2 tablespoons olive oil

1 shallot, minced

1 small clove garlic, minced

¼ teaspoon salt

⅛ teaspoon freshly ground black
pepper

1 chipotle chile in adobo, minced

18 to 24 Hog Island oysters or
other midsize, briny oysters

Minced fresh parsley leaves, for
garnish

For the sauce, put all the ingredients in a bowl and mix until just combined. Cover and refrigerate until needed.

For the spinach, remove the stems and wash the spinach well. Heat the olive oil in a large sauté pan over medium-high heat. Add the shallot and garlic and cook until soft, about 1 minute, making sure they don't brown. Add the spinach, salt, and pepper; cook, stirring, until the spinach is just wilted, 1 to 2 minutes, depending on how wide your pan is. Spread the contents of the pan out on a baking sheet and put it in the fridge immediately to cool quickly. When it is cool, squeeze the spinach mixture to get rid of any excess liquid, and chop coarsely. Place the spinach in a bowl, mix in the chipotle, and

taste. If you want a little more spice, stir in a little of the adobo sauce from the can. Set the spinach aside until needed.

To prepare the oysters, fill a large bowl with 2 to 3 inches of ice and water (heavy on the ice) and place a smaller bowl on top to hold the shucked oysters, with as much of their liquor as you can. Shuck the oysters, reserving the cupped sections of the shells. This can be done ahead, but be sure to keep the oysters and shells cold until you are ready for the final preparation.

Preheat the oven to 500°F. Unless you have one of those metal plates that have indentations for the oysters to sit nicely in, use a baking dish that will hold them snugly, or put a 1/2-inch layer of salt in a baking pan and nestle the oysters into the salt. This will keep them from tipping over when you move them in and out of the oven or under the broiler.

To cook the oysters, put 1 tablespoon of spinach in the bottom of each reserved shell and top with an oyster. Spoon any reserved liquor over the oysters, followed by about 3/4 tablespoon of sauce over each. Bake 6 to 8 minutes, keeping a close watch on them and removing them as soon as they are golden brown and bubbly. If they haven't reached this point when 8 minutes are up, pop them under the broiler for a moment or two.

Sprinkle with minced parsley and serve with cocktail forks.

Grilled Sea Scallops with Saffron Cream Sauce

Serves 6

saffron cream sauce

½ tablespoon butter

1 to 1½ medium shallots, minced

2 tablespoons Manzanilla or other dry sherry

½ cup white wine

8 to 10 strands saffron, crumbled

2 cups heavy cream

⅛ teaspoon salt

Several shakes of cayenne

⅛ teaspoon freshly ground white pepper

12 large sea scallops

Olive oil, for brushing

Salt and freshly ground black pepper

Torn chervil fronds, for garnish

Scallops and saffron have a special affinity for each other. When you match them up, you get outstanding flavors and striking colors. It's an extravagant combination, but worth it for the excitement it will create.

You want jumbo or day-boat sea scallops for this recipe, not the little bay scallops. For the skewers, try to get those flat Japanese bamboo skewers that are about four or five inches long and a quarter-inch wide. If you have to use traditional skewers, double them up and break off the excess.

The saffron sauce does well made ahead, even as much as the day before. Refrigerate it and reheat it before serving. This dish also works with jumbo prawns (6 to 8 count) or medallions of monkfish. For prawns, peel them, then make a tiny slit along the back and devein them. Don't cut in too deep or the prawns will dry out.

The scallops can be seared in a pan if you prefer (use high heat and a little oil).

Soak the skewers in enough water to cover at least 30 minutes.

***For the sauce**,* melt the butter in a medium saucepan over medium-low heat. Add the shallots and cook, stirring, until just tender, 3 to 5 minutes. Be careful not to caramelize them. Add the sherry and cook it down until the pan is almost dry. Add the wine and saffron; cook, stirring, until the alcohol has evaporated, another 2 or 3 minutes. Add the cream and cook, stirring, until the sauce has reduced at least by half. This might take another 2 minutes or so: you want about 1¹/₂ cups of sauce that is thick enough to coat the back of a spoon. Finish with the salt, cayenne, and white pepper. Keep the sauce warm while you grill the scallops or, if you're making it ahead, refrigerate it and reheat before serving.

Thread 2 scallops onto each skewer, keeping the scallops as flat as possible to ensure good contact with the grill. Brush the scallops with oil and sprinkle with salt and pepper. Grill over medium heat till caramelized nicely on the outside, $1\frac{1}{2}$ to 2 minutes each side for medium-rare. Rotating the skewers a quarter turn halfway through cooking on each side will give you nice crosshatch grill marks.

To serve, reheat the sauce, if necessary. Pour the sauce out onto 6 individual plates, top with the scallops, and sprinkle the chervil around.

Salmon Cakes with Corn-Mushroom–Piquillo Pepper Sauce

Serves 6

Two sauces might seem excessive, but this is one of the most beautiful dishes in this book. Tastes good, too, because the corn and salmon combination is a marriage made in heaven. So do it all: you only live once.

You need a cup and a half of cooked salmon for the cakes. If you don't have any leftover salmon, pick up about a pound of salmon fillets and panfry them in a nonstick pan with a little olive oil or butter. Or roast them, following the directions on page 204. You can make these cakes with leftover mashed potatoes if you have any. If not, just boil some fresh potatoes in salted water and mash them with one or two tablespoons of butter. Use a potato that has a nice flavor, like Yukon Gold or Rose Finn. Russet would also work well.

If you can't find piquillos in your local stores, they can be ordered from The Spanish Table (see page 362). Otherwise, substitute red or yellow bell peppers (they should be roasted, peeled, and seeded). Fish stock works best in the pepper sauce, but for most people it's not easy to come by. Clam juice makes a reasonably good substitute. In a pinch, I've used vegetable stock or even water. Chicken stock is okay, but be sure it doesn't have monosodium glutamate in it.

For the pepper sauce, heat the oil in a medium saucepan over medium heat and add the shallots, garlic, bay leaves, oregano, and tarragon. Cook for a couple of minutes, stirring everything

piquillo pepper sauce

1 tablespoon olive oil

2 or 3 shallots, sliced

2 or 3 cloves garlic, sliced

1 or 2 whole bay leaves

1 or 2 sprigs fresh oregano

1½ sprigs fresh tarragon

½ cup dry sherry

Pinch of cayenne pepper

1½ cups clam juice, vegetable stock, or chicken stock

1 to 1½ teaspoons salt

¼ to ½ teaspoon freshly ground white pepper

6 ounces (¾ cup) *piquillo* peppers, chopped

corn-mushroom sauce

3 ears sweet corn

1 tablespoon olive oil

2 cups sliced chanterelle or porcini mushrooms

1 Fresno chile, stemmed, seeded, and minced

1 tablespoon minced shallot

¼ cup white wine or vegetable stock

½ teaspoon salt

⅛ teaspoon freshly ground white pepper

2 tablespoons minced fresh chives

1 tablespoon butter

salmon cakes

1½ teaspoons olive oil, plus additional for frying

¼ cup minced fennel bulb or heart of celery

2 small scallions, white and light green parts only, minced

½ cup mashed potatoes

1½ teaspoons grated peeled fresh ginger

1 tablespoon minced fennel leaves or dill weed

½ teaspoon salt

¼ teaspoon freshly ground black pepper

1½ cups cooked salmon

well, then add the sherry and reduce by half, 3 to 5 minutes. Add the remaining ingredients and simmer 12 to 15 minutes, until the sauce is fairly thick. Allow it to cool, then puree it in a blender. Strain through a fine sieve and cook it down a little longer, until it is thick enough to coat the back of a spoon. Chill and reserve until needed.

For the corn sauce, grate or cut the kernels off the ears of corn into a bowl and set them aside. Heat the oil in a large pan over medium-high heat and sauté the chanterelles until they are tender and just beginning to caramelize, 5 to 8 minutes. Add the chile and shallot and cook 30 seconds more, then add the corn and get it mixed in well. Now pour in the wine and continue cooking until the sauce has reduced to a thick syrup. Add the salt, pepper, chives, and butter, and give everything a good stir. Remove from the heat and set aside.

For the cakes, heat the oil in a large sauté pan or skillet over medium-high heat and sauté the fennel until just tender, 2 to 3 minutes. Scrape the fennel into a medium-size bowl and allow it to cool. When it has cooled, add the scallions, mashed potatoes, ginger, fennel leaves, salt, and pepper; mix well. Add the salmon and mix it in gently so that it doesn't break up too much. You want recognizable chunks of salmon in the cakes. Form this mixture into 6 cakes, each about 2 inches in diameter and ³/₄ inch thick.

When you are ready to serve, put both sauces on to reheat as you cook the salmon cakes. Lightly oil a large pan or griddle and set it at medium-high heat. Cook the cakes until golden brown and crispy, 2 to 4 minutes per side. To serve, pour some of the corn-mushroom sauce out onto each of the plates, top with a salmon cake, and then drizzle some of the piquillo pepper sauce around. Pass any leftover sauces around on the side.

Grilled Swordfish with Roasted Cauliflower and Sweet-Sour Onions

Serves 6

1½ cups cauliflower flowerets (save the stems for soup)

½ to 1 red onion, julienned

3 tablespoons extra virgin olive oil

1 teaspoon salt

½ teaspoon freshly ground black pepper

vinaigrette

2 tablespoons freshly squeezed lemon juice

A few gratings of lemon zest

2 shallots, sliced

Salt and freshly ground black pepper

6 to 7 tablespoons extra virgin olive oil

salad

½ cup (loosely packed) finely chopped fresh parsley leaves, rinsed and squeezed dry in a towel

1 bunch celery, leaves only

½ to ¾ cup caper berries or 2 tablespoons capers, rinsed

16 to 20 ounces swordfish

Olive oil, for coating

Salt and freshly ground black pepper

Grilled fish with roasted vegetables—kind of a classy fish fingers recipe. I love this combination with swordfish, but it works with tuna or large sea scallops, too. To balance out the dish, it's served with a parsley–celery leaf–caper salad. It would also be super with Best Ever Tapenade (page 34) and a drizzle of any simple vinaigrette. You could also add a third of a cup of golden raisins that have been plumped in the vinaigrette for five to ten minutes.

Preheat the oven to 375°F.

Put the cauliflower and onion in a mixing bowl and add half the olive oil and the salt and pepper. Mix until the vegetables are well coated and evenly seasoned. Spread them in a roasting pan and roast, stirring occasionally, until tender, golden brown, and slightly caramelized on the edges. This should take 15 to 20 minutes.

For the vinaigrette, mix the lemon juice, zest, shallots, salt, and pepper together in a small bowl. Whisk in the olive oil in a slow, steady stream, and continue whisking till the dressing is well emulsified. Set this aside.

For the salad, combine the parsley, celery leaves, and caper berries in another bowl, and set this aside too. If you're going

(continued)

Cook the fish either in individual pieces or in one hunk, whichever is more convenient for you. You want two ounces or a bit more per person; if you're planning on cooking individual pieces, try to get thick pieces so you can sear them without overcooking them. If you panfry the fish as opposed to grilling it, any kind of pan should do the job, but cast iron works the best.

for the golden raisin option, plump the raisins in the vinaigrette while you finish the rest of the dish.

Coat the swordfish with olive oil, sprinkle with salt and pepper, and grill or pan-sear to medium doneness. This should take about 2¹/₂ minutes on each side for a 1-inch-thick piece of fish. Adjust the time according to the thickness of your fish.

For the final assembly, toss the salad with enough of the vinaigrette to coat everything lightly. If you cooked the fish in 1 large piece, cut it into serving-size pieces. Place a mix of cauliflower and onion on each plate, then lay down the swordfish and top with the salad (or with the raisins, if desired). Drizzle a little more dressing about and offer any remaining dressing on the side.

Wild Mushroom Tamales with Yucatecan Tomato Salsa

Serves 6

When we invented this tamale, we were trying for a new vegetarian entrée, and this is what we came up with. We used grits instead of masa for the dough, and chard leaves instead of corn husks for the wrapper to give a dark color contrast to the grits; then we used our imaginations when it came to the filling. It worked, people loved it, and it has been on Cindy's Backstreet Kitchen menu ever since.

All tamales are celebratory dishes, perfect for serving at parties, small or large. This recipe doubles and triples really well, which makes it a great choice for a big party or fiesta. Both the tamales and the sauce can be made a day ahead, which is another plus. Both should be refrigerated, and the tamales need to be well wrapped first. One tamale per person would be a nice three- to four-bite treat to serve along with two or three other small plates.

filling

1½ to 2 tablespoons olive oil

¾ cup sliced chanterelle
mushrooms

¾ cup sliced hen-of-the-woods
mushrooms

¼ onion, thinly julienned

1 teaspoon salt

Pinch of freshly ground black
pepper

¼ habanero chile, seeded and
minced

1½ to 2 serrano or jalapeño
chiles, seeded and minced

1 clove garlic, smashed and
minced

½ tomato, peeled and diced

1 tablespoon chopped toasted
almonds

1 to 1½ tablespoons golden
raisins

grits

1½ tablespoons butter

1 shallot, minced

1 or 2 slices habanero chile,
minced (optional)

1¼ cups (or more) water

¼ cup heavy cream

½ teaspoon salt

⅔ cup grits

⅓ cup finely grated Monterey
Jack cheese

1½ tablespoons finely grated
Parmesan cheese

yucatecan tomato salsa

3½ medium-size tomatoes

1½ tablespoons olive oil

(continued)

If you can't find hen-of-the-woods mushrooms for the filling, you could use dried or fresh porcinis, or all chanterelles—even simple button mushrooms would work. If you want a milder salsa, go for the jalapeño instead of the habanero. The habanero is my first choice, though, because it lends a great flavor—sweet and floral. Altogether you only need one habanero for the whole recipe.

When picking out the Swiss chard leaves you want ones that are perfect and, once the ribs are removed, about the size of your outstretched hand. If you can't find six like this, you will need extra for patching.

For the filling, heat the oil in a medium sauté pan or skillet over medium-high heat and sauté the mushrooms 6 to 8 minutes, until lightly caramelized. Add the onion and cook 5 minutes more, or until it is very tender. Season with the salt and pepper, then add the habanero and serrano chiles and garlic; cook 1 to 2 minutes more. Add the diced tomato, almonds, and raisins and simmer 5 minutes, until reduced but not dry. The sauce should coat the vegetables and not pool. Allow the mixture to cool.

To make the grits, heat the butter in a big pot over medium-high heat. Add the shallots and the chile, if desired, and sauté till tender and aromatic, 3 to 4 minutes. Add the water, cream, and salt; stir and bring to a boil. Pour in the grits in a slow stream, stirring as you go. Cook until the mixture has thickened and the grits are tender, 2 to 3 minutes for instant grits, 6 to 8 minutes for regular store-bought grits, and 20 minutes for stone-ground grits (check out the directions on the package). Add additional water if necessary. Remove from the heat, stir in the cheeses, and pour out onto a plate to cool.

For the salsa, griddle or broil the tomatoes until tender and well charred, turning to ensure all sides are done. At home I do this in a small cast-iron skillet over medium-high heat. You could probably use a nonstick pan, too. Whatever method you choose, don't use any oil. When cool to the touch, remove any very

(continued)

¼ to ⅓ medium onion, finely
   chopped
½ habanero or jalapeño chile
¾ teaspoon salt
½ cup vegetable stock or water

6 large, perfect Swiss chard
   leaves (a few extra if not
   perfect), tough ribs removed
6 large or 12 small fresh or dried
   corn husks
1 tablespoon butter, for the salsa
Minced fresh parsley leaves
Chopped toasted almonds

blackened pieces of skin, mash the tomatoes coarsely, and set aside. Heat the olive oil in a medium sauté pan over medium-high heat and sauté the onion 4 to 6 minutes without allowing it to brown, cooking until it is soft. Add the mashed tomatoes, chile, and salt and cook 1 to 2 minutes. Add the stock and cook about 6 minutes more over medium heat, until nice and saucy. Set aside until needed.

To prepare the tamale wrappers, bring a pot of water to a boil. Carefully (so as not to tear them) dunk a few leaves of chard into the water for 20 seconds or so, just till wilted. Remove them, and immediately dip them in an ice bath to keep them from cooking further. Repeat with the remaining leaves. Drain and reserve. Place the corn husks in the boiling water and boil until tender, about 6 minutes for fresh and 20 minutes for dried. Drain and reserve.

To make the tamales, lay out 1 large or overlap 2 small corn husks on the counter. Lay a chard leaf on top of the husks, overlapping the 2 edges of the leaf where you removed the tough rib. Spread a large spoonful (one-sixth of the batch) of grits on the bottom third of the leaf, leaving enough space at the bottom and on the sides to get a nice seal when rolling. Top the grits with some of the filling. Now fold up the bottom, fold in the sides, and roll from bottom to top. The tamales should be about 3 inches long and 1¹/₂ inches wide, though you could press them out into 3-inch squares. Repeat to make the rest of the tamales. If you're making them ahead, cover and refrigerate.

To finish the tamales, steam them over very slowly simmering water until nice and hot, 12 to 15 minutes. Reheat the salsa, swirling in 1 tablespoon of butter at the last minute and removing the chile. Unwrap the corn husks from around the tamales and set aside 6 of the husks (discard the rest if you used more). Fold husks in half and put one on each serving plate. Place a chard-wrapped tamale on top of each husk and spoon some hot salsa around the tamale (as shown on page 291). Sprinkle over some minced parsley and toasted almonds.

Rabbit Sausages with Sweet White Corn Grits and Sweet Pepper Relish

Serves 6

If you enjoy making sausage or want to give it a try for the first time, this is an excellent combination to work with. It's best to use a meat grinder to prepare the meat, but a food processor will work, too. Just "grind" the meat in small batches, pulsing it in short bursts, say three to five times. It's much better to end up with a mixture that is slightly too coarse than one that is too fine. Ideally, you're looking for a texture like that of coarse ground beef—a bit finer than a small dice. (Sausage-making novices may want to check out the additional information on stuffing sausage casings in the Glossary.)

There are lots of options with this recipe. If you're not interested in stuffing casings to make your own sausages, you can make patties with the sausage mixture and cook them on a grill or griddle. Or you could pack some of the mixture into a small loaf tin and bake at 325°F degrees to an internal temperature of 145°F (1½ to 2 hours), then chill it before slicing and serving it as a pâté. You can also substitute breast of chicken, turkey, duck, or any game meat for the rabbit. Simpler still, use a store-bought fresh sausage, such as chicken-apple, and skip the meat-grinding altogether.

I like to poach the sausages first, then brown them on the grill or griddle just before serving. This makes them juicier and reduces the time needed on the grill. If you skip this step and just cook them once, it should be done slowly over a much lower heat, otherwise your sausages will probably burst.

All the hard work for this recipe can be done well in advance (making the sausage and the grits). Final preparation just calls for quickly frying up the grits and sausages, and tossing the relish with its vinaigrette.

sausages

1 rabbit (about 3½ pounds)

6 ounces pancetta

2 chicken thighs, skinned and boned

⅓ cup golden raisins

⅓ cup shelled and coarsely chopped pistachios

1 tablespoon minced garlic

2 tablespoons brandy

½ bunch thyme or ¼ bunch rosemary, leaves only, minced

1 teaspoon ground toasted fennel seeds

1 teaspoon ground toasted cumin seeds

1½ tablespoons salt

2 teaspoons freshly ground white pepper

2 feet of sausage casing, rinsed

6 cups water

1 cup white wine

grits

3 cups water or chicken stock

1 teaspoon salt

1 cup quick-cooking grits

2 tablespoons butter

½ cup grated sharp Cheddar cheese (about 1½ ounces)

¼ to ½ teaspoon Tabasco sauce

(continued)

For the sausages, thoroughly wash the metal parts of your grinding equipment (using the $3/8$-inch plate), then put them in the freezer to get them well chilled. Disjoint the rabbit and cut the meat off the bones, removing any silver skin and connective tissue. Cut the rabbit meat, pancetta, and chicken into $1/2$-inch dice and spread this all out on a baking sheet. Place it in the freezer and chill till almost frozen. Grind the meat into a large mixing bowl. Mix the remaining sausage ingredients into the ground meat and panfry a couple tablespoons to taste for seasoning. Adjust it as you like. To make the sausages, remove the grinder blade and put on a sausage casing. Stuff the casing, being careful not to overfill it—it's better to err on the side of under- versus overstuffing. Twist off the sausages at 3-inch intervals and let the casing pull off at the end where the pressure naturally dictates. Tie the end in a knot. If you use a food processor for grinding the meat, you'll need to use a pastry bag. Fill the bag with some of the sausage mixture and put an appropriate nozzle on the end of the pastry bag. Stuff the casings as described above. You should get about a dozen sausages.

To poach the sausages, combine the water and wine in a large pot, bring it to a boil, and reduce to a simmer. Prick the sausage links a couple times with a skewer to keep them from bursting as they cook. Carefully drop them into the water and simmer till just cooked through, 2 to 5 minutes, depending on how firmly stuffed the sausage casings are. Refrigerate until needed, overnight if you like.

For the grits, bring the water and salt to a boil in a medium-size pot. Reduce the heat to medium and add the grits, stirring as they go in. Cook 5 to 8 minutes, stirring occasionally, till the grains are tender. Remove from the heat and stir in the butter,

(continued)

double mustard sauce

1 tablespoon good-quality
   prepared horseradish

1 tablespoon Dijon mustard

1 tablespoon coarse-grained
   mustard

vinaigrette

3 tablespoons red wine vinegar

1 shallot, minced

1 tablespoon Dijon mustard

1 to 1½ teaspoons salt

½ teaspoon freshly ground black
   pepper

½ cup plus 1 tablespoon extra
   virgin olive oil

sweet pepper relish

2 red, yellow, or orange bell
   peppers or pimientos, roasted,
   peeled, and julienned

1 Anaheim chile or green bell
   pepper, roasted, peeled, and
   julienned

½ sweet onion, sliced

2 tablespoons chiffonade of basil

Additional butter, for grilling
   the grits

cheese, and Tabasco sauce. Spray a baking sheet with pan spray and spread the grits out evenly on it to a ¹/₂-inch thickness. Chill at least 3 hours, until cool throughout and firm. This can be done a day ahead, too.

To prepare the mustard sauce, stir together the horseradish and the mustards. Cover and chill until needed.

To make the vinaigrette, mix the vinegar, shallot, mustard, salt, and pepper in a small mixing bowl. Add the olive oil in a slow steady stream, whisking all the while. Continue whisking until well emulsified. Set this aside until needed.

For the relish, in a separate bowl combine the peppers, chile, onion, and basil and reserve.

When you are ready to serve, cut out rounds of the grits with a cookie cutter—2-inch circles for small plates, 1-inch circles for hors d'oeuvres. You can take the trims, press them out into a ¹/₂-inch-thick sheet again, and cut more circles. Lightly butter a griddle or cast-iron pan and heat it over medium-high heat. Sauté the grits till hot through and light brown and crispy on both sides, 4 to 5 minutes. Keep in a warm oven till needed.

Grill the poached sausage over medium heat till they are hot throughout, turning to get nicely caramelized on all sides, 5 to 7 minutes. This might take longer if the sausages come straight from the refrigerator. The sausages can be griddled or panfried instead.

Gently toss the Sweet Pepper Relish with just enough vinaigrette to coat. Slice each sausage diagonally into 2 pieces. Place a grits cake on each plate and drizzle with mustard sauce. Arrange some sausage over that, and top off with some relish.

pictured on pages 296–297

Stuffed Pasilla Chiles with "Mole de la Suegra" and Cherry Tomato Salsa

Serves 6

In Spanish, mole de la suegra *means "mother-in-law's mole," and that's exactly what this mole is. Pablo learned the recipe from his mother-in-law, and when we opened Cindy's Backstreet Kitchen she actually came all the way from Mexico to make sure he did it right. I often make big batches of the mole sauce, as it freezes well and has many uses. It goes well with poultry and pork, and one of the very best ways I know of to use up leftover Thanksgiving turkey is to make turkey enchiladas with mole de la suegra. This recipe will make about a two quarts of sauce.*

There are a lot of parts to this recipe, but really, everything except roasting and stuffing the pasillas could be done up to a day ahead. Actually, some of the components have to be prepared ahead, such as the Cumin-Scented Black Beans and the rice, which are both needed for the stuffing.

When you get to toasting the chile seeds and the sesame seeds, toast them separately, as they are not the same size and will not cook evenly if they are done together. If you don't have a spice grinder, a coffee grinder is handy for grinding the seeds and spices.

(continued on page 298)

Stuffed Pasilla Chiles
with "Mole de la Suegra"
and Cherry Tomato Salsa
(page 295)

cherry tomato salsa

1 pint cherry tomatoes, halved

2 scallions, white and light green parts only, minced

1 shallot, minced

¼ bunch cilantro, leaves only, chopped

¼ to ½ teaspoon sea salt

⅛ teaspoon freshly ground black pepper

2 tablespoons extra virgin olive oil

cumin-lime crème fraîche

½ cup crème fraîche

½ cup sour cream

2 teaspoons finely ground toasted cumin seeds

Pinch of salt

Juice and grated zest of 1 lime

8 dried *chiles negros* (about 2 ounces)

8 dried ancho chiles (about 2 ounces)

6 tablespoons sesame seeds

1 tablespoon whole black peppercorns

6 whole cloves

5 to 6 tablespoons olive oil

2 slices French bread

1 large tomato, halved and cored

1 large onion, cut into 4 thick slices (lots of surface area for caramelizing)

1 large clove garlic

2 tablespoons salt

4 cups vegetable stock or water

3 ounces (1 disk) Mexican chocolate, coarsely chopped

For the salsa, combine all the ingredients in a mixing bowl and mix gently but well. Taste for seasoning and adjust as you like. Refrigerate until needed.

Combine the crème fraîche, sour cream, cumin, salt, and lime juice and zest in a small bowl. Mix well and keep chilled until needed.

Preheat the oven to 375°F. Stem the chiles, slit them, and carefully remove and save the seeds. Toast the chiles in the preheated oven 30 seconds to 1 minute, until a little soft and aromatic. Do not toast the chiles too much, or the sauce will be bitter. Put the chiles in a pan with enough warm water to cover and set them aside.

Heat a small skillet over high heat and toast the chile seeds lightly, 30 seconds to 1 minute, shaking the pan continuously and watching carefully so they do not burn. Put them in a small bowl. Using the same pan and shaking it all the while, toast the sesame seeds until they turn a nice golden brown. Set 2 tablespoons of the sesame seeds aside for a garnish. Put the rest in a spice grinder along with the chile seeds and grind them to a fine powder. In a separate batch, grind the peppercorns and cloves. Add the ground spices to the ground seeds and reserve.

In a large skillet, heat about 2 tablespoons of the olive oil over medium-high heat and fry the bread until it's nice and toasty on both sides. If the oil is hot enough, the bread will not soak up much of the oil. Scoop the bread out into a large bowl. Return the pan to the heat and add another tablespoon of oil to cover nicely the entire surface of the pan. Now fry the tomato, cut sides down first, till caramelized all around and heated through, 6 to 8 minutes. Scoop the tomato into the same bowl. Return the pan to the heat and coat it again with some of the remaining oil. Toss in the onion and garlic and cook until they are caramelized and tender throughout, 8 to 10 minutes. This goes into the bowl, too.

Drain the chiles, reserving the soaking water. Working in 2 or 3 batches, puree the chiles, bread, tomato, onion, garlic, ground seeds and spices, and salt in a blender. Blend until smooth,

stuffed *pasillas*

½ cup basmati rice

¾ cup water

¼ stick cinnamon

¾ teaspoon salt

6 *pasilla* chiles

1 recipe Cumin-Scented Black Beans (page 201), pureed

5 ounces Cheddar cheese, cut into ¼-inch dice

9 ounces soft fresh goat cheese or feta cheese, crumbled

¼ bunch cilantro, leaves and tender stems only, chopped

adding as much of the soaking water as needed to get a thick, saucelike consistency.

Heat the remaining oil in a heavy saucepan over high heat. When the oil is very hot (but not smoking), carefully pour the sauce into the pan and "fry" it 1 to 2 minutes, stirring. The sauce should bubble up on contact with the pan. This is the step that brings the sauce together. Reduce the heat, add the stock, and simmer 10 minutes. Stir in the chocolate. Simmer another 30 to 45 minutes, till dark, rich, and reduced. Set the *mole* aside, and refrigerate if not using within the hour.

To prepare the stuffed **pasillas**, preheat the oven to 350°F. Combine the rice, water, cinnamon, and salt in a small saucepan. Cover and bring to a boil over high heat, then turn the heat to low and steam, covered, for 20 minutes or until the water has evaporated. Meanwhile, place the chiles on a baking sheet and roast about 5 minutes, till the skins are blistered. Put them in a sealed plastic bag and let them rest. When they are cool enough to handle comfortably, peel them and cut out the stems as if you were carving a pumpkin. Remove the seeds and ribs from the insides of the chiles and the stems. Set the chiles and stems aside. Combine the black beans, rice, and Cheddar cheese in a medium-size bowl and mix well. Carefully fill each chile with some of this mixture, leaving enough space at the top to get the stems back in securely. The *pasillas* can be held overnight in the refrigerator at this point.

For the final preparation, start reheating the *mole*. Grill the chiles over medium heat, turning often to ensure they don't get burned. If you prefer, the *pasillas* can also be pan-sautéed or baked in the oven at 450°F, 20 minutes if the chiles have been refrigerated, 10 minutes if at room temperature. Whichever method you choose, cook until the chiles are hot through.

To serve, pour some hot *mole* into the center of each of the plates, and top with a stuffed chile and then some salsa. Finish off with a drizzle of the crème fraîche, followed by a sprinkle of goat cheese, the remaining toasted sesame seeds, and the chopped cilantro.

Stuffed Piquillo Peppers with Charred Tomato Sauce

Serves 6

I traveled to Spain for the first time in the early 1990s. At this time Spain was just beginning to introduce its food products to a broader United States audience. With seven other chefs, traveling as a guest of the Spanish government, I had a spectacular week of discovery, piquillo peppers being top of the list. They are flavorful but mild, and though not sold here fresh, they are available in cans and glass jars. They are roasted over wood fires, then cleaned up so they come ready to use.

Processed piquillos are slippery little devils. They'll come with a hole in the top, because the stem and seeds are removed for you. We drain them in a fine-mesh colander and save all the juices for sauce.

For tasty variations on this recipe, try stuffing them with salt cod or risotto. The tomato sauce is very versatile: you can use it with almost anything, from eggs to chicken to grilled pork tenderloin. It makes a great steak sauce, as well.

charred tomato sauce

1 or 2 dried *guajillo* chiles, stemmed and seeded

2 large tomatoes

3 cloves garlic

1 onion, thickly sliced

1 jalapeño chile, stemmed, seeded, and thickly sliced

2 cups chicken stock, vegetable stock, or water

½ teaspoon salt

¼ teaspoon pepper

(continued)

For the tomato sauce, toast the *guajillos* and put them in a medium-size saucepan. Core the tomatoes and cook them over charcoal or a gas flame, or under your broiler, until their skins are charred black and peeling, using a long barbecue fork or kitchen fork and turning them as they char. I poke them through the top and haven't lost any yet. Add the tomatoes to the *guajillos*. On a dry griddle or in a cast-iron pan, cook the

(continued)

stuffing

1¼ pounds hanger steak

¼ cup olive oil

1 medium onion, minced

1 tablespoon chopped garlic

¾ cup diced peeled tomato

2 tablespoons minced fresh
oregano leaves

1½ teaspoons ground toasted
cumin seeds

1 tablespoon kosher salt or sea
salt

1½ teaspoons freshly ground
black pepper

12 *piquillo* peppers

1 tablespoon olive oil

2 tablespoons sour cream

2 tablespoons Dijon mustard

¾ cup Lime Crème Fraîche
(page 199)

6 tablespoons toasted slivered or
sliced almonds

6 to 12 sprigs cilantro

garlic, onion, and jalapeño over medium-high heat until caramelized and almost black (black edges are okay). Put them in the saucepan, too, and add the stock. Bring to a boil, then reduce to a simmer. Add the salt and pepper and cook until all the vegetables are tender, 5 to 8 minutes. Allow the sauce to cool, then blend until smooth. Strain, if desired, and set it aside. Put the finishing touches on the sauce just before serving.

For the stuffing, mince the steak. Heat the oil over high heat in a large, flat sauté pan. Add the steak and cook until caramelized and brown, 8 to 10 minutes. Add the onion and garlic, reduce the heat to medium, and continue cooking until the onion is translucent, 8 to 10 minutes. Add the diced tomato, oregano, cumin, kosher salt, and pepper; simmer until the mixture is very thick and the steak is tender, 15 to 20 minutes. Chill the stuffing (this will make it easier to work with when you stuff the peppers).

Gently stuff the *piquillos*, being careful not to break them. We use a teaspoon, tuck some filling in through the top, then pull the spoon out gently, keeping slight pressure on the top of the pepper so the stuffing remains inside. You can do this a day ahead, cover, and refrigerate. Just don't stack the peppers, as they'll fall apart under the pressure.

For the final preparation, preheat the oven to 450°F. Heat the oil in an ovenproof sauté pan over medium-high heat. When both pan and oil are hot, carefully place the stuffed *piquillos* in the pan and put the whole pan in the oven; cook 4 to 6 minutes, until they are heated through. Meanwhile, bring the sauce back to a boil, remove it from the heat, and whisk in the sour cream and mustard.

To serve, spread some of the hot tomato sauce on each plate and top with 2 stuffed *piquillos*. Garnish with a drizzle of crème fraîche, toasted almonds, and cilantro sprigs.

6 gypsy peppers

¾ cup cream cheese

1½ cups feta cheese

2 cups cooked basmati, jasmine, or wild rice, chilled

¾ cup golden raisins

⅓ cup chopped fresh mint leaves

cherry tomato vinaigrette

1 to 1½ pints cherry tomatoes, halved

2 to 3 tablespoons minced fresh basil or whole baby basil leaves

1 tablespoon minced fresh parsley leaves

3 tablespoons rice vinegar or champagne vinegar

1 tablespoon freshly squeezed lemon juice

½ teaspoon salt

¼ teaspoon freshly ground black pepper

6 tablespoons extra virgin olive oil

¼ cup toasted sliced almonds

2 to 3 tablespoons crème fraîche, whisked until smooth and drizzleable

Grilled Goat Cheese–Stuffed Gypsy Peppers with Cherry Tomato Vinaigrette

Serves 6

When they're in season, gypsy peppers flood the farmers' markets here in Northern California. These sweet, thin-skinned peppers are a little smaller than a bell pepper, which makes them the perfect size for a small-plate serving. They come in many colors—white, light yellow, gold, red—so you can work out a pretty dramatic color scheme with them. If you can't get gypsy peppers, use drained, canned piquillo peppers. If you do, use gold or orange tomatoes in the vinaigrette and cook the piquillos not on the grill but in the oven. Ten to twelve minutes at 350°F to 375°F should do it.

For the stuffing, you'll need two cups of cooked rice that has been chilled, so figure that into your time plan.

You can use large tomatoes instead of cherry tomatoes in the vinaigrette: Cut out the stem end and cut an x in the bottom of each. Blanch in boiling water for thirty seconds, then shock in an ice bath. Peel them and cut them in half; remove the seeds, and dice. Then carry on with the recipe.

To prepare the gypsy peppers, cut around the base of each stem the way you would with a pumpkin, and gently pull the stem out. Trim off the seeds and keep the tops to hold the stuffing in. Blanch the peppers in rapidly boiling water 60 to 90 seconds, until just tender but not collapsing. Drain and shock in an ice bath. Drain again very well before stuffing.

To make the stuffing, fit a mixer with the paddle attachment and beat the cream cheese until light and fluffy. Crumble the feta into this and beat until they are well mixed and there are no more big chunks of feta. Quickly mix in the rice, raisins, and mint, breaking up any raisins that are sticking together. Do not overmix.

Divide the filling into 6 equal portions. Moisten your hands, then roll each into a lozenge about the same shape as the peppers. Slip the lozenges into the peppers, pressing them gently to get the filling into all the nooks and crannies. Put the tops back on and set the peppers aside.

To make the vinaigrette, combine the cherry tomatoes, basil, and parsley in a medium bowl. In a small bowl, whisk together the vinegar, lemon juice, salt, and pepper until the salt is dissolved. Whisk in the oil, then pour over the tomatoes and herbs and mix gently. The vinaigrette should be made no more than 20 minutes or so in advance of serving.

For the final preparation, grill the peppers over a medium-high flame until caramelized nicely on all sides and hot through. You could also heat them up in a ridged or flat cast-iron pan. To serve, place a few spoonfuls of vinaigrette on each plate. Top with a stuffed pepper, sprinkle with almonds, and drizzle with crème fraîche.

"pizza" sauce

1 teaspoon cornstarch

2 tablespoons water, at room temperature, plus ¼ cup more

1 tablespoon soy sauce

1 teaspoon *ketjap manis* or other dark soy sauce

1 tablespoon Worcestershire sauce

¼ teaspoon sugar

¼ teaspoon rice vinegar

"pizza" batter

1 cup all-purpose flour

½ teaspoon baking powder

¼ cup water

4 large eggs

½ teaspoon salt

1 teaspoon freshly ground white pepper

¼ teaspoon *shichimi togarashi* or cayenne pepper (optional)

½ cup (firmly packed) finely shredded cabbage

¼ cup coarsely chopped peeled cooked shrimp

¼ cup cooked crabmeat, pieces as large as possible

1 or 2 scallions, white and light green parts only, thinly sliced

Peanut oil or vegetable oil, for coating the griddle

1 generous tablespoon toasted sesame seeds

2 sheets toasted nori, julienned

Japanese Crab and Shrimp "Pizzas"

Serves 8

I first had this dish in Osaka, Japan, and it was quite an experience. My host, Ikira, said he was taking me out for Japanese pizza. We sat in a crowded restaurant, and at the center of each table was a griddle. We were armed with chopsticks, a spatula, a platter of vegetables, a platter of seafood, a bowlful of batter that looked just like ordinary pancake batter, and some sauce to drizzle on the top. My favorite! Interactive food! The real name for these "pizzas," I learned, is okonomiyaki, and the restaurants that specialize in them are very popular throughout Japan.

Shichimi togarashi, the seven-spice pepper mix that goes into the batter, is a very common Japanese seasoning. It is made up of a combination of togarashi (a Japanese dried red chile pepper—very hot), san sho pepper (from the prickly ash shrub—not really a pepper), poppy seeds, white sesame seeds, black hemp seeds, dried orange peel, and crumbled nori. Some brands are hotter than others, so use a little caution. You can add some daikon sprouts or julienned carrots to the batter, too.

You should get about two dozen two- to three-inch "pizzas" out of this recipe. I recommend serving three or four per person, depending on what else is on the menu.

For the sauce, combine the cornstarch and 2 tablespoons of water in a tiny bowl and stir until the cornstarch has dissolved. Put this slurry into a small saucepan along with the ¼ cup of water, soy sauce, *ketjap manis*, Worcestershire sauce, sugar, and vinegar; bring to a boil. Reduce the heat to a simmer and

Nori is dried seaweed that has been pressed into flat sheets. The sheets of nori, which look a lot like handmade paper, usually measure about six by eight inches. You can find packages of nori at Asian markets, and maybe even at your local market. Nori is most often used for rolling sushi, but it is also julienned or crumbled and used as a garnish or flavoring. It should be toasted on one side to bring out its flavor and aroma. To toast it, pass it quickly back and forth just above a gas flame (use tongs). There are other fun Japanese "rice seasonings" on the market, like *wasabi fumi furikake*, that would make colorful and tasty garnishes for this dish.

cook until the sauce thickens. This sauce is usually served at room temperature or cold, so you can make it ahead.

For the batter, mix the flour and baking powder together in a medium-size bowl. Put the water and eggs in another bowl and whisk to combine well. Form a well in the center of the dry ingredients and pour the egg mixture into it. Whisk the wet ingredients into the dry, and continue whisking until smooth. Add the salt, pepper, and *shichimi togarashi*, if using. Fold in the cabbage, shrimp, crab, and scallions.

To cook, heat a griddle or a flat-bottomed pan over medium-high heat and coat with the oil. Spoon a generous tablespoonful of the batter onto the griddle and spread it to an even thickness with the back of the spoon. Continue spooning out batter, and try to fill up the cooking surface in order to avoid smoking. Cook about 2 to 3 minutes on each side, depending on how hot your griddle is. Flip the "pizzas" over when they are golden brown on the bottom and you see bubbles forming on the top. The "pizzas" should be cooked through, and golden brown on both sides. They will take a little longer than ordinary pancakes, so be patient.

To serve, spread a generous amount of sauce on top of each "pizza," then sprinkle with some toasted sesame seeds and julienned nori.

piquillo pepper sauce

2 tablespoons olive oil

1 tablespoon butter

1 tablespoon all-purpose flour

½ teaspoon salt

¼ teaspoon freshly ground black
pepper

1½ cups fish or chicken stock

6 piquillo peppers

garden greens

½ pound rainbow chard or red
chard

½ pound mustard greens or
spinach

2 tablespoons olive oil

½ onion, finely diced

3 cloves garlic, minced

¼ heaping teaspoon salt

¼ teaspoon freshly ground black
pepper

12 to 16 ounces sea bass

½ teaspoon salt

¼ teaspoon freshly ground
black pepper

2 tablespoons olive oil

2 tablespoons minced parsley
leaves or minced chives

Sea Bass with Piquillo Pepper Sauce and Garden Greens

Serves 6

Pan-seared chunks of fish served on a bed of sautéed greens, and topped with a velvety, vibrant red sauce—it's a beautiful combination, easy to prepare, and delicious, too. The sauce keeps well, so you can make it up to three days ahead of time, and reheat it before serving.

Halibut makes a good substitute for sea bass. For the greens, chard is ideal, but any peppery watercress or mustard green would work. You could substitute spinach but, if you do, cook it till it's just wilted. Don't overcook it.

For the sauce, melt the oil and butter in a saucepan over medium heat, and whisk in the flour. Cook, stirring constantly, until the flour no longer smells raw, about 2 minutes. Season with the salt and pepper. Whisk in the stock and cook till the sauce is thick enough to coat the back of a spoon. Add the *piquillo* peppers and simmer for a couple of minutes. Allow the mixture to cool slightly, then puree it in a blender till smooth. Return the sauce to the pan, and keep it warm until ready to serve. (If you make it ahead, reheat it before serving.)

To prepare the greens wash them thoroughly. Tear the chard leaves into bite-size pieces, and chop up the stems. If you are using spinach, remove and discard the stems. Heat the olive oil over medium-high heat in a large sauté pan. Add the onion and

(continued)

garlic, and cook, stirring, until caramelized. Add the greens and cook, stirring, until wilted and tender, 3 to 6 minutes. Season with salt and pepper, and set aside.

To prepare the fish, cut it into 6 equal-size portions, season with salt and pepper, and brush with olive oil. Heat a cast-iron pan over high heat and quickly sear the fish on each side, about 2 minutes on each side for 1-inch-thick pieces of fish. The fish can also be cooked on the grill. Whichever method you use, don't overcook it.

To serve, place some greens in the center of each plate, top with a piece of fish, and pour several tablespoons of Piquillo Pepper Sauce over everything. Sprinkle with parsley and serve.

Crab-Stuffed Gypsy Peppers with Red and Green Salsas

Serves 6

This dish is so beautiful with its two salsas. It's fine with one, but so much better with both of them, especially if these crab-stuffed peppers are going to be the highlight of the meal. For the crabmeat, the ideal is to buy freshly cooked Dungeness or blue crab and pick out the meat yourself, keeping the meat in big chunks as best you can. One Dungeness crab ought to provide enough meat for this dish: if you're using blue crab, you'll need four or five. Otherwise, buy fresh crabmeat sold by the pound. Either way, before mixing the crabmeat in with the other stuffing ingredients, you should check it one last time for any renegade shell or cartilage fragments.

This dish is prepared pretty much like the recipe on page 304, but the stuffings are completely different.

This dish is prepared pretty much like the recipe on page 304

red salsa

8 dried *guajillo* chiles

2 tomatoes, stem end cut out

½ bunch oregano, leaves only

½ teaspoon ground toasted cumin seeds

Juice of ½ lime

1 tablespoon rice vinegar

3 tablespoons extra virgin olive oil

½ teaspoon salt

¼ teaspoon freshly ground black pepper

green salsa

1 pound tomatillos, peeled and halved

1 avocado, peeled and pitted

1 jalapeño chile, stemmed, with seeds

4 cloves garlic

½ bunch cilantro

Juice of 1 lime

¾ teaspoon salt

¼ teaspoon freshly ground black pepper

To make the red salsa, stem and seed the *guajillos*, then toast them till soft. Soak them in just enough hot water to cover 15 minutes. In a dry cast-iron skillet or on a griddle, sear the tomatoes till almost black, then put them in a blender. Drain the chiles, reserving the water, and put them in the blender, too, along with the oregano, cumin, lime juice, vinegar, olive oil, salt, and pepper. Blend until smooth. If you find the salsa too thick for your liking, add some of the chile soaking water, a little at a time, and pulse until you reach the consistency you like. Taste, and add additional salt and pepper if needed. Refrigerate until ready to use.

To make the green salsa, combine all the ingredients in a blender and blend until smooth. Refrigerate until ready to use.

6 gypsy peppers

2 ears sweet corn

1½ tablespoons butter

1 shallot, thinly sliced

2 cloves garlic, minced

1¾ cups fresh crabmeat
(about 1 pound)

1 jalapeño chile, stemmed,
seeded, and minced

½ cup mayonnaise

Scant ¼ teaspoon salt

⅛ teaspoon freshly ground black
pepper

Cilantro sprigs

Toasted pumpkin seeds

To prepare the gypsy peppers, cut around the base of each stem the way you would with a pumpkin stem, and gently pull it out. Trim off the seeds and membranes. Clean off the tops, put them back on the peppers, and reserve.

For the stuffing, cut the kernels off the corn cobs. Heat the butter in a sauté pan over medium heat, being careful not to brown the butter. Sauté the shallot, garlic, and corn until just tender. Pour everything out onto a large plate to cool. In a large mixing bowl, combine the crabmeat, jalapeño, mayonnaise, salt, and pepper. Mix gently but well. When the corn mixture is cool, add it to the bowl and mix well.

Stuff each pepper gently with the crab mixture using a small spoon. Make sure you get some stuffing all the way to the bottom of the peppers and that you leave enough room to get their stems back on top securely, but don't overstuff them, as the filling is rich and will expand a bit when hot. The peppers may be made to this point and refrigerated for several hours or as long as overnight, if you wrap them well.

To finish the peppers, fire up the grill, and when the coals have a nice white ash covering, place the peppers on the grill and cook 2 minutes, rotating them a quarter turn halfway through the cooking to get nice crosshatch grill marks. Turn the peppers over and do the same thing on the other side. Make sure the peppers are nicely caramelized and tender before you take them off the grill. To serve, place a pepper in the center of each plate; spoon out 3 to 4 tablespoons of the red salsa on 1 side and 3 to 4 tablespoons of the green salsa on the other. Garnish with a sprig of fresh cilantro and a sprinkle of toasted pumpkin seeds.

something
sweet

. . . just dive in and swim through the calories, happy as a clam.

chapter 6: Something Sweet

learned from my dad that all you need to end a meal is just a bite or two of something sweet. Following that philosophy, most of the desserts in this chapter are small. They range from homemade chocolate cookies (good with ice cream or berries) to the Mini Tres Leches Cakes (a rich make-ahead dessert) and mini banana splits. Almost any dessert you fancy can be baked in individual serving-size portions. That's how we came up with the Mini Tres Leches Cakes, for instance. Not only are these tiny treats more fun, but people can indulge without feeling too guilty. However, if you need to go wacko, as I do every once in a while, make the Double Trouble Chocolate Mousse Torte, then just dive in and swim through the calories, happy as a clam.

You don't always have to "make" dessert. Sometimes the most satisfying way to end a meal is with fresh fruit—perfectly ripe peaches, or melons, or sweet oranges, whatever happens to be in season. Cheeses also make a great dessert. When I serve cheeses, I try to get a contrast—a soft ripe cheese with a sharp Cheddar, for instance—or an interesting combination, such as a fresh goat cheese, a sheep's milk cheese, and a cheese made with cow's milk. Cheese and fruit together is another option. Ripe figs pair beautifully with Camembert or with a nice blue cheese, such as Roquefort or Gorgonzola. Another great combination is sharp Cheddar with apples and walnuts. To add a little interest, embellish the fruit or cheese platters with some dried fruit and nuts.

When all else fails, run to the nearest chocolate shop and splurge on some fancy treats to set out for everyone's after-dinner enjoyment.

Anne's Chocolate Biscuits

Makes about 3 dozen

Anne Baker—our pastry chef at Mustards—perfected this recipe for us. These crispy, waferlike cookies are so addictive, don't count on one batch lasting very long. They are excellent for making ice cream sandwich cookies. They are also the perfect foil for Raspberries Romanoff (page 320). When we were testing these recipes, we put some whipped cream on each biscuit, topped it with six to eight berries, and then ate them as open-faced sandwiches.

1¾ cups all-purpose flour

⅓ cup cocoa powder, plus additional for dusting

1 teaspoon baking powder

11 tablespoons unsalted butter

2 tablespoons vegetable oil

¾ cup sugar

1 large egg

1 teaspoon vanilla extract

½ teaspoon salt

Line a baking sheet with parchment paper, spray it with a pan spray, or grease it lightly with a little butter or vegetable oil smeared on with a paper towel.

Stir the flour, ¹/₃ cup of the cocoa powder, and the baking powder together in a bowl, and set this aside. Put the butter, oil, and sugar in the bowl of a mixer fitted with a paddle attachment and beat until light and fluffy. Add the egg, vanilla, and salt; continue to beat till well blended and smooth. Add the flour mixture and stir it in by hand until evenly incorporated.

Preheat the oven to 350°F.

Roll the dough out about ¹/₂ inch thick between large sheets of parchment or waxed paper. Place the sheet of dough, still encased in the parchment paper, on a baking sheet and put it in the refrigerator. Refrigerate until chilled and firm, about 35 minutes.

Using a 2-inch round or square cookie cutter, cut out the cookies. Bake on the prepared baking sheet 6 to 8 minutes. Let them cool, then dust with cocoa powder.

Raspberries Romanoff

Serves 6

M. F. K. Fisher, the famous food writer, was the inspiration for this dessert. One summer, we did a benefit dinner for the Napa Valley Symphony at Fisher's St. Helena home. I devised a menu from her Alphabet for Gourmets, and this dish stood for the letter R.

This is the world's simplest, most wonderful dessert. It's all about the quality of the liqueur you use, so don't skimp there. Use a high-quality crème de cassis, such as the GE Massenez Crème de Cassis de Dijon. Or use a good framboise or kirsch. These liqueurs are all made from fruits: crème de cassis from black currants, framboise from raspberries, and kirsch from cherries. You don't need much—it's a little over a table-spoon per person. If you really want to spoil your guests, serve the raspberries with Anne's Chocolate Biscuits (page 319).

1 cup heavy whipping cream
1 teaspoon vanilla extract
⅓ cup powdered sugar

3 pints ripe raspberries
7 to 8 tablespoons crème de cassis, framboise, or kirsch

In a medium bowl, lightly beat the cream, then add the vanilla and sugar. Whip till firm but not buttery: it should just hold peaks.

Serve in 8-ounce wineglasses, 6-ounce sherry glasses, or some other attractive glass. Do a layer of berries, then liqueur, then cream. Repeat, making 2 to 3 layers of each.

Baked Peach Crisps

Serves 6

You can bake these either on a parchment-lined baking sheet or tucked snugly into a ceramic casserole dish. Either way, the trick is not to overbake. Garnish with sweetened whipped cream or a small scoop of vanilla ice cream and a tablespoon or so of warm caramel sauce (page 329).

¼ cup old-fashioned oats

½ cup all-purpose flour

¼ cup dark brown sugar

¼ teaspoon salt

⅛ teaspoon ground cinnamon

4½ tablespoons butter, chilled and cut into small pieces

3 peaches

3 tablespoons rum

½ cup sliced almonds

Preheat the oven to 375°F.

For the topping, spread the oats out on a baking pan and heat in the oven 7 to 10 minutes. Remove the pan when the oats smell nice and toasty and are lightly golden in color. Let the oats cool, then put them in a mixing bowl along with the flour, sugar, salt, cinnamon, and butter. Mix gently till crumbly, as if you were making a pie dough. I use my fingers, but you could use a mixer fitted with the paddle attachment.

Do not peel the peaches, as the skin will help them hold their shape after they are baked. Just cut the peaches in half and remove the pits, then slice a tiny bit off the bottom of each half so they will sit nicely and won't wobble around. Place the peaches on a parchment-lined baking sheet or in a casserole dish and drizzle each with a little of the rum. Spoon about 3 tablespoons of the topping onto each peach half, then sprinkle on some almonds. Bake 10 to 15 minutes, until the top is crisp and golden brown.

Serve as is or with a little sweetened whipped cream or vanilla ice cream with a drizzle of Caramel Sauce.

Date Candy

Makes 40 to 45 pieces

This is a great item to have in your fridge to make an instant dessert. It keeps well for up to three months in the refrigerator— if you don't start snacking on it, that is. I often serve it with of a nice cheese such as a Gorgonzola or a nutty Comté from France to make a cheese or dessert course. Or serve the Date Candy with chocolate truffles or candied orange peel dipped in chocolate for a sweet ending to a meal.

I usually make this with almonds, but I've used pistachios or walnuts with good results. Like the almonds, pistachios and walnuts need to be toasted first.

2½ cups sliced almonds

1 scant cup sesame seeds

2 pounds Medjool dates, pitted

2 to 3 tablespoons butter, melted

Preheat the oven to 375°F. Spread the almonds out on a baking pan, toast 7 minutes, and allow to cool. Toast the sesame seeds in a skillet over medium-high heat and set aside.

It is best to process the dates and almonds in small batches, as you will have better control and will get a more even texture. Put about a third of the dates, almonds, and butter in a processor and pulse to chop the dates and almonds. Be sure not to overprocess or you will end up with a pureed mass. You want chopped nut and date pieces evenly distributed throughout the mixture, and you should still be able to tell what's what. As each batch is processed, scoop it out into an ungreased 9 by 9-inch metal or glass pan. If you're feeling energetic, all the chopping and mixing can be done by hand. Mix with a strong wooden spoon.

Press the whole date-nut mixture down firmly so that it is smooth and even. Pour the sesame seeds over the top and press them into the dates as evenly as possible. Pour off all the loose seeds. If you like, you may turn the whole date-nut sheet over and press sesame seeds into the other side, too. Chill it well, then cut it into finger-width slices about 1¹/₂ inches long. It will help to wet the knife first, or spray it with oil. Wrap the slices in parchment paper and store in a sealed plastic bag in your refrigerator.

This is a great dessert to do ahead, as the cakes are best if they are allowed to soak overnight.

Mini Tres Leches Cakes with Mexican Chocolate Sauce

Makes about 30

In Spanish, tres leches *means "three milks," and the three milks in this cake are sweetened condensed milk, evaporated milk, and heavy cream. These milks don't go into the cake batter, though. Instead, the cake is first baked and then saturated with the* tres leches, *the way a rum cake gets soaked with rum. Usually the cake would be baked in a single cake pan, but I like to bake them in tiny muffin tins and serve them topped with Mexican Chocolate Sauce, two or three mini cakes per person. Some people are sure to want seconds. My stepson, for instance, can eat eight of these. You could also bake the cakes in three-inch muffin tins and serve one or two per person.*

This is a great dessert to do ahead, as the cakes are best if they are allowed to soak overnight. If the recipe is bigger than you need, instead of trying to cut it in half, you can make the whole recipe, bake all the cakes, then soak only those you want to use immediately. Freeze the others in freezer bags. When you are ready to use the frozen cakes, simply defrost them thoroughly, then carry on with the recipe from the "prick the cakes all over their tops" step. If you're doing this, make half portions of both the chocolate sauce and the tres leches *soaking mix.*

Here are a few helpful hints regarding the chocolate sauce. The Mexican chocolate called for in it is made with a coarse sugar and is a lot less processed than most chocolates. It's a sweet chocolate flavored with almonds, cinnamon, and vanilla. It can be found in most large groceries. As for the espresso, if you don't have an espresso machine you could use a tablespoon of espresso powder mixed with a tablespoon of water. And finally, a coffee grinder works great for grinding the nuts. The sauce is sinfully good, but you need only a tablespoonful per cake.

(continued)

cake

1½ cups cake flour

¼ teaspoon baking powder

½ teaspoon salt

5 large eggs, separated

1¼ cups sugar

1½ teaspoons vanilla extract

2½ teaspoons freshly squeezed
    lime juice

½ cup whole milk

los tres leches

12 ounces evaporated milk

14 ounces sweetened condensed
    milk

1¾ cups heavy cream

mexican chocolate
sauce

2 ounces unsweetened chocolate

1 (3⅓-ounce) disk Mexican
    chocolate

2 tablespoons butter

3 tablespoons Kahlúa

½ cup sweetened condensed
    milk

2 tablespoons finely ground
    almonds

¼ teaspoon ground cinnamon

2 tablespoons corn syrup

1 tablespoon espresso

3 to 4 tablespoons whipping
    cream (optional)

Whipped cream, slightly
    sweetened with vanilla if
    desired

Powdered sugar

Raspberries or strawberries
    (optional)

Butter or pan-spray the muffin tins, dust with flour, and set them aside. Preheat the oven to 350°F.

Combine the cake flour, baking powder, and salt in a small bowl and set aside. Put the egg whites in the bowl of a mixer and whip them to the soft-peak stage. With the mixer still running, slowly add the sugar and beat till stiff peaks form. On the lowest speed, add the egg yolks, vanilla, and lime juice. Still on slow speed, mix in half the flour, then half the milk, beating after each addition till the mixture is just combined. Do not overmix, or else the cakes will be tough. Repeat with the remaining flour and milk.

Pour the batter into the muffin tins, filling them about two-thirds full. Bake 20 to 25 minutes, until lightly golden brown. While the cakes are baking, make the *tres leches* mixture by stirring the evaporated milk, condensed milk, and cream together in a pitcher or bowl. When the cakes are done, turn them out into a glass baking dish or some other nonaluminum casserole dish. Prick the cakes all over their tops using bamboo skewers or toothpicks.

While the cakes are still warm, pour or ladle some of the *tres leches* over the cakes, getting it all over the tops. Wait for the cake to absorb that milk and add more. Continue in this manner until all the milk has been absorbed. Chill the cakes overnight.

To make the chocolate sauce, put the unsweetened chocolate, Mexican chocolate, and butter in the top of a double boiler and heat until melted. Whisk in the Kahlúa, condensed milk, almonds, cinnamon, corn syrup, and espresso, whisking until the sauce is smooth. If it is too thick to pour easily, add up to 4 tablespoons of whipping cream to thin it. Reserve until needed. Reheat over gently simmering water or in a microwave before serving.

Serve with a dollop of whipped cream, a sprinkling of powdered sugar, and a drizzle of warmed Mexican Chocolate Sauce. Scatter raspberries or strawberries about, if you are using them.

pineapple sauce

1½ cups chopped fresh
 pineapple

1 to 2 tablespoons sugar

A few drops of freshly squeezed
 lemon juice

strawberry sauce

1½ cups chopped fresh
 strawberries

1 to 2 tablespoons sugar

A few drops of freshly squeezed
 lemon juice

caramel sauce

1 cup sugar

½ cup light corn syrup

⅓ cup water

2 teaspoons vanilla extract

½ cup butter

¾ cup heavy cream

Tiny pinch salt

2 tablespoons rum (optional)

3 regular bananas or 6 small red
 bananas

¾ cup sugar

1 quart vanilla ice cream, or your
 favorite flavor

Whipped cream

Candied pecans or toasted flaked
 coconut

Fresh Bing cherries or dried
 sweet cherries

Teeny-Weeny Bikini Banana Splits

Serves 6

For this recipe you will need a one-ounce ice cream scoop and a butane torch, both of which are available at well-stocked kitchenware stores. You need the scoop to make mini balls of ice cream for the banana split, and the torch is for making a hard candy shell around the bananas. One of the tricks to a nice, hard sugar shell is to start with an even layer of sugar. I find shaking the sugar from a salt shaker to be extremely helpful in this task. Also, be sure to leave enough time between the caramelizing and the serving because the sugar needs to cool completely in order to develop that nice crispness. (You can skip the sugaring-the-bananas step if you really don't want to deal with a butane torch, but the dish won't have quite the same effect.)

Vanilla ice cream is called for here, but a really rich, homemade chocolate ice cream would be spectacular, too. If you want to get crazy, go for three different flavors. Chocolate, vanilla, and pistachio would be fabulous, as would dulce de leche, vanilla, and chocolate. (Dulce de leche, or cajeta, is caramelized sweetened milk. You can get it at Latin American markets.) The Caramel Sauce should be served warm. It can be made ahead and reheated just before you need it.

To make the pineapple sauce, combine the pineapple, 1 tablespoon of the sugar, and the lemon juice in a food processor and process to a rough puree. Taste, and add more sugar if needed.

(continued)

Using a butane torch is fun, but don't get too carried away. I've had pastry and pantry cooks accidentally burn holes in the kitchen walls when they set a torch down *before* turning it off. You don't want to set the kitchen curtains or walls on fire. Keep your hair out of the way as well!

For a more rustic sauce, simply chop the pineapple by hand to the desired consistency, then combine it with the sugar and lemon juice.

Prepare the strawberry sauce in the same manner. Reserve both sauces until needed.

For the caramel sauce, combine the sugar, corn syrup, and water in a large stainless steel saucepan. Bring to a boil and cook till a rich caramel color develops. Do not stir as it cooks, but swirl the pan as the edges brown to achieve an even color. Remove from the heat immediately. Wrap your hand in an oven mitt or a towel (there will be lots of steam) and whisk in the butter, vanilla, and cream. Add the salt and rum, if desired, and stir. Set this aside.

Peel and cut the bananas in half crosswise, then split them in half lengthwise. (Small red bananas just need to be split in half lengthwise.) If you are going to caramelize the bananas, arrange them cut side up on a pizza tray. Sprinkle an even layer of sugar over the flat cut surfaces of the bananas and caramelize the sugar with a butane torch until it is golden brown and melted. Set aside to cool. While the bananas are cooling, get the sauces lined up and set up your dishes with 3 small scoops of ice cream in each. Reheat the caramel sauce. Carefully arrange two slices of banana alongside the scoops of ice cream; top with spoonfuls of caramel, pineapple, and strawberry sauces. Finish with a dollop of whipped cream, a sprinkling of nuts, and a cherry on top.

For a more rustic
sauce, simply chop the
pineapple by hand...

Rhubarb, Lemongrass, and Ginger Sauce over Vanilla Ice Cream

Serves 6

This is a really beautiful, light spring dessert. The lovely pink of the cooked rhubarb over creamy white vanilla ice cream looks great, especially if you serve it in black or dark brown bowls. The hidden flavors of ginger and lemongrass in the rhubarb sauce are surprisingly refreshing, especially welcome after a round of intensely flavored small plates.

You don't need to peel the ginger or the lemongrass for this sauce, as everything will get strained out. You just need to "smash" them, which means to hit and flatten them with the broad side of a chef's knife or cleaver. This will open up the fibers and begin the release of juice and flavor. If the rhubarb is very wide, split it in half lengthwise before cutting it up further.

2 stalks lemongrass, smashed and chopped

3-inch piece of fresh ginger, smashed and chopped

1½ cups sugar

2 cups water

1 vanilla bean

1½ pounds rhubarb, chopped into ½-inch pieces

1 quart really good vanilla ice cream

To make the syrup, combine the lemongrass, ginger, sugar, and water in a big pot. Split the vanilla bean and scrape the seeds into the pot. Toss in the pod, too, and bring to a boil. Reduce to a simmer and cook 5 minutes. Remove from the heat and let steep 20 to 30 minutes.

Remove the vanilla bean pod, and strain the syrup to remove the bits of ginger and lemongrass. Don't worry about the vanilla seeds passing through the strainer. Return the syrup to the pot and add the rhubarb. Bring to a boil and cook 10 to 15 minutes, till the rhubarb is soft, but not so long that it dissolves. The sauce can be held at this point and reheated before serving. To serve, ladle hot sauce over scoops of really good vanilla ice cream.

Yummy Sherried Figs

2 tablespoons wildflower honey

½ cup Pedro Ximénez sherry or other cream sherry

8 fresh ripe figs, halved

Vanilla ice cream, mascarpone cheese, soft ricotta, *fromage blanc*, crème fraîche, or plain yogurt, for topping

Serves 4

You have your choice of toppings for the figs. Whichever you choose, scoop it over the figs while they are still hot. It makes for a nice cold-hot yumminess.

When it's not fig season, try this recipe using halved peaches or quartered pears. For peaches, you would bake five to eight minutes, until lightly caramelized and fork-tender. Firm but ripe pears need ten to fifteen minutes. In rhubarb season, try using chunked rhubarb with port instead of the sherry.

Preheat the oven to 375°F.

Combine the honey and sherry in a small bowl and mix well. Place the figs, cut side up, in individual gratin dishes or in a casserole dish. Drizzle with some of the sherry-honey mixture, saving some for additional basting while the figs are cooking. Bake, basting occasionally, till the liquid has reduced to a syrupy consistency, about 20 minutes. Be careful not to over-bake. Serve hot with a dollop of the topping of your choice. With vanilla ice cream, you can reverse the order, if you like; ice cream on the bottom and hot figs as the topping.

Oranges and Smashed Cherries

Serves 6

At the end of orange season here in Northern California, the cherries start coming in. This very simple and refreshing dessert is one of the ways I take advantage of the abundance. It's great following a meal of many different flavors. When they're available, I've made this with raspberries, too.

Nanami togarashi is a spice mix from Japan that has a little bit of a kick to it. It can be found at Asian markets and other specialty foods stores. If you can't find it, use shichimi togarashi plus a few gratings of orange zest. You could also substitute two teaspoons of freshly grated ginger mixed with the zest and juice of one lime, or a tiny sprinkle of cayenne pepper and toasted sesame seeds to dress the orange slices.

6 navel oranges

30 or so fresh cherries

⅛ teaspoon ground cinnamon

6 shakes *nanami togarashi*

¼ teaspoon freshly ground black pepper

Grate the zest of 1 of the oranges into a bowl. Now peel the rest of the oranges and cut the pith from all of them, catching any juice you can and adding it to the zest. Cut the oranges into slices about ¼ inch thick, again saving as much of the juice as you can and adding it to the zest. Arrange the slices on plates. Pour the zest and juice evenly over the orange slices.

Smack the cherries with the side of a knife to pop them open, and remove the pits. Arrange 5 or 6 per serving on the orange slices. Lightly sprinkle with cinnamon, *nanami togarashi*, and pepper.

Double Trouble Chocolate
Mousse Tortes (page 340)

It's a cool recipe for making in interesting molds, too.

Double Trouble Chocolate Mousse Torte

Serves 12

1 recipe Anne's Chocolate
Biscuits (page 319)

2 tablespoons butter, melted

dark chocolate mousse

12 ounces semisweet chocolate
bits

½ cup (1 stick) butter

8 large egg yolks

4 tablespoons sugar

¾ cup whipping cream

2 tablespoons sour cream

2 large egg whites

white chocolate mousse

9 ounces white chocolate

2½ cups whipping cream

3 large egg yolks

2½ tablespoons sugar

2 large egg whites

meringue cookies

3 large egg whites

¾ cup sugar

1 teaspoon coffee extract

Make this very special torte for your next family gathering or dinner party, and everyone will be so impressed. It features a layer of white chocolate mousse and layer of dark chocolate mousse on top of a chocolate cookie crust, topped by crunchy coffee-flavored meringue cookies. This torte is rich, yet light in texture, and it just, as they say, melts in your mouth! It can be made in a round springform pan or a low rectangular pan. It's a cool recipe for making in interesting molds, too.

If it seems like too much trouble, you can skip the fancy meringue cookie garnish, and the torte will still be delicious. It's just nice to have something crisp with all the rich mousse. The torte can be made ahead and frozen overnight. And, if stored in a well-sealed jar, the meringue cookies should keep for a day. Check out the recipe before you separate the eggs, and get enough bowls out so you can organize the egg yolks and egg whites. You need eight yolks and two whites for the dark mousse, three yolks and two whites for the light mousse, and three whites for the meringue cookies. That's eleven eggs in all, with egg whites to spare.

Finely crumble enough of the chocolate biscuits to measure 2 cups. You can crush them on a cutting board using a rolling pin, or in a food processor. (You may have cookies to spare. Good for a later snack.) Line a 10-inch springform pan with parchment paper. Scoop out ¹/₂ cup of the cookie crumbs and set it aside. Combine the remaining 1¹/₂ cups of crumbs with the butter and pour this mixture into the pan, pressing it in to form a crust.

To make the Dark Chocolate Mousse, melt the chocolate bits and the butter in the top of a double boiler. In a large mixin bowl, whip the egg yolks and 3 tablespoons of the sugar together until light and thick. Whisk the chocolate into the yolk mixture and cool to room temperature. In a separate bowl, whip the cream with the sour cream until stiff peaks form, then fold this into the chocolate mixture. In a clean bowl and using a clean whisk or egg beater, whip the egg whites to soft peaks and whip in the remaining 1 tablespoon sugar. Beat until firm but not dry. Fold the whites into the mousse. Pour the mousse over the biscuit crust, spreading it out as evenly as you can, and sprinkle evenly with the reserved cookie crumbs. Put in the freezer to chill 10 to 15 minutes.

In the meantime, make the White Chocolate Mousse. Melt the white chocolate in the top of a double boiler with a few drops of the cream. In a large mixing bowl, whisk the egg yolks and 1^1/$_2$ tablespoons of the sugar until light, then whisk in the chocolate until thick. Whip the remaining cream to stiff peaks in a stand mixer or mixing bowl and fold it into the chocolate in 3 batches. In a clean bowl, whip the egg whites to soft peaks and whip in the remaining 1 tablespoon sugar. Continue beating until firm but not dry. Fold the egg whites into the chocolate mixture, and pour this over the layer of dark chocolate mousse. Freeze solid.

To make the meringue cookies, line a baking sheet with parchment paper and preheat the oven to 200°F. Put the egg whites in the bowl of a mixer and whip them to the soft-peak stage. With the mixer still running, very slowly sprinkle in ^{1}/$_2$ cup of the sugar. Beat 2 to 3 minutes, then gradually sprinkle in the rest of the sugar, beating until it is well incorporated. Pipe half of the meringue in long strips onto the baking sheet. Fold coffee extract into the remaining meringue and pipe this in long strips alongside the other strips. Bake for 1^1/$_2$ to 2 hours, until crispy. Allow the meringues to cool, then break them into erratic pieces. Reserve in an airtight container.

About 30 minutes before serving, move the torte to the refrigerator to temper. Cut into 12 portions. Sprinkle randomly with meringue cookies.

Lemon-Buttermilk
Pudding Cakes
(page 344)

Lemon-Buttermilk Pudding Cake with Chantilly Cream and Berries

cake

⅔ cup plus ¼ cup sugar

½ cup all-purpose flour

½ cup freshly squeezed lemon juice

2 tablespoons finely grated lemon zest

1½ cups buttermilk

4 tablespoons (½ stick) butter, melted

3 large eggs, separated

1 cup heavy cream

1 teaspoon vanilla extract

2 tablespoons powdered sugar, plus extra for dusting

2 pints fresh raspberries or blueberries, mashed

¼ cup sugar

3 tablespoons Cointreau or other liqueur

Serves 6 to 8

I got the recipe for this cake from my cousin Joan years ago. You can bake it in an eight-inch-square glass baking dish or, for individual servings, in eight 4-ounce ramekins.

Preheat the oven to 350°F.

In a large bowl, whisk together ²/₃ cup of the sugar and the flour. Add the lemon juice, zest, and buttermilk and whisk until smooth. In a separate bowl, whisk together the butter and the egg yolks. Stir the egg yolk mixture into the buttermilk mixture. Using the whisk attachment of a mixer, whip the egg whites until frothy. Sprinkle in the remaining ¹/₄ cup sugar and whip until soft peaks form, about 1 minute. Fold the egg whites into the egg yolk and buttermilk mixture. The batter should be smooth and thick.

Pour the batter into a baking dish and place the dish in a water bath with the water halfway up the sides of the dish. Bake 23 to 30 minutes, until slightly brown and beginning to crack but still jiggly. The smaller the baking dish, the less time will be needed to reach this stage. Cool to room temperature.

While the cake is in the oven, make a chantilly cream by whipping together the cream, vanilla, and 2 tablespoons of the powdered sugar in a bowl until fluffy. Keep chilled until needed.

To serve, turn the cake out onto a serving platter. (Individual ramekins do better in low, rimmed soup dishes). Spoon on mashed berries, sprinkle with sugar, and drizzle with Cointreau. Finish with a dollop of cream and a dusting of powdered sugar.

N-WAFFLE

DINNER   50¢

R DAY

LING WORKERS

suggested menus for small-plates meals

If you're not sure how to set up a sit-down small-plates meal, start with a few of the sample menus below. When you get a little more confident about working with small plates, try substituting dishes on the suggested menus, and pretty soon you'll be creating whole menus on your own. The sample menus are organized by season, and are designed to serve six to eight people. Small-plates meals are very flexible, though: you can add a dish or adjust recipe quantities up or down.

If you want some ideas for larger parties, skip to the end of this section, and check out the menus for the Fish Tostada Fest, Summer Barbecue Fest, and Burger Fest.

spring

Seared or Grilled Asparagus with White Truffle Oil Aioli | 134, Morel Mushroom– and Goat Cheese Stuffed Crêpes with Corn Cream | 264, Rhubarb, Lemongrass, and Ginger Sauce over Vanilla Ice Cream | 334

Pablo's Boquerones | 49, Garlic Soup | 153, Seared or Grilled Asparagus with Brown Butter Vinaigrette | 134, Crispy Fried Rabbit with Dijon-Madeira Sauce | 268, Spanish cheeses and fresh fruit

Pan-Roasted Hazelnuts | 15, Grilled Baby Leeks and Spring Onions with Garlicky Romesco Sauce | 126, Roasted Artichokes with Tarragon-Basil Dipping Sauce | 40, Gaucho Empanadas | 84, Mini Tres Leches Cakes with Mexican Chocolate Sauce | 326

Hard-Boiled Eggs with Green Garlic Cream | 38, Hearts of Romaine, Watercress, and Avocado Salad with Erasto's Red Jalapeño–Lime Vinaigrette | 113, Spiced Ahi Tuna Sticks, New Year's Eve | 44, Halibut "Stew" with Saffron Broth | 150, Oranges and Smashed Cherries | 337

summer

Corn Soup with Double-Basil Tomatoes | 172, Halibut Tostadas with Jicama Slaw | 203, Avocado-Papaya Salad with Papaya Seed Dressing | 116, Baked Peach Crisps | 322

Onion-Tomato-Bread "Soup" | 162, Grilled "Street" Corn | 26, Black Pepper and Garlic Chicken Wings | 105, Ken Hom's Pork Riblets | 76, Ripe stone fruit on ice

Bix Steak Tartare | 180, Roasted End o' Summer Tomatoes with Red Wine–Honey Vinaigrette | 240, Crisp-Fried Squash Blossoms with Tomatillo–Ancho Chile Salsa | 250, Salmon, Halibut, and Scallop Ceviche with Coconut | 156, Wild Mushroom Tamales with Yucatecan Tomato Salsa | 288, Mini Tres Leches Cakes with Mexican Chocolate Sauce | 326

fall

Grilled Oysters—Easy as Pie | 84, Grilled Beef on Potato Rafts with Salpicón | 190, Raspberries Romanoff with Anne's Chocolate Biscuits | 320

Stuffed Piquillo Peppers with Charred Tomato Sauce | 301, Grilled Scallops Amandine | 274, Avocado-Papaya Salad with Papaya Seed Dressing | 116, Date Candy | 323

Oysters Pablo | 278, Stuffed Pasilla Chiles with "Mole de la Suegra" and Cherry Tomato Salsa | 295, Teeny-Weeny Bikini Banana Splits | 329

Papas Bravas | 24, Roasted Peppers with Anchovies and Capers | 243, Morel Mushroom "Casseroles" with Pedro Ximénez Sherry and Thyme | 169, Rabbit Tostadas with Cumin-Scented Black Beans and Lime Crème Fraîche | 197, Yummy Sherried Figs | 336

winter

Duck and Mustard Green Wontons with Vietnamese-Style Sauce | 148, Dungeness Crab–Sweet Potato–Corn Fritters | 48, Mongolian Barbecued Lamb Chops | 86, Lemon-Buttermilk Pudding Cake with Chantilly Cream and Berries | 344

Wilted Winter Greens on Bruschetta | 244, Baked Goat Cheese and Tomato Fondue | 163, Serrano Ham–Wrapped Prawns with Piquillo Vinaigrette and Living Watercress | 50, Anne's Chocolate Biscuits and fresh ripe pears | 319

Gougères | 10, Braised Portobello and Porcini Mushrooms with Spiced Flatbread | 188, Cindy's Supper Club Escargots | 236, Grilled Swordfish with Roasted Cauliflower and Sweet-Sour Onions | 287, My Very First Beef Satay | 102, Fancy chocolates

party menus

FISH TOSTADA FEST

Chile-Garlic Peanuts | 17, Squash Blossom Quesadillas with Homemade Tortillas and Queso Oaxaca | 56, Tuna Tostadas with Watermelon and Tomatillo Salsas | 208, Halibut Tostadas with Jicama Slaw | 203, Salt-Roasted Salmon Tostadas with Cindy's Backstreet Tomatillo-Avocado Salsa | 204, Double Trouble Chocolate Mousse Torte | 340

SUMMER BARBECUE FEST

Avocado-Papaya Salad with Papaya Seed Dressing | 116, Chicken "Satay" in a Lettuce Cup with Lemon Olive Oil Vinaigrette | 90, Mustards' Vietnamese-Style Pork Lettuce Wraps | 94, Black Pepper and Garlic Chicken Wings | 105, Summer King Salmon Kebabs | 66, Mongolian Barbecued Lamb Chops | 86, Lemon-Buttermilk Pudding Cake with Chantilly Cream and Berries | 344

BURGER FEST

Mustards' Famous Onion Rings with House-Made Ketchup | 18, Sunday Supper Burgers with Thousand Island Dressing | 216, Mini Beef Burgers with Roasted Chile Relish and Pablo's Pickled Onions | 222, Mini Duck Burgers with Shiitake Mushroom Ketchup and Chinese-Style Mustard Sauce | 226, Spicy Lamb Burgers with Vietnamese Herb Salad and Tamarind Vinaigrette | 232, Double Trouble Chocolate Mousse Torte | 340

glossary

asian ingredients

Black bean sauce or paste is a Chinese condiment made from fermented black beans, used in cooking and in marinades. Some varieties are flavored with chiles and/or garlic. Make sure there is no MSG (monosodium glutamate) or shrimp paste in whichever black bean sauce you choose, as many people are allergic to these additives. For garlic-flavored black bean sauce, we use the Lan Chi brand.

There are many brands of **chile-garlic sauce** or paste available, each with its own heat level and flavor. We use the Heavenly Chef Vietnamese Garlic Sauce.

Hoisin sauce is a thick, sweetish soybean-based Chinese condiment commonly used in marinades, or as a dipping sauce. I use it a lot in marinades for duck, pork, quail, and squab. I've heard it referred to as Chinese barbecue sauce.

Most **soy sauces** are made with soy beans plus wheat (in some cases as much as 40 percent to 50 percent wheat) and salt. There are two classic kinds of soy sauce—light and dark. Dark soys are often colored with caramel or molasses, and are less salty than light soys. Dark soy sauce is usually used in cooking, whereas the saltier light soy is generally used as a dipping sauce. Note: when I say "light" soy, I do not mean the reduced-salt "lite" soy sauces you may see in the market. I do not recommend these at all. There is also a mushroom soy sauce, which is flavored with essence of straw mushrooms. It is good in marinades and for use as a dipping sauce. (See also tamari and *ketjap manis*, below.)

Tamari is a thick, dark Japanese soy sauce with a very low wheat content. Some brands are made by very strict traditional methods, and you can even get some Japanese tamaris that are 100 percent soybean. These special tamaris can be very pricey.

Another type of soy sauce is **ketjap manis** (also *kecap manis*) from Indonesia—dark brown and syrupy, it's much thicker and sweeter than Chinese soy sauce. A decent substitute for it would be a mix of two parts tamari to one part molasses.

Kaffir lime leaves are very aromatic and, when cut, give off a little essential oil that adds a nice background flavor and aroma. There's a tiny bitterness to them that cuts the richness of a dish in just the right way. Fresh kaffir lime leaves may be difficult to find, but many Asian markets carry frozen leaves. It's worth a little legwork to find the real thing, but if you can't, it's okay to substitute a little lime or lemon zest. The fruit itself is a hard little warty thing that you don't actually get much juice out of. They are probably used by somebody for something, but I don't know what that might be.

Lemongrass is a Southeast Asian herb that looks like a dried-up foot-long reed or overgrown scallion. Peel away the tough outer stalks until you get to the smooth, pale yellow inner stalks. This bulblike part can be minced up and added to stir-fries, marinades, sauces, soups, and more. Lemongrass has a very delicate lemon flavor but is not at all sour.

bread

The next-best thing to baking your own breads is to seek out local bakeries that make what I call "artisanal," "rustic," "country," or "*levain*-style" breads. By this I mean bread with a great crust and an airy but structurally sound crumb, the kind that makes crispy toast that won't turn soggy immediately when topped with something saucy, yet will not cut you up when you bite into it.

Good bread can't be made by shortcut methods. Artisanal breads require slow, low-temperature rises of the dough (as much as fifteen hours). There are many bakeries around now that make these great European-style breads, some with rye and whole wheat flours in varying ratios to white flour, resulting in loaves with excellent texture and structure. In Northern California, there is the Acme Bakery, a company that was a leader in the artisanal bread revolution. Acme supplies many of the restaurants in this area, and its breads are sold in many of the local markets. In New York City there is Amy's Bread, which has several shops. Just do a little exploring wherever you live. Check out the smaller bakeries, too, as you never know. Della Fratoria in our area does breads in a wood-fired oven. Its sesame seed–olive loaf is one of my all-time favorites.

To make **toasts** (also known as bruschetta), brush both sides of the bread with olive oil and place on a baking sheet. Bake in a 375°F oven until the bread begins to turn golden, and is crispy on the outside but still a little soft in the middle. If you already have the grill going, you could toast the bread on the grill. You can also pop the slices in a traditional toaster and coat them with olive oil or butter as soon as they come out (do it while they're still hot).

You can make **croutons** any size or shape you like. It all depends on what you're serving. Sometimes I garnish soups with tiny croutons, cut into quarter-inch dice or smaller; for finger foods, I like two-bite-size toasts. For diced croutons, toss with a little olive oil and spread out on a baking sheet. Bake in a 350°F oven for five to ten minutes, until golden brown and crisp through. Stir once or twice to ensure even cooking. For flat croutons, brush with olive oil and bake until toasty and crispy all through.

A true *levain* is a sourdough starter made from wild yeasts. A *levain*-style bread may not have a wild yeast starter but is made by the older, slower methods of breadmaking that a *levain* requires.

A *bâtard* is a one-pound loaf of sourdough French bread.

chiles and peppers

I use a lot of chiles and peppers in my cooking, even now that Miramonte has been transformed into Cindy's Backstreet Kitchen. Both Latin and Asian markets carry an amazing variety of fresh and dried chiles, and local farmers' markets are a good source, too.

In general, the smallest chiles are the hottest ones of all. The little **Thai bird chiles**, for instance, can take your head off. Much of the heat of a chile is held in its seeds, so if you want a less spicy result, remove the seeds as part of the chile preparation. Be sure to wash your hands thoroughly after handling chiles, and do not rub your eyes.

Roasting and peeling fresh chiles and peppers. Place the chiles or peppers over an open flame on a gas stove or a grill, or place them in a heavy flat skillet over an electric element. Turn them as needed to char and blister the skins evenly. When the skins are nicely blackened all over, put the chiles in a plastic bag or a large bowl. Seal the bag or cover the bowl, and allow the chiles to cool. Once they are cool, the skin should slip off easily.

Toasting and rehydrating dried chiles. I always toast dried chiles before using them, as this brings out their flavor. You can toast chiles in a number of ways. Start off by stemming and seeding them, then place the chiles on a baking sheet and put them in a 375°F oven for two to three minutes, until aromatic; or, using tongs, hold the chiles over a direct flame for about a minute, turning as you toast; or toss the chiles around in a skillet over medium-high heat for one or two minutes. The main point is to warm them enough to release their oils and to soften them up a little. You'll know when you've accomplished this by the aroma they give off. Be careful not to toast them too long, as they will become bitter.

To rehydrate dried chiles, soak them in warm water to cover for ten to fifteen minutes, until they are soft. Sometimes I weight the chiles down with a saucer to make sure they are completely submerged.

A note on *piquillo* **peppers**: Once I discovered these sweet, richly flavored pimiento-style Spanish peppers, I was hooked. I even began inventing recipes for them. *Piquillos* are smallish red peppers, about two inches long and one inch across at the top, tapering to a little hook at the bottom. (In Spanish, *piquillo* means "little beak.") Fresh *piquillos* are not currently available in the United States, but you can find cans or jars of them at specialty foods stores, or get them through a mail-order source such as The Spanish Table. They are fire-roasted and peeled and come ready to stuff, slice, or puree.

miscellaneous ingredients

Epazote is a spiky-leafed green herb frequently used in Mexican cooking. It is pungent and a little bitter. Some say it tastes like musty mint or basil. Once you get used to it, you become addicted. It is always used in cooking black beans, maybe because it is said to have antiflatulent properties. It will grow like a weed in a less-than-perfect environment. Only use fresh epazote, as the dried is like sawdust. If you can't find epazote, use some Mexican oregano and mint or basil instead. It won't be the same, but it should be delicious anyway.

My favorite type of **salt** is Maldon sea salt from England, made by a special process that involves boiling seawater. The salt comes in the form of delicate pyramid-shaped flake crystals (they remind me of snowflakes). It is most often used as a finishing salt, but I use it in cooking as well. Try crumbling a little over grilled fish or meats just before serving. It adds a little crunch but is not overly salty. One of my greatest pleasures is to eat lunch in my garden, munching on tomatoes right off the vine, with a kitchen towel on my lap and a box of Maldon salt by my side.

To really boost the flavors of **nuts**, toast them briefly before using them. Pre-heat the oven to 350°F, spread the nuts out on a baking sheet, and toast until lightly browned.

For the oyster recipes in this book I recommend using live in-the-shell **oysters** only. To shuck an oyster, wrap the hand that's going to hold the oyster in a thick towel or wear a glove; using the other hand, place the tip of an oyster knife in the hinge at the back of the oyster shell, and work the knife side to side until you feel or hear a pop. Slide the knife along the deeper bottom shell to cut the muscle that attaches the oyster to the shell. Be careful not to cut through the oyster itself. When your meal is over, toss the oyster shells in the compost—pure calcium.

Because it is made strictly with smoked Spanish pimientos, *pimentón* (Spanish) paprika tastes quite different from Hungarian paprika. The two can be used interchangeably, but when I make Spanish dishes, I go for authenticity (unless I'm stuck). In a pinch, I've mixed a little ground chipotle (smoked dried jalapeños) with Hungarian paprika to a get a touch of smokiness. There are three types of *pimentón*: sweet and mild (it may be labeled *pimentón de la Vera*, *dulce*, or simply *dulce*), bittersweet medium-hot *(agridulce)*, and hot *(picante)*. La Chinata and Chiquilín are the two brands most commonly sold by specialty stores and mail-order firms.

There aren't any stand-alone green salads in this book, but I use various combinations of **greens** tossed with different light vinaigrettes to add a finishing touch to many of the plates. Each of these mini salads is designed to complement, highlight, or balance the flavors in a particular dish, and to make it attractive as well.

If you're willing to experiment, there are many different kinds of greens available in the markets, especially at farmers' markets; or try growing your own. I am partial to arugula (also known as *rucola* or rocket). My latest fad is growing "wild" *rucola*, which is a slower-growing, more pungent variety with a sturdy but not tough texture and beautiful spiky dark green leaves. I'm not sure why wild *rucola* is more expensive in the markets, because it grows like a weed in my garden, reseeding itself and popping up all over.

Always give your greens a thorough rinse in cold water, and dry them in a salad spinner or in towels. Greens should never be dressed until just before serving, so if you're not going to use them right away, store them in the refrigerator in plastic bags, or in a bowl covered with a damp towel.

Before cooking **sea scallops**, check them over to see if there is a tiny white ligament attached to them on one side. This "little hard knobblies bit," as Jane Grigson called it in her great *Fish Book*, is what connects the scallop to its shell. It is tougher than shoe leather, and should be removed. Pull it off gently so you don't tear the scallop apart. If you can't find it, your fish purveyor has already taken care of it for you.

To toast seeds, heat a small dry skillet over medium-high heat. Pour in the seeds and cook till they are aromatic and lightly browned, stirring or shaking them continuously. Keep a close eye on them, as they can go from perfect to burned all at once. Remove from the hot pan as soon as they reach the desired doneness.

You can often find **squash blossoms** in Latin American, Mexican, or Italian markets, and at farmers' markets, too. Or plant a bunch of zucchini and harvest your own flowers. The male flowers, which are attached to a vine, are the best for stuffing: the females are attached to baby squash, and they are beautiful and delicious cooked together. Peel off the small sharp points around the base of the blossom, and remove the center pistil. Check them for ants and bees, too. For soups, omelettes, and stuffings, I tear the blossoms rather than cut them, as they are so delicate.

The simplest **vinaigrette** of all is three parts olive oil whisked together with one part vinegar or lemon juice until well emulsified, and seasoned to taste with salt and pepper. Sometimes that's all you need, especially if the salad is accompanying a complicated or very flavorful dish. Once you've mastered the basic vinaigrette, you can become creative and experiment with different oils and vinegars, herbs, garlic, mustards. Just be sure to use really good-tasting stuff. There is no hiding poor-quality oil or highly acidic vinegars, and either one will ruin all your hard work.

Lately I've been using a lot of **sherry vinegars**. These vinegars are made from sherry wine, and there are dozens of different kinds, so you have a lot to explore. Try to find ones that have 8 percent acidity or less. Buy small bottles and taste. My favorites come from Jerez, Spain. These are nutty and rich in flavor, great with poultry and all sorts of greens. I will often add a few drops to a sauce just before serving.

Another staple to keep on hand for making vinaigrettes is Japanese **rice vinegar**, which is very mild-flavored and has low acidity. Most regular grocery stores stock it: be sure to get the unsweetened kind.

Sausage casings are made from the intestines of pork. My butcher buys them by the hunk. They have been thoroughly cleaned and salted to preserve them. I can buy as many feet as I need. They do keep for a long time if you need to buy the whole hunk. Rinse well in cold running water to desalt before using. We always coat the stuffing nozzle with vegetable oil before sliding the casings on. We keep a skewer handy as we go to pop air bubbles. I find it easiest to work in 3 feet lengths at home. I let the sausage coil onto a baking sheet, then pinch and twist the links after all the sausage meat has been cased.

cooking tips and cooking equipment

To caramelize means to cook food so that it is nicely browned on the surface. Whether you are grilling, panfrying, or griddling, the heat level needs to be quite high in order to caramelize food.

The purpose of **deglazing** is to take advantage of all the tasty goodies stuck to the pan after you have panfried, stir-fried, or sautéed food. Deglazing is usually done with wine or vinegar, but broth or water can also be used. To deglaze, remove the cooked food from the pan and pour off any excess fat or oil; raise the heat, and add the deglazing liquid to the hot pan, scraping to loosen up all the browned bits on the bottom and sides. Stir to dissolve, and boil to reduce the mixture to a thickish glaze.

Deep-frying is best done in an electric deep-fat fryer for automatic heat control, but a heavy-bottomed, deep-sided pan will do if you use a candy or deep-fry thermometer to monitor the heat. It's very important to get your oil really hot, but never so hot that you exceed the oil's smoke point, the temperature at which the oil begins to burn and put off smoke and acrid odors. The higher the smoke point, the better the oil's ability to fry without burning. If oil is heated past its smoke point, it will develop an off odor and bad flavor, which will transfer right over to any food that's fried in it.

The ideal temperature for deep-frying is 365°F–375°F. Safflower, soybean, sunflower, cottonseed, and corn oils all work well, as they have high smoke points (about 450°F). Peanut oil also has a high smoke point and has the best flavor of all, but peanut allergies are common, so beware. Olive oil is good for shallow panfries below 400°F.

Be sure not to overcrowd the fryer, or the food will not crisp up properly. When frying in batches, make sure you skim out any bits of food or coating that have fallen into the oil, and let the oil return to the cooking temperature between batches. A fryer basket makes life easier when you're cooking small items.

Erasto, Pablo, and I prefer **grilling** over wood fires. It's not the easiest way, but the flavor is the best. We use hardwoods like oak or almond, which are both very easy to get here in California. Stay away from pine or other woods high in pitch. They will send up an acrid smoke that will permeate the food you are grilling, which will ruin its flavor, leave a sooty coating on it, and keep it from crisping and caramelizing properly.

Our next favorite choice is charcoal, but we *never* use lighter fluid to get it going. We just roll up some newspaper into cones, stack some kindling and a few small logs on top, followed by the charcoal, and light. You should be able to do it with one match. Let the fire burn down to coals; it's much easier to control your foodstuffs over an even fire than a blazing inferno.

Wear work gloves or cooking mitts unless you have chef's hands (impervious to heat, but you don't want them—trust me). Long tongs (never a fork), a spatula or two, a squirt bottle for controlling flare-ups, some clean platters for the cooked foods to be placed on, and you are ready to go.

A Jaccard tenderizing machine is an inexpensive hand-operated tool that does an excellent job of tenderizing meat and poultry. It has tiny steel blades that "pin" the meat as you run the machine across the surface. Available from specialty kitchenware stores or by mail order, this is a great investment, especially if you're into hunting.

An indispensable device for slicing vegetables thinly and evenly (and quickly) is the **mandoline**. There are many different kinds for sale, with varying accessories and adjustment capabilities. I favor the Japanese mandolines with carbon steel blades.

A spice grinder is a handy tool for grinding up seeds and spices. Clean it out with a dry brush after every use, to keep the flavors from transferring from one batch to another. An electric coffee grinder also works well.

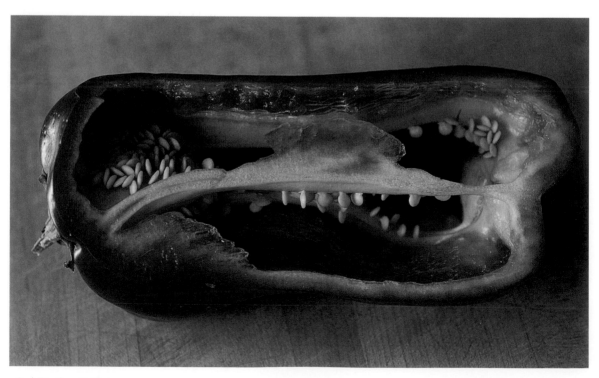

sources

Penzeys Spices
P.O. Box 924
Brookfield, WI 53008
p   800-741-7787
f   262-785-7678
www.penzeys.com
  • *Spices*

Spice Islands Marketplace and
  Campus Store
The Culinary Institute of America
  at Greystone
2555 Main Street
St. Helena, CA 94574
p   888-424-2433
f   877-967-2433
www.prochef.com/marketplace
ciaprochef@culinary.edu
  • *Kitchen equipment*

Shackford's Kitchen Store
1350 Main Street
Napa, CA 94559
p   707-226-2132
f   707-226-5924
  • *Kitchen equipment*

Napa Nuts, Etc.
1755 Industrial Way, Suite 7
Napa, CA 94558
p/f 707-226-6083
www.napanuts.com
maxine@napanuts.com
• *Assorted nuts*

Hobbs' Smoked Meats
P.O. Box 637
El Cerrito, CA 94530
p   510-232-5577
f   510-234-2577
hobbsco2002@aol.com
  • *Assorted smoked meats*

Wine Forest Mushrooms
6493 Dry Creek Road
Napa, CA 94558
p   707-944-8604
f   707-944-2334
wineforest@earthlink.net
  • *Wild mushrooms*

Pacific Gourmet
1060 Marin Street
San Francisco, CA 94124
p   415-641-8400
f   415-641-8309
www.pacgourmet.com
info@pacgourmet.com
• *Gourmet foods*

Hog Island Oyster Company
20215 Highway 1
Marshall, CA 94940
p   415-663-9218
f   415-663-9246
www.hogislandoysters.com
michael@hogislandoysters.com
• *Assorted oysters*

The Spanish Table
1814 San Pablo
Berkeley, CA 94702
p   510-548-1383
www.spanishtable.com
berkeley@spanishtable.com
• *Spanish and Portuguese foods
  and cookware*
(There are also branches in Seattle,
Santa Fe, and Mill Valley, CA.)

**Point Reyes Farmstead Cheese
Company**
P.O. Box 9
Pt. Reyes Station, CA 94956
p   800-591-6878
f   415-663-8881
www.pointreyescheese.com
• *Cheeses*

Mozzarella Company
2944 Elm Street
Dallas, TX 75226
p   800-798-2954
f   214-741-4076
www.mozzco.com
contact@mozzco.com
• *Cheeses*

Laura Chenel Chevre
4310 Fremont Drive
Sonoma, CA 95476
p   707-996-4477
f   707-996-1816
• *Aged and fresh goat cheeses*

index

Tangerine Broth, Mussels and Clams with Andouille Sausage in, 154–55
Tapenade, Best Ever, 33–34
Tarragon-Basil Dipping Sauce, 40–41
Teeny-Weeny Bikini Banana Splits, 329–31
Tenderizing, 362
Thai-Style Fish Cakes, 54–55
Thousand Island Dressing, 216
Three-Cheese Croquettes, 28–29
Tomatillos
    Cindy's Backstreet Tomatillo-Avocado Salsa, 207
    Green Salsa, 312
    Tomatillo–Ancho Chile Salsa, 250–51
    Tomatillo Salsa, 208–9
Tomatoes
    Baked Goat Cheese and Tomato Fondue, 163–64
    Brava Sauce, 24
    Charred Tomato Sauce, 301–2
    Cherry Tomato Salsa, 295, 298
    Cherry Tomato Vinaigrette, 304–5
    Cindy's Supper Club Escargots, 236–37
    Coquilles St. Jacques, 194–95
    Double-Basil Tomatoes, 172–73
    Fried Green Tomatoes with Spicy Rémoulade, 234–35
    Halibut "Stew" with Saffron Broth, 150
    Heirloom Tomato Sauce, 36–38
    heirloom varieties of, 37
    House-Made Ketchup, 18–19
    Onion-Tomato-Bread "Soup," 162
    Pablo's Boquerones, 49
    Red Salsa, 312
    Roasted End o' Summer Tomatoes, 240–41

Shrimp, Crab, and Octopus–Stuffed Avocado, 122–23
Tomato-Lemongrass Salsa, 100–101
Wild Mushroom Stew, 167–68
Yucatecan Tomato Salsa, 288–90
Torte, Double Trouble Chocolate Mousse, 340–41
Tortillas
    Halibut Tostadas, 203
    Pacific Halibut Soft Tacos, 210–11
    Rabbit Tostadas, 197–99
    Salt-Roasted Salmon Tostadas, 204–5
    Squash Blossom Quesadillas, 56–58
    Tortilla Dough, 56–57
    Tuna Tostadas, 208–9
Tostadas, 205, 207
    Halibut Tostadas, 203
    Rabbit Tostadas, 197–99
    Salt-Roasted Salmon Tostadas, 204–5
    Tuna Tostadas, 208–9
Tres Leches Cakes, Mini, 326–28
Truffle Oil Aioli, White, 137
Tuna
    Ahi and Shiitake Mushroom Wontons in Broth, 146–47
    buying, 112
    Spiced Ahi Tuna Sticks, New Year's Eve, 44–45
    Tuna Tartare with Cucumber Salad and Avocado, 111–12
    Tuna Tostadas, 208–9

V
Vietnamese Herb Salad, 232–33
Vietnamese-Style Sauce, 148
Vinaigrettes
    Apple Balsamic Vinaigrette, 44–45
    basic, 360

Brown Butter Vinaigrette, 136
Champagne Vinaigrette, 66–67
Cherry Tomato Vinaigrette, 304–5
Erasto's Red Jalapeño–Lime Vinaigrette, 113
Lemon Olive Oil Vinaigrette, 90–91
Lime-Cumin-Dijon Vinaigrette, 210
Lime Vinaigrette, 122–23
Piquillo Vinaigrette, 50–51
Red Wine–Honey Vinaigrette, 240–41
Sherry Vinaigrette, 133
Tamarind Vinaigrette, 232–33
Walnut Oil Vinaigrette, 140–41
Vinegars, 360

W, Y
Walnuts
    Chiles en Nogada, 254–57
    Herbed Goat Cheese and Walnut Log, 140–41
    Walnut Oil Vinaigrette, 140–41
    Walnut Sauce, 256
Watercress, 50
    Hearts of Romaine, Watercress, and Avocado Salad, 113
    Serrano Ham–Wrapped Prawns with Living Watercress, 50–51
Watermelon Salsa, 208
White Chocolate Mousse, 340–41
White Truffle Oil Aioli, 137
Wontons
    Ahi and Shiitake Mushroom Wontons in Broth, 146–47
    Duck and Mustard Green Wontons, 148–49
    wrappers for, 146
Yummy Sherried Figs, 336